Voter Suppression and Disenfranchisement

Other Books in the Contemporary Debates Series:

Domestic Violence
Police Abuse and Reform in America
Consumer Rights and Protections
Media Bias
American Foreign Policy
Women's Equality in America
Human Trafficking
Political Control of America's Courts
America's National Debt
Energy Resources
Vaccination
Sexual Assault and Harassment in America
LGBTQ Life in America
Public and Private Education in America
Guns in America
Race Relations in America
Voting in America

Voter Suppression and Disenfranchisement

Examining the Facts

James A. Beckman

BLOOMSBURY ACADEMIC
NEW YORK • LONDON • OXFORD • NEW DELHI • SYDNEY

BLOOMSBURY ACADEMIC
Bloomsbury Publishing Inc, 1359 Broadway, New York, NY 10018, USA
Bloomsbury Publishing Plc, 50 Bedford Square, London, WC1B 3DP, UK
Bloomsbury Publishing Ireland, 29 Earlsfort Terrace, Dublin 2, D02 AY28, Ireland

BLOOMSBURY, BLOOMSBURY ACADEMIC and the Diana logo are
trademarks of Bloomsbury Publishing Plc

First published in the United States of America 2026

Cover design: Holly Capper
Cover image © Megan Varner / Stringer via Getty Images

A catalog record for this title is available from the Library of Congress.

ISBN: HB: 979-8-7651-3367-5
ePDF: 979-8-7651-3370-5
eBook: 979-8-7651-3369-9

Series: Contemporary Debates

Typeset by Integra Software Services Pvt. Ltd.
Printed and bound in the United States of America

For product safety related questions contact productsafety@bloomsbury.com.

To find out more about our authors and books visit www.bloomsbury.com
and sign up for our newsletters.

Contents

How to Use This Book

Voter Suppression and Disenfranchisement: Examining the Facts is the latest volume in ABC-CLIO/Bloomsbury Publishing's Contemporary Debates reference series. Each title in this series, which is intended for use by high school and undergraduate students as well as members of the general public, examines the veracity of controversial claims or beliefs surrounding a major political and cultural issue in the United States. The purpose of the series is to give readers a clear and unbiased understanding of current issues by informing them about falsehoods, half-truths, and misconceptions—and confirming the factual validity of other assertions—that have gained traction in America's political and cultural discourse. Ultimately, this series has been crafted to give readers the tools for a fuller understanding of controversial issues, policies, and the laws that occupy center stage in American life and politics.

Each volume in this series identifies thirty to forty questions swirling about the larger topic under discussion. These questions are examined in individualized entries, which are in turn arranged in broad subject chapters that cover certain aspects of the issue being examined, that is, history of concern about the issue, potential economic or social impact, findings of latest scholarly research, and so on.

Each chapter features three to ten individual entries. Each entry begins by starting an important and/or well-known **Question** about the issue being studied. The entry then provides a concise and objective one- or two-paragraph **Answer** to the featured question, followed by a more comprehensive, detailed explanation of **The Facts**. This latter portion of each entry uses quantifiable, evidence-based information from respected sources to fully address each question and provides readers with the information they need to be informed citizens. Importantly, entries will also acknowledge instances in which conflicting data exists or data is incomplete. Finally, each entry concludes with a **Further Reading** section providing users with information on other important and/or influential resources.

The ultimate purpose of every book in the Contemporary Debates series is to reject "false equivalence," in which demonstratable false beliefs or statements are given the same exposure and credence as the facts; to puncture myths that diminish our understanding of important policies and positions; to provide needed context for misleading statements and claims; and to confirm the factual accuracy of other assertions. In other words, volumes in this series are being crafted to clear the air surrounding some of the most contentious and misunderstood issues of our time—not just add another layer of obfuscation and uncertainty to the debate.

1

Foundational Issues Pertaining to Voter Suppression and Disenfranchisement

Unlike outright disenfranchisement, which explicitly bars individuals from voting, voter suppression often operates through indirect means that restrict access to the ballot box. A state's laws and practices pertaining to regulating elections can have the effect of suppressing the vote among certain groups or even disenfranchising certain groups altogether. Voter suppression may occur through a variety of practices and often occurs subtly and indirectly through administrative or logistical obstacles to the individual act of voting. The harder it is for a citizen to access the ballot box and exercise their constitutional right to vote, the more voter suppression occurs.

Examples of indirect state practices or laws that might suppress the vote can be found in restricting the time and/or place of voting conditions, requirements for voter registration and the procedure of registration roll purges, and restrictions on early voting or the use of no-excuse absentee ballots. State governments justify revisions to their election laws based upon sometimes-nebulous factors such as fiscal responsibility or administrative efficiency or sometimes to prevent perceived fraud in the electoral process. However, these laws and practices tend to target people with certain socioeconomic characteristics such as poverty, lack of mobility, illiteracy, and age. Thus, these laws disproportionately impact these particular groups.

The states have the primary role in setting election rules not only for state offices but also for elections pertaining to the US Congress and the Presidency. The US Constitution, in Article 1, Section 4, empowers each state to generally determine the "time, place, and manner" of elections. Article 2, Section 1 empowers the state the authority to set the conditions of appointing presidential electors as well. As such, there are a variety of different approaches to elections by the states, and sometimes there is a wide divergence of practices among states. Beyond the basic empowerment of states to set the election rules, Article

I, Section 4 also indicates that the "Congress may at any time by Law make or alter such Regulations" pertaining to elections, giving Congress some authority, and change election-related rules having previously been set by the states. This means there is also a layer of federal law to consider when accessing elections. The result is a sometimes-bewildering assortment of rules and restrictions on the subject of voting. Because of overlapping state and federal laws, there tends to be confusion among voters and citizens about things like voter registration list maintenance and voter name removals (i.e., colloquially referred to as purges), including how and when list maintenance and revisions can be lawfully done, and confusion about groups of people disenfranchised altogether (e.g., felons in some states, individuals with a mental incompetency in others) and other groups adversely impacted as a result of various state practices (or restrictions), or federal protections against certain state practices.

In addition to laws that may operate to suppress the vote, there are also several federal constitutional principles that improve access to the ballot box. Historically, these have ameliorated the effects of state-level practices that might otherwise negatively have impacted one's ability to freely vote or even outright disenfranchised voters. Hence, the Constitution has been amended to allow for the franchise through the Fifteenth, the Nineteenth, and the Twenty-Sixth Amendments.

Congress has also acted to prevent voter suppression and/or disenfranchisement through federal legislation on several occasions, most notably the Voting Rights Act of 1965, the National Voter Registration Act, and the Help America Vote Act. These core federal protections, however, have been heavily debated and in the case of the Voting Rights Act dramatically weakened by the US Supreme Court in the years since 2013.

Q1: Has there always been universal suffrage and the right to vote in America?

Answer: No. Prior to the Fifteenth and Nineteenth Amendments, there was no provision granting or guaranteeing the right of vote in the U S Constitution. The concept of universal suffrage did not exist. Instead, the original Constitution gave the states the power to determine election rules. Using this discretion, states established different criteria, such as property ownership, to limit who could vote. As a result, vast demographic segments of society were denied the right of suffrage throughout much of early US history.

The "Election Clause" in Article I, Section 4 of the Constitution states, "The Times, Places and Manner of holding Elections for Senators and Representatives, shall be prescribed in each State by the Legislature thereof." It goes on to specify that "the Congress may at any time by Law make or alter such Regulations, except as to the Places of choosing Senators." The first part of the Election Clause establishes that each state legislature has the primary authority to determine when, where, and how federal elections are held. The second part grants to the US Congress a supervisory role, allowing it to override or supplement state-issued election rules when it so chooses. Article 2, Section 1, gives states the discretion to set rules for choosing presidential electors.

The Facts: On August 7, 1787, in the waning days of the Constitutional Convention, James Madison, considered by many to be the Father of the US Constitution, stated that "the right of suffrage is one of the fundamental articles of republican Government" (Ferrand, 1911, 201). Much more recently, during oral arguments at the US Supreme Court in 2017 (in a voting rights gerrymandering case entitled *Gill v. Whitford*), Justice Ruth Bader Ginsburg characterized the right to vote as one of America's most cherished freedoms, calling it a "precious right."

The right to vote is viewed as a "fundamental" principle of republican government and is embedded in the country's self-image as the "standard bearer of democratic values on the stage of world history" (Keyssar, 2009, xix). In the American Revolution, the battle cry of "no taxation without representation" suggested an expectation of colonist suffrage in the election of individuals to represent their interests in England. The Declaration of Independence includes such sweeping statements as "all men are created equal" and asserts that the government derives "their just powers from the consent of the governed," implying the right to vote. During the American Civil War, in his Gettysburg Address delivered on November 19, 1863, President Abraham Lincoln stated that the Union war efforts were necessary so that the "government of the people, by the people, for the people, shall not perish from the earth." This statement, too, connotes that voting is a necessary part of any government "of the people" and "by the people."

Yet, this "precious right" to vote in the United States was not included in the main text of the Constitution, and the framers opted to avoid any express pronouncement regarding it. During the Constitutional Convention of 1787, in fact, the delegates struggled with which classes of individuals should be granted the right to vote. These delegates adopted the then-prevalent views that a voter needed to be independent, and that this independence was best guaranteed by being a landholder and not being beholden to the wealthy elite. This idea of voter independence and its connection to landownership had its moorings in the writings of William Blackstone in his *Commentaries on the Laws of England* (1765–9). Virtually all the early federal leaders were well read and versed in the writings of Blackstone. On the issue of voting and property ownership, Blackstone wrote as follows:

> The true reason of requiring any qualification, with regard to property, in voters, is to exclude such persons as are in so mean a situation that they are esteemed to have no will of their own. If these persons had votes, they would be tempted to dispose of them under some undue influence or other. This would give a great, an artful, or a wealthy man, a larger share in elections than is consistent with the general liberty. If it were probable that every man would give his vote freely and without influence of any kind, then, upon the true theory and genuine principles of liberty, every member of the community, however poor, should have a vote in electing those delegates, to whose charge is committed the disposal of his property, his liberty, and his life. But, since that can hardly be expected in person of indigent fortunes, or such as are under the immediate dominion of others, all popular states have been obliged to establish certain qualifications; whereby some, who are suspected to have no will of their own, are excluded from voting, in order to set other individuals, whose wills may be supposed independent, more thoroughly upon a level with each other. (Keyssar, 2009, 8–9)

During the Convention, much of the debate on voting qualifications occurred in July and August 1787. The Delegates disagreed on the issue and displayed a tendency to defer to state governments and state laws on the subject.

On August 7, 1787, Oliver Ellsworth of Connecticut (who would later serve as the third Chief Justice of the US Supreme Court) stated that "the right of suffrage was a tender point, and strongly guarded by most of the State Constitutions … [and] the States are the best judges of the circumstances and temper of their own people" (Ferrand, 1911, 201). Prominent delegate John Dickinson considered property ownership "the best guardians of liberty [as to the right to vote]; and the restriction of the right to them as a necessary defence [*sic*] against the dangerous influence of those multitudes without property & without principle, with which our Country like all others, will in time abound" (Ferrand, 1911, 202). Gouverneur Morris, another influential member of the Constitutional Convention, came closest to articulating the views of William Blackstone when he stated:

> Give the votes to people who have no property, and they will sell them to the rich who will be able to buy them. We should not confine our attention to the present moment. The time is not distant when this Country will abound with mechanics & manufacturers who will receive their bread from their employers. Will such men be the secure & faithful Guardians of liberty? (Ferrand, 1911, 202)

Morris went onto equate propertyless individuals as children not to be trusted with the right to vote. "Children do not vote. Why? [B]ecause they want prudence [and] because they have no will of their own. The ignorant & the dependent can be as little trusted with the public interest" (Ferrand, 1911, 203). Finally, as to those of "wealth & value" subject to taxations, Morris opined that "if [individuals] have wealth & value they can acquire it" [i.e., property] [and] "if not they don't deserve it [i.e., the right to vote]" (Ferrand, 1911, 203).

Even James Madison, considered to the chief architect of the Constitution and future US President, and one who considered the right of suffrage to be one of America's most fundamental articles of republican government, had a dim view of the exercise of the right to vote by the propertyless classes. Madison stated that "viewing the subject in its merits alone, *the freeholders of the Country would be the safest depositories of Republican liberty*" (italics added; Ferrand, 1911, 203). Madison further envisioned:

> In future times a great majority of the people will not only be without landed, but any other sort of, property. These will either combine under the influence of their common situation; in which case, the rights of property and the public liberty, will not be secure in their hands: or which is more probable, they will become the tools of opulence & ambition, in which case there will be equal danger on another side. (Ferrand, 1911, 204)

Therefore, what emerged from the Constitutional Convention largely failed to expand the right to vote beyond those practices of England or to codify a broader and more universal right to vote. Because the universal right to vote was not viewed as a right of citizenship as recognized under the Constitution, and since only the propertied class could exercise the right to vote in most states, "only about half of the free adult male population was eligible to vote at the time the Constitution was adapted" (Kernell et al., 2012, 492). Per the Constitution, the right to vote, if any, was wholly dependent on state laws on the topic.

If one visited the United States in the early 1800s, much like today, one would find a variety of restrictions placed upon the right to vote, with significant differences from state to state. At least six states maintained freeholder status (i.e., the requirement of property ownership) as a precondition to voting: Virginia, Massachusetts, Rhode Island, Connecticut, Delaware, and South Carolina (Keyssar, 2000, 18). Other states had variations to the freeholder prerequisite to voting. One example can be seen in North Carolina where the state allowed those who paid taxes to vote for the lower state legislative chamber but still required a fifty-acre property ownership requirement to vote in elections for the state senate (Keyssar, 2000, 17). Georgia permitted any 21-year-old white male to vote who could establish a net worth of "ten pounds value," paid taxes in the state, or was a member of any "mechanic trade" (Keyssar, 2000, 17). Only Vermont allowed voting by any white, adult, male voter regardless of property ownership (or lack thereof) or the payment of taxes (Keyssar, 2000, 17–18).

Yet, in the first five decades following the ratification of the Constitution from 1790 to 1840, state governments, one after another in rapid succession, uniformly eliminated property requirements and the payment of taxes as prerequisites to voting. "Why was the franchise broadened—and broadened so dramatically?," asked one scholar. "Why were property requirements jettisoned almost everywhere and taxpaying requirements abandoned in most states? Why were men who were not even citizens permitted to vote? Why, in sum, was the suffrage enlarged nearly everywhere in the United States, North and South, along the coast and island?" (Keyssar, 2000, 33–4).

Political scientists and historians still debate the exact reasons for this expansion. Some scholars have opined that the expansion of voting rights in this period was the culmination and "triumph of Jacksonian democracy" (Kernell, et al., 2012, 493). This expansion of voting rights occurred by virtue of the removal of property ownership requirements in order to vote, an expansion to suffrage and voting which occurred both during and in the immediate aftermath of the presidency of Andrew Jackson (1829–37). Others point to a more complex convergence of factors, including "significant changes in the social structure and social composition," the "formation of broadly based political parties that competed systematically for votes," and the appearance of "conditions under which the material interests of the enfranchised could be served by broadening the franchise" (Keyssar, 2000, 34).

This broad expansion of suffrage was not unforeseeable by the nation's founders. As early as 1776, in a letter to James Sullivan, John Adams wrote that once the populace became accustomed to a "right" to vote, there would then be no "end of it" (Keyssar, 2000, 13). Madison defended these developments in The Federalist Papers, Number 57, writing: "Who are to be the electors … ? Not the rich more than the poor, not the learned, more than the ignorant, not the haughty heirs of distinguished names, more than the humble sons of obscure and unpropitious fortune. The electors are to be the great body of the people of the United States."

Alexis de Tocqueville, in his highly influential book *Democracy in America* (1835), observed the same after visiting and studying the United States in the early 1830s. He wrote: "There is no more invariable rule in the history of society: the further electoral rights are extended, the greater is the need of extending them, for after each concession the strength of the democracy increases, and its demands increase with its strength. … Concession follows concession, and no stop can be made short of universal suffrage" (de Tocqueville, 1990, 57). Although white, adult males without landholdings benefited from the expansions to suffrage between 1790 and 1840, the right to vote was not yet extended to other groups, such as women and Black Americans.

Further Reading

de Tocqueville, Alexis. *Democracy in America*. Vol. *I*. (Originally published in 1835) Vintage, 1990.

Ferrand, Max, ed. *Records of the Constitutional Convention of 1787*. Vol. *II*. Yale University Press, 1911.

Kernell, Samuel, Gary C. Jacobson, and Thad Kousser. *The Logic of American Politics*. 5th edition. Sage & Congressional Quarterly Press, 2012, pp. 492–531.

Keyssar, Alexander. *The Right to Vote: The Contested History of Democracy in the United States*. Basic Books, 2000.

Keyssar, Alexander. *The Right to Vote: The Contested History of Democracy in the United States*. Revised edition. Basic Books, 2009.

Lichtman, Allan J. *The Embattled Vote in America: From the Founding to the Present*. Harvard University Press, 2018.

Madison, James. The Federalist No. 57 (1788), in The Federalist Papers, ed. Clinton Rossiter. New American Library (1961), p. 351.

Oral Arguments. *Gill v. Whitford*, No. 16–1161, October 3, 2017, p. 24. https://www.supremecourt.gov/oral_arguments/argument_transcripts/2017/16-1161_mjn0.pdf

Q2: Does the Fifteenth Amendment guarantee the right to vote regardless of race?

Answer: Yes, but it was not enforced right away and only became so after a lengthy period and litigation. Section 1 of the Fifteenth Amendment provides that "the right of citizens of the United States to vote shall not be denied or abridged by the United States or by any State on account of race, color, or previous condition of servitude." The Fifteenth Amendment did not absolutely guarantee the right to vote but rather indicated that states were precluded to deny the right to vote solely on those grounds. This meant that the states could still deprive the right to vote based upon other considerations. The implementation of the Fifteenth Amendment was met with widespread opposition throughout the southern United States for close to a century. Many states developed a variety of tactics to circumvent the Fifteenth Amendment and deny the vote on other grounds not prohibited by the express terms of the Fifteenth Amendment. These tactics had the intended effect of disenfranchising non-white racial groups, especially Black Americans.

The Facts: The Reconstruction-era Amendments (the Thirteenth, Fourteenth, and Fifteenth Amendments) were passed by Congress in response to the Supreme Court's infamous *Dred Scott v. Sanford* (1857) decision. Included in an opinion authored by Chief Justice Roger Taney in *Dred Scott* is what many considered to be one of the most pernicious lines of Supreme Court history, stating that Black Americans "had no rights that a white man was bound to respect." This statement clearly included the right to vote.

The Thirteenth Amendment took President Abraham Lincoln's Emancipation Proclamation and extended the prohibition of slavery nationwide. The Fourteenth Amendment ensured that no state government would deprive citizens of the right of "due process of law" or the "equal protection of laws." The Fifteenth Amendment dealt directly with the right to vote. Section 1 of the Fifteenth Amendment stated, "The right of citizens of the United States to vote shall not be denied or abridged by the United States or by any state on account of race, color, or previous condition of servitude." Section 2 of the Amendment specified that "the Congress shall have power to enforce this article by appropriate legislation."

Several northern states had permitted Black Americans to vote in the first few years of the American Revolution only to disavow that practice in the early 1800s (Keyssar, 2000). In 1855, there were five northern states that did not restrict the right to vote to just white males but allowed for Black males to vote. Those states were Massachusetts, Vermont, New Hampshire, Maine, and Rhode Island (Keyssar, 2000). However, state governments and the federal government denied Black Americans, even free Black Americans, the right to vote prior to the end of the American Civil War.

On the surface, the Fifteenth Amendment seemed to settle the issue regarding race-based restrictions to the ballot box. Immediately after the Civil War, and federal soldiers protecting polling places during Reconstruction (1865–76), Black voter registration and voting rates soared across the South. According to author Farrell Evans, more than 500,000 Black men voted during Reconstruction (Evans, 2021). The inclusion of Black Americans helped approximately two thousand Black Americans win election to state and federal offices (Evans, 2021).

The impact of these changes was evident in places like South Carolina, one of the very first places that a Black man could vote in the southern United States following the Civil War. Toward the end of the war and after Union Army occupation, over 123,000 people registered to vote in an election to approve of a constitutional convention needed to add the Fourteenth Amendment to South Carolina's constitution. Over 80,000 of those registered voters were Black Americans voting for the first time in the history of South Carolina (Burke, 2006, 863). According to historian and University of South Carolina Distinguished Professor Emeritus W. Lewis Burke:

> For the first in South Carolina history, a constitution was ratified by the voters, and the majority of those voters were black. For the first time in the state's history, black candidates were elected to office. Numerous Black Americans were elected to local offices, a black majority was elected to the State House of Representatives, and ten Black Americans were elected to the state Senate. Francis L. Cardozo was elected secretary of state, becoming the first African American elected to any statewide office in the nation. (Burke, 2006, 863–4)

These electoral successes in integrating the ballot were not limited to South Carolina. Evidence of racial integration in the voting booth and ballot box could be seen throughout the South. In Louisiana, more than 130,000 Black Americans were registered to vote by 1896, and in Alabama, over 180,000 Black Americans were registered to vote in the same period (Anderson, 2020, 4).

However, at the end of Reconstruction, and when federal troops were pulled out of the South through the Compromise of 1876, election protection for Black voters disappeared. This left Black Americans subject to the whims and prejudices of local sheriffs and belligerent townspeople. Townspeople harassed and threatened violence toward those Black voters who had previously attempted to exercise their right to vote. As author Carol Anderson wrote in her book *One Person, No Vote*, "what states could not accomplish by law, they were more than willing to achieve by violence. The wholesale slaughter of African Americans in Colfax, Louisiana (1873), Wilmington, North Carolina (1898), and Ocoee, Florida (1920) resulted in the loss of hundreds of lives simply because whites were enraged that black people had voted" (Anderson, 2020, 14). And this does not even consider the tens of thousands who stayed home to protect themselves and their families against violence. While these acts of violence and intimation are tragically too numerous to delineate, Anderson describes one such incident in Taylor County, Georgia, in 1946. In Anderson's retelling of the incident, whites in the county made numerous verbal threats leading up to a primary election and even posted signs advising Black Americans not to vote. One such sign nailed to a church door read: "The first Negro to vote will never vote again" (Anderson, 2020, 15). Second World War combat veteran Maceo Snipes cast his ballot in July 1946. Several days later, he was summoned out of his house by a mob and killed on his front porch because he tried to exercise his right to vote—a freedom he fought for in the battlefields of Europe. According to Anderson, Snipes was the only Black voter to cast a ballot in that county's election (Anderson, 2020, 15).

In addition to the extrajudicial violence and terrorism, virtually every state in the South passed laws to circumvent the spirit and purpose of the Fifteenth Amendment. While the Fifteenth Amendment specified that no state shall abridge the right to vote "on account of race, color, or previous condition of servitude," this did not stop states from contriving other methods of abridging or denying the right to vote to Black Americans. These methods included the use of poll taxes, literacy tests, a so-called understanding test (often utilized in concert with literacy tests), and "grandfather" exemption clauses. While seemingly race neutral on their face, these various mechanisms were implemented to eviscerate the Black vote down to almost nonexistent levels.

Adopted by all eleven states comprising the former Confederacy, the poll tax required payment of a fee, usually one or two dollars, to vote. While this might not sound like much money in 2025, in the late 1800s, such a fee might discourage a father who struggled to put food on the table for his family. As historian C. Vann Woodward pointed out, additional barriers were created in the procedures for paying the poll tax, which were "artfully devised to discourage payment" (Woodward, 1966, 84). These included unclear payment instructions and the collection of fees by law enforcement, which intimidated many potential voters, especially since many Black voters who showed up at the sheriff's office were subject to physical abuse (Anderson, 2020, 8; Woodward, 1966, 84). Anderson recounts the intimidation suffered by Black voters trying to register at police stations:

> Over and over again those who tried to register to vote would be photographed by the police and harassed and threatened. … They would soon receive a visit from the sheriff, endure arrest on some trumped-up charge, and face jail time or an exorbitant fine. In Rankin County, Mississippi, the sheriff stopped a black man from registering to vote at the courthouse by beating him. "I hit him and kept on hitting him," the sheriff bragged, "and if he hadn't run I would have kept on hitting him." The beating was not just about stopping this one man; "it was meant to send a message" that this "was the fate for others seeking this precious right." (Anderson, 2020, 14)

The poll tax was also assessed months before the actual election and sometimes as far in advance as two full years. As described by one voter, "paying a poll tax in February to vote in November is to most folks in Texas like buying a ticket to a show nine months ahead of time, and before you know who's playing or really what the thing is all about. It is easy to forget to do, too" (Anderson, 2020, 9). Finally, the poll tax was cumulative in the sense that payment was due every year a person was eligible to vote, even if the person did not vote. As described by Anderson, "if after twenty years of not voting or having been unable to vote, an African American in Alabama in 1944 was finally able to pay, he or she would need not $1.50 to do so but rather $30," which would be the equivalent of a paying a poll tax of $538.90 in 2025. Given that many sharecroppers, mechanics, farm hands, and other manual laborers might be paid than $100 for the year, it is no wonder why many Black voters decided to forego the vote (Anderson, 2020, 9).

Literacy tests and educational requirements were another method to disenfranchise Black voters in the South. Because of unfunded or nonexistent schools for Black children, a large segment of the Black population in the late 1800s and early 1900s were illiterate. According to W. Lewis Burke, roughly 76 percent of southern Black Americans could not read in the 1880s (Burke, 2006). As there were illiterate white voters as well, many states augmented the literacy test with an "understanding" test. This allowed prospective illiterate white voters to explain their knowledge of a particular passage in a way that would ensure that they passed the test. Of course, the test administrators were white, and the tests were administered subjectively. Many denied Black would-be voters complained that simple text or questions would be asked to white applicants, but aspiring Black voters would be given obscure or overly convoluted questions to answer. As one civil rights lawyer described at the time, "Local boards or registrars readily found highly educated Negroes unable to pass literacy tests and just as readily registered illiterate or semiliterate whites. When all else failed, local registrars resorted to slow-downs, in which one or two Negroes per day were permitted to take tests, or suddenly resigned, leaving no registration machinery available" (Miller, 1966, 299–300).

Finally, so-called grandfather clauses exempted whites from any new voting requirements. Such clauses were as simple as a provision in the state code specifying that "any man eligible to vote before 1867 (or his descendants) is exempt" from any new voting requirements that might be enacted. Phrased another way, if a prospective voter's father or grandfather had voted prior to 1867, no literacy text was required and/or no poll tax was due Practically speaking, this meant that illiterate or poor whites (who would have failed literacy test or could not pay the poll tax) could still register if their ancestors voted before the Civil War. Grandfather clauses allowed white individuals to vote, while denying the exact same right to vote to similarly situated Black individuals.

The result of these state laws circumventing the Fifteenth Amendment was the disenfranchisement and decimation the Black vote. A few examples will illustrate this point. In Louisiana, while more than 130,000 Black Americans were registered to vote in 1896, that number dropped to 1,324 by 1904 (Anderson, 2020, 4; Woodward, 1966, 85). In 1896, registered Black voters were a majority in twenty-six different parishes in the state, but by 1900, none (Woodward, 1966, 85). Similarly, in Alabama, 180,000 Black Americans registered to vote plummeted to fewer than 3,000 in less than three years (Anderson, 2020, 4). In Mississippi and Alabama, less than 2 percent of all eligible Black voters were registered to vote (Evans, 2021). Finally, across the Deep South in 1953, "'eleven counties where the black population equaled or exceeded that of whites' had only 1.3 percent of all eligible Black Americans registered to vote. Two counties had no African American voters at all" (Anderson, 2020, 7).

In response to the problems with Black and other minority voter disenfranchisement in the South, Congress promulgated the Voting Rights Act of 1965, which finally and successfully prompted the expansion of the electorate as it relates to minority groups. The full scope of the Voting Rights Act will be covered in Question 5 in this book, and the Supreme Court's controversial decision regarding the Voting Rights Act in *Shelby County v. Holder* (2013) will be covered in Question 6.

Poll taxes, literacy tests, and grandfather clauses eventually lost favor and were curtailed by legislation and court decisions in the twentieth century. The Twenty-Fourth Amendment (ratified in 1964) abolished the use of poll taxes in any federal election. In *Harper v. Virginia State Board of Elections*, 383 U.S.

663 (1966), the Supreme Court ruled that poll taxes to vote for local officials in non-federal elections was also impermissible. The Voting Rights Act (1965) prohibited the use of literacy tests. And, in *Guinn v. United States*, 238 U.S. 347 (1915), the same Court that had held the use of literacy tests to be constitutional overturned the use of grandfather clauses.

Further Reading

Anderson, Carol. *One Person, No Vote: How Voter Suppression Is Destroying Our Democracy*. Bloomsbury Publishing, 2020.

Bentele, Keith G., and Erin E. O'Brien. "Jim Crow 2.0? Why States Consider and Adopt Restrictive Voter Access Policies." *Perspectives on Politics, American Political Science Association, 11*, no. 4 (December 2013), 1088–116.

Burke, W. Lewis. "Killing, Cheating, Legislating, and Lying: A History of Voting Rights in South Carolina after the Civil War." *University of South Carolina Law Review, 57* (2006), 859–88.

Evans, Farrell. "How Jim Crow-Era Laws Suppressed the African American Vote for Generations: In the Wake of the Passage of the 15th Amendment and Reconstruction, Several Southern States Enacted Laws That Restricted Black Americans' Access to Voting." History.com, 2021. https://www.history.com/articles/jim-crow-laws-black-vote

Gillette, William. *The Right to Vote: Politics and the Passage of the Fifteenth Amendment.* Johns Hopkins University Press, 1965.

Keyssar, Alexander. *The Right to Vote: The Contested History of Democracy in the United States*. Basic Books, 2000.

Kousser, J. Morgan. *The Shaping of Southern Politics: Suffrage Restriction and the Establishment of the One-Party South, 1880–1910*. Yale University Press, 1974.

Lineberry, Robert L., and George C. Edwards III. *Government in America: People, Politics, and Policy*. 4th edition. Scott, Foresman, 1989, pp. 184–90, 391–418.

Miller, Loren. *The Petitioners: The Story of the Supreme Court of the United States and the Negro*. Pantheon Books, 1966.

Teach Democracy. "BRIA 12 2 b Race and Voting in the Segregated South." Accessed May 14, 2025. https://teachdemocracy.org/bill-of-rights-in-action/bria-12-2-b-race-and-voting-in-the-segregated-south

Valelly, Richard M. *The Two Reconstructions: The Struggle for Black Enfranchisement.* University of Chicago Press, 2004.

Woodward, C. Vann. *The Strange Career of Jim Crow*. Oxford University Press, 1966.

Q3: Have women always enjoyed the right to vote?

Answer: No. Women were excluded from the right to vote until the ratification of the Nineteenth Amendment on August 18, 1920. The first clause of the Nineteenth Amendment states that "the right of citizens of the United States to vote shall not be denied or abridged by the United States or by any State on account of sex." Like the Fifteenth Amendment before it, the Nineteenth Amendment did not affirmatively bestow a right to vote upon women, but rather only precluded state governments from denying the right to vote based upon gender, leaving open the possibility that states would use other factors as proxies to deny women the vote. Tellingly, women composed a minority of overall voters from 1920 to 1980.

The Facts: Women clearly constituted the biggest segment of adults disenfranchised in the first half of US history. It was only with the passage and ratification of the Nineteenth Amendment in 1920 that the Constitution was expanded to include the right to vote in America "regardless of sex." The Nineteenth Amendment immediately doubled the voting electorate after its ratification, at least in theory. Generally speaking, women did not meet with the same level of overt opposition and stonewalling by state governments that Black citizens experienced with the implementation of the Fifteenth Amendment. However, Black women in the South were subject to the same "Jim Crow" types of disenfranchisements discussed in Question 2. Even for some white women, in states hostile to women voting, or when a prospective woman voter encountered a prejudiced misogynistic male poll worker, the right to vote could be denied. White women in some states were disenfranchised by poll taxes and literacy tests as well as other subtle disenfranchisement efforts. Not until the 1980s would female voters surpass male voters at the ballot box.

Section 1 of the Nineteenth Amendment provides that "the right of citizens of the United States to vote shall not be denied or abridged by the United States or by any state on account of sex." Like each of the three Reconstruction-era Amendments (Thirteenth, Fourteenth, and Fifteenth), the Nineteenth Amendment also contains an additional provision that "Congress shall have power to enforce this article by appropriate legislation." As noted by historian Christine Stansell, the Nineteenth Amendment represented the "single greatest act of mass enfranchisement" in American history (Graves, 2020). Distinguished Professor Emerita Nancy Hewitt concurred, stating that the Nineteenth

Amendment in theory "added the largest number of voters to the electorate of any measure in American history" (Hewitt, 2020).

Despite Abigail Adams plea to John Adams during the Continental Congress to "remember the ladies," women were largely forgotten and excluded as part of the US electorate for well over a century. In the early years of lobbying for the right to vote, women worked with Republican leaders and abolitionists to include gender neutral language in the text of the Fifteenth Amendment. These efforts were rebuffed even by some civil rights advocates. In the words of abolitionist Wendell Phillips (known as the "Golden Trumpet" for his passionate abolitionist rhetoric), activists should focus on only "one question at a time" and "this hour belongs to the negro" (Keyssar, 2000, 177). Years of campaigning and hard work by suffragettes ensued, finally ensuring the ratification of the Nineteenth Amendment in 1920.

As suggested by Stansell, the immediate effect of the Nineteenth Amendment was a massive enlargement of those Americans eligible to vote. Because of the inclusion of women, the overall size of the electorate increased by over eight million in 1920. And yet, while many women did vote in that election, their numbers were a far cry from the twenty-six million newly eligible women voters. As author Meilan Solly wrote, contemporary studies of the 1920 election have suggested that only around 36 percent of eligible women voted, compared with 68 percent of eligible men (Solly, 2020). One newspaper ran the headline "Is Woman Suffrage a Failure?" in 1924 (Solly, 2020). In his book *The Right to Vote* (2000), Alexander Keyssar wrote that, despite the huge influx of potential new voters, "it is a very well-known irony in American history that politics did not change very dramatically after women were enfranchised" (Keyssar, 2000, 218).

Women voters continued to lag far behind their male counterparts until the 1980s, but since that decade, women have outpaced men. What were the reasons for the initial lower voter turnout among female voters after the ratification of the Nineteenth Amendment? In the decades after 1920, various forces, some subtle and some overt, acted to disenfranchise or suppress women's right to vote, these included legal and political limitations as well as social and cultural norms.

While some states rushed to include women as registered voters, many other states did not. Some of the same tools (e.g., poll taxes, literacy tests) that states used to disenfranchise Black voters in the South and to circumvent the spirit of the Fifteenth Amendment were also utilized to disenfranchise female voters. For example, Arkansas, Georgia, Mississippi, and South Carolina did not permit women to vote in the 1920 presidential election because deadlines to register or pay the required poll taxes had already expired by August 1920 (Corder and

Wolbrecht, 2021). In addition to a literacy text, "Massachusetts added a poll tax, while Connecticut piled on a morals clause and a long residency requirement" as a means of keeping the number of women voters low (Corder and Wolbrecht, 2021). The implementation of these measures in Connecticut and Massachusetts in 1920 resulted in a female turnout barely over 20 percent, which was far below the turnout in many other states post-1920 (Corder and Wolbrecht, 2021).

The Nineteenth Amendment did little to help Black women in southern states, as these potential voters were subject to same barrage of lengthy residency clauses, literacy tests, poll taxes, and even "morals" qualifications to which Black males were subject. The tests were administered and the rules enforced by the same election officials who hindered voting access for Black men. The result was a disproportionate negative impact on Black women voters as compared to white women.

Some states failed to fund and allocate registrars and poll workers needed to register the large influx of new voters. Evidence from Richmond, Virginia, in 1920 shows that election officials added staff to handle the surge of white women registrants but refused to add staff for the registration of Black women. The result was that Black women were forced to wait in long lines and were subjected to rigorous literacy tests (Corder and Wolbrecht, 2021). These practices resulted in a 5 percent turnout for women voters in Virginia, as compared to other states like Kentucky that reported a 50 percent turnout (Corder and Wolbrecht, 2021). The same disenfranchisement methods foisted upon Black men of the South seemed to work with equally efficiency as it related to Black women. Not until the Voting Rights Act of 1965 were literacy tests and similar devices outlawed.

The Expatriation Act of 1907 was the subject of a final little-known legal barrier to women's voting in the 1920s. Under the law, if a woman married a man who was not a US citizen, her citizenship might be revoked. The loss of citizenship also meant the loss of the right to vote. Tens of thousands of women who married foreign nationals in the early twentieth century suffered revocation of citizenship, while American men who married foreign women did not (Brown, 2017). Tens of thousands of women found themselves ineligible to vote in 1920 because of this legislation. It was not until Congress passed the Cable Act in 1922 that the law was revised to allow women to keep their citizenship upon marriage to an alien.

Much like with the implementation of the Fifteenth Amendment for Black Americans, women had won the right to vote in principle, but not in fact. Various state laws continued to treat potential women voters differently than men even after ratification of the Nineteenth Amendment. The struggle to operationalize the full meaning of the amendment occurred over an extended period.

Further Reading

American Experience. "Not All Women Gained the Vote in 1920." July 6, 2020. https://www.pbs.org/wgbh/americanexperience/features/vote-not-all-women-gained-right-to-vote-in-1920/

Anderson, Carol. *One Person, No Vote: How Voter Suppression Is Destroying Our Democracy*. Bloomsbury Publishing, 2020.

Brown, Tanya Ballard. "That Time American Women Lost Their Citizenship Because They Married Foreigners." NPR: Code Switch, March 17, 2017. https://www.npr.org/sections/codeswitch/2017/03/17/520517665/that-time-american-women-lost-their-citizenship-because-they-married-foreigners

Cahill, Cathleen D. *Recasting the Vote: How Women of Color Transformed the Suffrage Movement*. University of North Carolina Press, 2020.

Corder, J. Kevin, and Christian Wolbrecht. "Did Women Vote Once They Had the Opportunity?" American Bar Association, October 21, 2021. https://www.americanbar.org/groups/public_education/publications/insights-on-law-and-society/volume-20/issue-1/did-women-vote-once-they-had-the-opportunity-/

Graves, Kristina. "Women's Political Participation after 1920: Myth and Reality." National Women's History Museum, September 10, 2020. https://www.womenshistory.org/articles/womens-political-participation-after-1920-myth-and-reality

Hewitt, Nancy. "What Did Ratification of the 19th Amendment Mean to Women?" Rutgers-Newark School of Arts and Sciences, August 26, 2020. https://sas.rutgers.edu/about/news/faculty/faculty-news-detail/what-did-ratification-of-the-19th-amendment-mean-towomen

HistoryHub. "How Many Women Voted in the 1920 Presidential Election?" March 11, 2019. https://historyhub.history.gov/suffragist/f/discussions/27521/how-many-women-voted-in-the-1920-presidential-election

Keyssar, Alexander. *The Right to Vote: The Contested History of Democracy in the United States*. Basic Books, 2000.

Solly, Meilan. "What the First Women Voters Experienced When Registering for the 1920 Election." *Smithsonian Magazine*, July 30, 2020. https://www.smithsonianmag.com/history/what-first-women-voters-experienced-when-registering-1920-election-180975435/

Terborg-Penn, Rosalyn. *African American Women in the Struggle for the Vote, 1850–1920*. Indiana University Press, 1998.

Tetrault, Lisa. *The Myth of Seneca Falls: Memory and the Women's Suffrage Movement, 1848–1898*. University of North Carolina Press, 2014.

Ware, Susan. *Why They Marched: Untold Stories of the Women Who Fought for the Right to Vote*. The Belknap Press of Harvard University Press, 2019.

Wolbrecht, Christina, and J. Kevin Corder. *A Century of Votes for Women: American Elections since Suffrage*. Cambridge University Press, 2020.

Q4: Can examples of significant voter fraud be found in US history?

Answer: Unfortunately, yes, there have been numerous examples of voter fraud throughout US history. Further, multiple historians and scholars have argued that not only did instances of voter fraud occur, but the scope of some fraud also impacted electoral results and the ultimate "winners" and "losers" of certain races. However, instances of voter fraud waned significantly after the Watergate scandal (1972–4), and there has been no evidence to suggest that post-Watergate voter fraud (if it did exist) was sufficiently large in scope to influence electoral results. (See Question 8 regarding claims of voter fraud in the first two decades of the twenty-first century and the 2020 election in particular.)

The Facts: Fraud has always existed at some level in elections in the United States. To completely deny the existence of voter fraud is to suggest a superficial (or nonexistent) reading of American history. Examples of bribery, voter impersonation, ballot stuffing, and the like can be found from even before the United States became a country. In 1758, future president George Washington ran for a seat in the Virginia House of Burgesses, and during his campaign saw to it "that the 391 voters and their friends received 160 gallons of rum, beer, and cider on election day" (Boller, 1984, 6). The papers derisively said Washington was "swilling the planters with bumbo," and one paper reported that "the Voice of the People, was the Voice of Grog" (Boller, 1984, 6).

In the 1800s, in large cities, a practice called "cooping" was an unfortunate occurrence. Cooping involved criminal gangs working with rogue political actors to prey upon vulnerable individuals (alcoholics, immigrants, the homeless). These individuals would be surreptitiously drugged or plied with drinks to the point of gross inebriation and moved around to different political polling locations. The largely incapacitated individuals were made to vote multiple times under different names and aliases, often being changed into different clothes, and sometimes given wigs, to further ensure the success of the fraud. The term "cooping" derived from the practice of imprisoning these unfortunate individuals in small rooms, or coops, where more drugs or alcohol could be administered and clothes could be changed before moving the person onto a different polling station. During the 1800s, people were also being unjustly prosecuted for voter fraud, with officials employing "heavy-handed tactics to intimidate voters, especially immigrants" (Tumulty, 2024).

The famous writer Edgar Allen Poe may have been a victim of cooping, leading to his death on October 7, 1849. Poe was found in a delirious state outside a polling place in Baltimore on the day of the election, purportedly wearing someone else's poor-quality clothes that did not fit properly. He was largely incoherent and unable to explain his situation. Taken to a local hospital, he died a few days later without ever being able to describe what had happened to him. The possibility of Poe being a victim of the practice of cooping was put forth shortly after his death and discussed in various sources (Walsh, 1998).

In the infamous Rutherford B. Hayes (Republican) and Samuel Tilden (Democrat) presidential election of 1876, fraud was seen at levels arguably never witnessed before in the United States. Samuel Tilden had won the popular vote, and he was leading Rutherford B. Hayes in the Electoral College as well, with Tilden being only a single vote short of being elected president. However, because of massive fraud and electoral shenanigans, the electoral votes for three states (South Carolina, Florida, and Louisiana) were in dispute. The states carried a total of twenty electoral votes. If Tilden won just one of these states, he would win the presidency. Hayes needed all three to secure victory. But "palpable frauds" were occurring (Boller, 1984, 135). In each of the three contested states, "the voting had been accompanied by bribery, forgery, violence, intimidation, and ballot-box stuffing" (Boller, 1984, 135). Ultimately Congress set up an Electoral Commission, composed of eight Republicans and seven Democrats. Despite Tilden needing only one of the twenty electoral votes to be elected president, the Electoral Commission (by a vote of eight to seven along party lines) gave all twenty votes to Republican Rutherford Hayes, making Hayes the president. As a result, critics called Hayes names such as "Rutherfraud Hayes," "the Fraudulent President," the "Usurper," and the "Boss Thief" (Boller, 1984, 137).

President Chester A. Arthur (1881–5) was known as a "spoilsman's spoilsman," meaning that he was adept at participating in a system of rewards for political support (Boller, 1984, 173). Before he eventually became vice president and then president after the assassination of President James Garfield, Arthur had first come to prominence as the collector of the Port of New York. This position involved collecting customs duties and managing thousands of employees, and Arthur became a key player in US Senator Roscoe Conkling's notorious New York political machine, known for its egregious graft, bribery, and fraudulent practices. A few months before Garfield's assassination, Vice-President Elect Arthur drew national attention with a speech he gave referencing the usage of fraudulent voters and paid votes in the 1880 Presidential election of the Garfield-Arthur ticket, specifically in winning Indiana, which leaned Democratic, for the Republican Party. Arthur jokingly remarked, "I don't think we had better go into the minute secrets of the campaign, so far as I know them, … still if I should get to going about the secrets of the campaign, there is no saying what I might say to make trouble between now and the fourth of March" (when the inauguration was to occur) (Boller, 1984, 173–4). Arthur further remarked that "Indiana was really, I suppose, a Democratic State. It has always been put down in the book as a State that might be carried by close and careful and perfect organization and a great deal of …, " but he did not finish the sentence. The listening crowd finished it for him, yelling "soap" (meaning purchased votes), after which Arthur reportedly just laughed (Boller, 1984, 174).

In the 1960 election between John F. Kennedy and Richard Nixon, Kennedy won by a razor thin margin. The outcome separating Kennedy and Nixon was a mere difference of slightly over 100,000 votes out of roughly 68 million votes cast or less than one-tenth of 1 percent (Cummings, 2007, 218). Some Republicans charged fraud in voting, and *New York Herald Tribune* writer Earl Mazo began publishing a series of investigatory stories alleging fraud, including strong evidence of fraud in Texas and Illinois. In Texas, according to Mazo, there was widespread evidence of stolen ballots, dead men voting, and phony voting registrations (Cummings, 2007, 218). Mazo wrote "a minimum of 10,000 votes for the Kennedy Johnson ticket were simply nonexistent," with several polling stations reporting thousands more votes than they had registered voters (Cummings, 2007, 218). In Illinois, Mazo discovered evidence of cash payments for votes, duplicate voting, and pre-primed ballot machines, which would automatically record three votes for every one vote cast (Cummings, 2007, 219). Mazo had published four investigatory articles out of a proposed twelve-part series. However, Nixon, to his credit, met with Mazo and convinced him to stop the investigation, reportedly saying, "Earl, no one steals the presidency of the United States," and further explaining how impractical such a claim would be given the size of the country, as well as the damage that would be done to the nation's reputation abroad (Boller, 1984, 300). No conclusive evidence pointed to fraud to an extent that would have influenced the results of the election.

Perhaps one of the most well-known examples of election fraud also involved Richard Nixon. About six months after his victory over George McGovern in 1972, details began to emerge of a break-in at the Democratic National Committee headquarters at the Watergate complex in Washington, DC, orchestrated by the Committee to Re-Elect the President (CREEP). During the ensuing investigations in 1973 and 1974, "the efforts of grant juries, investigative reports, and Congressional committees looking into the Watergate incident gradually unraveled an unsavory tale of intimidation, forgery, sabotage, bribery, and perjury running in the White House itself" (Boller, 1984, 338).

Yet, in the decade before the Watergate scandal, "the legal underpinnings of the right to vote were transformed more dramatically than they had been at any earlier point in the nation's history" (Keyssar, 2000, 256). This transformation came about, in large part, because of the passage of the Voting Rights Act of 1965, explored in the next question (Question 5) in this book. As a result of this legislation, and corresponding enforcement actions under the legislation, "virtually all formal restrictions on the suffrage rights of adult citizens were swept away, and the federal government assumed full responsibility for protecting and guaranteeing those rights" (Keyssar, 2000, 256).

Further Reading

Boller, Paul F., Jr. *Presidential Campaigns.* Oxford University Press, 1984.

Cummings, Joseph. *Anything for a Vote: Dirty Tricks, Cheap Shots, and October Surprises in U.S. Presidential Campaigns.* Quirk Books, 2007.

Keyssar, Alexander. *The Right to Vote: The Contested History of Democracy in the United States.* Basic Books, 2000.

Silverman, Kenneth. *Edgar A. Poe: Mournful and Never-Ending Remembrance.* Harper Perennial, 1991.

Tumulty, Karen. "Voter Fraud Hysteria Isn't New. Just Ask My Ancestors." *The Washington Post,* October 8, 2024. https://www.washingtonpost.com/opinions/2024/10/07/immigrants-texas-vote-fraud-ken-paxton/

Walsh, John Evangelist. *Midnight Dreary: The Mysterious Death of Edgar Allan Poe.* St. Martin's Press, 1998.

Q5: Was the Voting Rights Act of 1965 passed to combat voter disenfranchisement and voter suppression?

Answer: Yes. The Voting Rights Act of 1965 was desperately needed to curb the almost complete disenfranchisement of otherwise eligible Black voters throughout the southern United States (and a few isolated pockets elsewhere) before 1965. The legislation was heralded as the "crown jewel" of the Civil Rights Movement (Lopez, 2015) and President Lyndon B. Johnson declared it "one of the most monumental laws in the entire history of American freedom" (Department of Justice, 2024).

The Facts: The following simple statistics show the overall effectiveness of the Voting Rights Act in a relatively short time period. In 1957 (before enactment), 25 percent of eligible Black Americans in the South were registered to vote. By 1970, five years after enactment, this number had risen to 65 percent (Gordon, 1970, 325). In thirteen years, registration of eligible Black voters had improved by 40 percent.

Despite the promises and hopes in ratifying the Fifteenth Amendment in 1870, the end of Reconstruction in the southern states ushered in the lowest point of race relations in the post-Civil War South. This directly resulted in the evisceration of the right to vote for southern Black Americans. Several examples illustrate the depth of the problem prior to 1965 and the corresponding need for the Voting Rights Act. In Selma, Alabama, out of approximately 15,000 eligible Black voters, only 335 individuals were registered to vote (Gordon, 1970, 325). In Dallas County, Alabama (a county with over 50 percent Black residents) only 156 of 15,000 eligible Black voters were registered before 1965 (Joint Center for Political and Economic Studies, 2019). Because of poll taxes, literacy tests, and other state ploys, the number of registered Black Americans fell from 130,334 in 1896 to a mere 1,342 in 1904 (Woodward, 1966, 85). In Alabama, the number of Black Americans registered to vote plummeted from 180,000 to less than 3,000 in less than three years after implementation of these disenfranchisement measures (Anderson, 2020, 4). The fact that less than 2 percent of all eligible Black voters were registered to vote in Alabama (Evans, 2021) demonstrates the purpose and effectiveness of the state's efforts and the need for the Voters Rights Act. Similarly, registered Black voters in Louisiana dropped from 44.8 percent in 1896 to a slight 4 percent by 1900 (ACLU, 2025). Finally, across the Deep South in 1953, "'eleven counties where the Black population equaled or exceeded that of whites' had only 1.3 percent of all eligible Black Americans registered to vote. Two counties had no African American voters at all" (Anderson, 2020, 7).

In another survey completed by the US Civil Rights Commission, the Commission selected seventeen "black belt" counties wherein Black Americans made up a clear majority of the population. Despite a large Black population, the Commission reported that only 3 percent of the Black Americans were registered to vote in these counties (Curry, et al., 2003, 267). But after the Voting Rights Act passed in 1965, registrations skyrocketed throughout the South. For instance, in Mississippi, only 6.7 percent of Black Americans were registered to vote in

1965, but this number shot up over forty percentage points to a 59.8 percent registration rate by 1967 (Lopez, 2015) and up to 67.4 percent by 1976 (Curry, et al., 2003, 268). From 1964 through 1976, the following states substantially increased their voter registering of Black voters: Alabama (23 in 1964 to 58.1 percent in 1976); Georgia (44 in 1964 to 56.3 percent in 1976); Louisiana (32 in 1964 to 63.9 percent in 1976); Mississippi (6.7 in 1964 to 67.4 percent in 1976); South Carolina (38.8 in 1964 to 60.6 percent in 1976); and Virginia (45.7 in 1964 to 60.7 percent in 1976) (Curry, et al., 2003, 268).

Congress (and the country) became aware of the abysmal registration figures in the early 1960s. The low rates became a focus of the Civil Rights Movement and various voter registration efforts. Coming on the heels of the Civil Rights Act of 1964, the Voting Rights Act of 1965 was passed by Congress on August 6, 1965. As the Supreme Court explained in *South Carolina v. Katzenbach*, 383 U.S. 301, 327–8 (1966), after "nearly a century of systematic resistance" to the Fifteenth Amendment, Congress finally adopted "strong medicine" that "shift[ed] the advantage of time and inertia from the perpetrators of evil to its victims." The Voting Rights Act gave the federal government the power to review and reject state schemes that were discriminatory in nature before states could implement their law. The Voting Rights Act also empowered the federal government and private actors with the power to enforce fair voting practices and challenge discriminating voting practices through the courts. While all the provisions of the legislation cannot be detailed here, the major sections protecting against voter disenfranchisement and suppression are briefly highlighted in the following paragraphs, illustrating the potency of this law.

Section 2 of the Act restated the Fifteenth Amendment in a sweeping statement indicating that any state or local voting law or procedure that discriminated on the basis of race or color was prohibited and that it was a criminal offense for individuals to engage in such voting discrimination. Section 2 also authorized both the Department of Justice and private citizens to challenge discriminatory voting laws in any federal district court. As a result of Section 2, other methods of disenfranchisement such as racially biased voter purges and racially gerrymandered districts, among other things, could be challenged in federal court after 1965.

Section 4 of the Voting Rights Act was meant to police and supervise the historically worst offenders among the state and local governments. That is, all states and localities with deep histories of disenfranchising minority voters would be subject to several federal remedial measures (measures that were in effect for over a half-century thereafter). Section 4A of the Act terminated all literacy tests and similar voting tests meant to circumvent the plain meaning of the Fifteenth Amendment and to disqualify minority voters. Most of the effected jurisdictions under Section 4A were in the Deep South and included Alabama, Georgia, Florida, Louisiana, Mississippi, South Carolina, North Carolina, and several parts of other states (e.g., South Dakota, New York, Arizona) where Black registration had been abysmally low due to discriminatory practices. States that employed these measures had to eliminate all their discriminatory laws and conduct elections in a racially neutral fashion. Elections could also be directly observed by federal officials if deemed necessary.

The legislation also contained a test to determine what jurisdictions were subject to deeper scrutiny by the federal government. Section 4(b) contained a "coverage formula" specifying that any state or county that, in November 1964, had maintained a "test or device" (e.g., a literacy or knowledge test) as a prerequisite to voting and had voter registration or turnout below 50 percent of those old enough to vote in the 1964 presidential election, was deemed a "covered" jurisdiction. While the elimination of literacy tests applied in each of the targeted jurisdictions, Congress also amended the Voting Rights Act in 1970 to extend this ban nationwide to every jurisdiction throughout the United States. Like Section 2, Section 4 allowed for the Department of Justice and private citizens to challenge state created proxy assessments for the literacy tests in court (e.g., the usage of "grandfather clauses") or through a "preclearance procedure."

The preclearance procedure was delineated in Section 5. Section 5 specified that any covered jurisdiction (as defined under Section 4) was required to obtain federal approval before implementing any changes to its existing voting-related laws. The provision meant that covered states and counties had to submit all proposed changes to the Department of Justice or to a federal court in Washington, DC, for approval. Preclearance applied regardless of the type of change proposed by the state/county (e.g., a new voter registration rule, a different polling place location, a redistricting plan, changes to voter identification laws, etc.). The proposed plan would need to be certified, ensuring that the change was not discriminatory, before the jurisdiction could adopt the changed voting plan.

Under Section 5, the Department of Justice reviewed thousands of proposed changes to voting laws in the covered states/jurisdictions before the changes could be implemented. Between 1965 and 2006, Department of Justice objected to over a thousand proposed voting changes that it found would have discriminated against minority voters, blocking those laws from ever taking effect. Examples of blocked laws under preclearance ranged from racially discriminatory redistricting plans that diluted Black voting strength to restrictive voter identification laws that would disproportionately burden minority voters

(Brennan Center, 2013; Strossen, 2006). According to Department of Justice, because of the Section 5 pre-clearance requirement, "more than 800 proposed changes were altered or withdrawn in the period after 1982 alone" (Department of Justice, 2023).

And while Sections 2–5 received a lion share of the focus, other provisions of the Act are also relevant in policing against disenfranchisement or voter suppression. Sections 6 and 7 authorized the appointment of federal voting examiners (through the US Civil Service Commission) in covered areas to directly take over voter registration if local officials refused to register eligible Black voters. The US Attorney General was also empowered to send federal observers to monitor polling places and ensure elections were conducted fairly.

Section 10 of the Act addressed poll taxes. While the Voting Rights Act did not outright ban poll taxes in state elections (the Twenty-Fourth Amendment banned poll taxes in federal elections in 1964 but did not address elections for state government officials), Congress declared in Section 10 that poll taxes were an unjust barrier and instructed the Department of Justice to challenge those laws. This in turn led to the Supreme Court's 1966 decision in *Harper v. Virginia Board of Elections*, wherein the Court deemed state poll taxes to be unconstitutional. Section 11 of the Act imposed criminal penalties for intimidation, threats, or coercion aimed at interfering with someone's right to vote and made it a federal offense to harass or retaliate against voters (or would-be voters).

The Voting Rights Act was amended and extended multiple times after 1965, with notable amendments to the law occurring in 1970, 1975, 1982, 1992, and 2006 that added protections for voters into the statute and extended how long the law would be in effect. Some notable provisions included in these various amendments to the Voting Rights Act included a ban on literacy tests nationwide, lowering the voting age to 18 years in federal elections (a protection made mute by passage of the Twenty-Sixth Amendment in 1971), increasing the number of pre-clearance states and counties based upon low turnout in the 1968 election, and requiring bilingual ballots in places with large non-English-speaking populations. The requirement for bilingual ballots and registration matters illustrates that Voting Rights Act protections were meant to protect other marginalized groups beyond Black Americans and extend to such groups as Native Americans, Asian Americans, and Alaskan Natives, groups who historically faced English-only language voting barriers.

Facing a 2007 expiration of Section 5, Congress conducted extensive hearings and found that while great progress had been made, voting discrimination was "not yet fully conquered." The legislative record included roughly 15,000 pages documenting continued efforts by states and counties to suppress and disenfranchise the vote. As a result of congressional hearings and the voluminous congressional record, Congress determined that more time was needed to eradicate voter suppression and disenfranchisement still existing throughout the country. As such, in 2006, Congress reauthorized the Voting Rights Act for another twenty-five years, extending the law through 2032. The law's extension passed in overwhelming numbers (390–33 in the House of Representatives and 98–0 in the Senate), but this extension was later partially invalidated in *Shelby County v. Holder* (2013), as discussed in more detail in Question 6. Therefore, Section 5 of the Act no longer provides an effective way to prevent voter disenfranchisement.

Further Reading

American Civil Liberties Union (ACLU). "Voting Rights Act: Major Dates in History." Accessed May 15, 2025. https://www.aclu.org/voting-rights-act-major-dates-in-history

Anderson, Carol. *One Person, No Vote: How Voter Suppression Is Destroying Our Democracy*. Bloomsbury Publishing, 2020.

Brennan Center for Justice. "The Voting Rights Act: Protecting Voters for Nearly Five Decades." February 26, 2013. https://www.brennancenter.org/our-work/research-reports/voting-rights-act-protecting-voters-nearly-five-decades

Coleman, Kevin J. "The Voting Rights Act of 1965: Background and Overview." Congressional Research Service, CRS Report R43626, July 20, 2015.

Curry, James A., Richard B. Riley, and Richard M. Battistoni. *Constitutional Government: The American Experiment*. 5th edition. Kendall/Hunt Publishing, 2003.

Davidson, Chandler, and Bernard Grofman. *Quiet Revolution in the South: The Impact of the Voting Rights Act, 1965–1990*. Princeton University Press, 1994.

Department of Justice. "Reflecting on the 10th Anniversary of Shelby County v. Holder." June 23, 2023. https://www.justice.gov/archives/opa/blog/reflecting-10th-anniversary-shelby-county-v-holder

Department of Justice. "The Enduring Work of Protecting Voting Rights: 59 Years and Counting." August 6, 2024. https://www.justice.gov/archives/opa/blog/enduring-work-protecting-voting-rights-59-years-and-counting

Evans, Ferrell. "How Jim Crow-Era Laws Suppressed the African American Vote for Generations: In the Wake of the Passage of the 15th Amendment and Reconstruction, Several Southern States Enacted Laws That Restricted Black Americans' Access to Voting." History.com, 2021. https://www.history.com/articles/jim-crow-laws-black-vote

Gordon, Irving L. *Review of American History*. AMSCO, 1970.
Joint Center for Political and Economic Studies. "50 Years of the Voting Rights Act: The State of Race in Politics." 2019. https://jointcenter.org/wp-content/uploads/2019/11/VRA-report-3.5.15-1130-amupdated.pdf
Lopez, German. "How the Voting Rights Act Transformed Black Voting Rights in the South." *Vox*, August 6, 2015. https://www.vox.com/2015/3/6/8163229/voting-rights-act-1965
May, Gary. *Bending toward Justice: The Voting Rights Act and the Transformation of American Democracy*. Basic Books, 2013.
Menendez, Jose A. *The Voting Rights Act: Securing the Ballot*. ABC-CLIO, 2021.
National Archives. "Milestone Documents: Voting Rights Act (1965)." Accessed May 17, 2025. https://www.archives.gov/milestone-documents/voting-rights-act
Strossen, Nadine. "Statement of ACLU President Nadine Strossen Submitted to the Subcommittee on the Constitution Regarding the Voting Rights Act." American Civil Liberties Union, March 8, 2006. https://www.aclu.org/documents/statement-aclu-president-nadine-strossen-submitted-subcommittee-constitution-regarding-voting
Voting Rights Act of 1965 (as amended), Pub. L. 89-110, 79 Stat. 437 and codified in the US Code as follows: 52 U.S.C. § 10101; 52 U.S.C. §§ 10301-10314; 52 U.S.C. §§10501-10508; and 52 U.S.C. §§ 10701-10702.
Woodward, C. Vann. *The Strange Career of Jim Crow*. Oxford University Press, 1966.

Q6: What was the impact of the Supreme Court's *Shelby County v. Holder* (2013) decision on voting rights and voter suppression?

Answer: The Voting Rights Act, initially set to expire in 2007, is still in effect in 2026, as Congress extended the Act in 2006 for twenty-five additional years, until 2032. In its *Shelby County v. Holder* (2013) decision, the Supreme Court did not invalidate the entire Voting Rights Act of 1965 as being unconstitutional, but it did weaken the overall force and effect of the law by invalidating its preclearance provision, Section 4(b). This decision immediately opened the floodgate for states to pass legislation which might restrict voting access in a variety of ways. While the Voting Rights Act of 1965 remains valid law, the Supreme Court significantly weakened the government's ability to combat newly enacted state and local laws that disenfranchise voters or operate to suppress the vote.

The Facts: The Voting Rights Act was last renewed by overwhelming numbers in 2006 (390–33 in favor of renewal in the House of Representatives and 98–0 in favor of renewal in the Senate). After hearing and considering voluminous evidence, Congress extended the entire Voting Rights Act by twenty-five years (until 2032), finding that attempted discriminatory practices, voter suppression, and voting disenfranchisement were still occurring four decades after the law's initial passage. Despite this fact, Shelby County, Alabama, sued the US Attorney General (at the time, Eric Holder) claiming that Section 4(b) and Section 5 were unconstitutional.

On September 11, 2011, a federal district court ruled in favor of the federal government determining that the voluminous evidence before Congress in 2006 was sufficient to justify reauthorizing both Sections 4(b) and 5. Shelby County, Alabama, appealed the decision, and on May 18, 2012, a federal appellate court also ruled in favor of the federal government, holding that Sections 4(b) and 5 were constitutional. Like the federal district court before it, the Court of Appeals examined the evidence submitted to Congress in 2006 and determined that Congress had ample reason to conclude that the rights of minority voters still needed the protection provided by Sections 4(b) and 5.

Shelby County, Alabama, then appealed to the US Supreme Court, and the Court agreed to hear the case in order to decide the specific question of "whether Congress's decision in 2006 to reauthorize Section 5 of the Voting Rights Act under the pre-existing coverage formula of Section 4(b) of the Voting Rights Act exceeded its authority under the Fourteenth and Fifteenth Amendments and thus violated the Tenth Amendment and Article IV of the United States Constitution." The Supreme Court heard oral arguments on February 27, 2013, and issued its decision in the case on June 25, 2013. Despite a congressional record involving approximately 15,000 submitted documents that had convinced both a federal district court and a federal appellate court in DC that preclearance was still needed, the Supreme Court held otherwise. In a fractured 5–4 ruling, the Court declared Section 4(b) to be unconstitutional. Chief Justice John Roberts, writing for the majority, indicated that the legislation no longer aligned with "current conditions." He specified that the Voting Rights Act (and Section 4[b]) was "based on 40-year-old facts having no logical relationship to the present day." Roberts emphasized that the country had changed significantly since 1965, citing the confluence of voter registration rates and turnout between Black and white voters in the Section 4(b)-covered jurisdictions. He opined that "our country has changed, and while any racial discrimination in voting is too much, Congress must ensure that the legislation it passes to remedy that problem speaks to current conditions." Phrased another way, while Congress can limit state autonomy to remedy racial disenfranchisement through the enforcement clause of the Fifteenth Amendment, it must do so with up-to-date evidence and not with evidence that had not been updated. While the Supreme Court did not invalidate Section 5 in *Shelby*, its ruling had the effect of disabling the operation of the Section 5 preclearance, as preclearance was premised on covered jurisdictions identified through Section 4(b).

In a caustic dissent, Justice Ruth Bader Ginsburg (writing for three other justices), chastised the majority for supplanting its views in place of Congress's view. Ginsburg commented that Congress, in 2006, had compiled an extensive legislative record showing persistent voting discrimination and that the majority of the Court brushed aside that evidence. Ginsburg noted that "voting discrimination still exists; no one doubts that." Yet, according to the dissent, the Court's ruling "terminates the remedy that proved to be best suited to block that discrimination," a remedy best determined by Congress and not the courts. Justice Ginsburg's dissent famously chastised the majority, saying the decision was akin to "throwing away your umbrella in a rainstorm because you are not getting wet."

Chief Justice Roberts optimistically wrote that times had changed and alleged state disenfranchisement efforts no longer aligned with "current conditions," although he cited no evidence supporting his view. But within hours and days of the ruling, officials from different states started to show that discriminatory impulses in election policy were alive, or at least there was a demonstrated pent-up frustration within those states previously covered by preclearance. A 2023 Justice Department review noted that on June 25, 2013 (the day of the *Shelby* decision), Texas officials announced they would implement a previously blocked strict photo identification law. The day after that, North Carolina legislators moved forward with an omnibus (covering many items) voting bill that would place multiple new restrictions on voting access. In another law that went into effect one day after the *Shelby* decision, Alabama implemented a "strict voter ID law that eliminated utility bills, bank statements and other documents as viable proof of residency and instead required government-issued photo IDs to cast a ballot" (Anderson, 2020, 124). Alabama already had this legislation drafted prior to the *Shelby* decision and immediately implemented the draft law on the day *Shelby* was decided.

These states became early examples of post-*Shelby* curtailment on voting rights on the part of previous preclearance jurisdictions. Other states (e.g., Mississippi, Georgia) soon also followed suit. According to author Carol Anderson, a mere three years after the ruling, 868 polling places had closed (Anderson, 2020; Lopez, 2016). Five years after the ruling, nearly 1,000 polling places had closed, many of them reportedly in predominantly Black counties (McCarthy, 2019).

In an article entitled "States Have Added Nearly 100 Restrictive Laws Since SCOTUS Gutted the VRA 10 Years Ago," Jasleen Singh and Sara Carter highlighted the rapid pace in which states have enacted restrictive voting laws following *Shelby*. According to these authors, at least ninety-four restrictive laws have been passed in twenty-nine states by 2023, with many of those laws adopted in states that had previously been subject to preclearance and Department of Justice approvals (Singh and Carter, 2023). These new laws run the gamut and involve "a rash of voter ID laws, purged voting rolls, redrawn district boundaries, and closed and moved polling places" (Anderson, 2020, 42). Other examples of state changes include the removal of online voter registration, the elimination of same-day voter registration, limits on early voting, a prohibition on Sunday voting (which adversely impacted "Souls to the Polls" drives popular in states like Florida, North Carolina, and Georgia), as well as a bevy of other limitations which tend to restrict access to the ballot box.

Further Reading

Anderholm, Paige. "Battered by the Storm: 10 Years since Shelby County in North Carolina." Democracy Docket, June 23, 2023. https://www.democracydocket.com/analysis/battered-by-the-storm-10-years-since-shelby-county-in-north-carolina/

Anderson, Carol. *One Person, No Vote: How Voter Suppression Is Destroying Our Democracy*. Bloomsbury Publishing, 2020.

Brennan Center for Justice. "Effects of Shelby County v. Holder on the Voting Rights Act." June 21, 2023. https://www.brennancenter.org/our-work/research-reports/effects-shelby-county-v-holder-voting-rights-act

Department of Justice, Office of Public Affairs. "Reflecting on the 10th Anniversary of Shelby County v. Holder." June 23, 2023. https://www.justice.gov/archives/opa/blog/reflecting-10th-anniversary-shelby-county-v-holder

Epstein, Richard A., and Richard H. Pildes, eds. *The Future of the Voting Rights Act*. Russell Sage Foundation, 2006.

Karlan, Pamela S. *Democracy and Disdain*. Harvard University Press, 2012.

Lopez, German. "Southern States Have Closed Down at Least 868 Polling Places for the 2016 Election." Vox, November 4, 2016. https://www.vox.com/policy-and-politics/2016/11/4/13501120/vote-polling-places-election-2016

McCarthy, Tom. "More than 1,000 US Polling Sites Closed since Supreme Court Ruling, Report Finds." *The Guardian*, September 11, 2019. https://www.theguardian.com/us-news/2019/sep/11/us-polling-sites-closed-report-supreme-court-ruling

Shelby County v. Holder, 570 U.S. 529 (2013).

Shelby County v. Holder, 570 U.S. 529, 557–602 (2013) (Ginsburg, J., dissenting).

Singh, Jasleen, and Sara Carter. "States Have Added Nearly 100 Restrictive Laws since SCOTUS Gutted the VRA 10 Years Ago." Brennan Center for Justice, June 23, 2023. available at https://www.brennancenter.org/our-work/analysis-opinion/states-have-added-nearly-100-restrictive-laws-scotus-gutted-voting-rights

Tokaji, Daniel P. *The Supreme Court and the Voting Rights Act*. University Press of Kansas, 2016.

Tucker, Don. *The Voting Rights Act of 1965: An Interpretive History*. University of Alabama Press, 2017.

Voting Rights Lab. "Polling Place Consolidation: Negative Impacts on Turnout and Equity." July 2020. https://votingrightslab.org/report/polling-place-consolidation-negative-impacts-on-turnout-and-equity/

Q7: Which states passed restrictive voting suppression laws after *Shelby County v. Holder*?

Answer: As of 2025, twenty-nine states have passed what have been characterized as restrictive voting laws since *Shelby County v. Holder*. The Brennan Center for Justice, a nonprofit organization, has provided a useful definition of "restrictive" in this context, characterizing a law as "restrictive" if it "contains one or more provisions that would make it harder for eligible Americans to register, stay on the voter rolls, or vote as compared to existing state law" (Brennan Center for Justice, 2023). Eleven of the twenty-nine states that have passed restrictive voting laws since 2013 were previously subject to the Voter Rights Act preclearance provisions made invalid by the *Shelby* decision. Of those eleven, at least seven states have passed five or more restrictive laws. States that have passed numerous or omnibus laws restricting voting includes Texas, Arizona, Florida, Georgia, North Carolina, South Carolina, Mississippi, and Alabama, among others.

The Facts: As discussed in Question 6, the Supreme Court's *Shelby County v. Holder* decision in 2013 struck down the preclearance formula of the Voting Rights Act. This in turn resulted in many states revising their existing voting laws. The Brennan Center for Justice has been "tracking and cataloging this trend of restrictive voting legislation" on a state-by-state basis since the *Shelby* case was decided (Singh and Carter, 2023). It is unlikely that these states would have been able to pass the legislation with such rapidity absent the decision in *Shelby*.

In a Brennan Center report, at least twenty-nine states (a majority under Republican control) have enacted ninety-four new laws since 2013 that restrict voting access. Broadly speaking, these various laws promulgated post-*Shelby* included stricter photo voter identification laws, aggressive voter registration list purges, restrictions on previously allowed early voting (i.e., a reduction of early voting days), and restrictions to how or when one might vote by mail. The Brennan Center also alleges that the post-*Shelby* legislation includes racially gerrymandered redistricting maps (Singh and Carter, 2023), although it is unclear to which jurisdictions this comment references. The Brennan Center report characterized the rush by states pass laws post-*Shelby* as a "barrage" and reaching a "fever pitch" after the 2020 presidential election. The report also indicates that the promulgation of these laws "show no signs of abating" (Singh and Carter, 2023).

Of the twenty-nine states identified in the Brennan Center report, only eleven were formerly preclearance jurisdictions: Arizona, Texas, Louisiana, Mississippi, Alabama, Georgia, Florida, South Carolina, North Carolina, New York, and South Dakota. Seven of these states enacted five or more voting laws that might be classified as restrictive in nature. Texas, North Carolina, Georgia, and Florida are four of these states that will serve to illustrate the types of laws promulgated post-*Shelby* (Singh and Carter, 2023). Texas, North Carolina, and Florida appeared to restrict access to voting, while Georgia's new voting laws were restrictive in certain areas but also expanded access in at least one area (i.e., extended early voting to a longer period).

Perhaps no state illustrates the post-*Shelby* trend better than Texas. Texas announced that it would be imposing stricter voting laws on the very same day that *Shelby* was decided, and the law was passed a mere two hours after the *Shelby* decision was announced. Those changes to Texas election law included multiple aspects of voting. First, the 2013 law tightened up what identification may be used to vote. Prior to 2013, a voter in Texas did not have to provide a government-issued photo identification card to vote and could use documentation like utility bills and bank statements to substantiate the voter's identity. Under the prior law, a birth certificate could also be used. The 2013 law, as codified in Texas's Election Code at Title 6, Chapter 63, lists seven types of government issued photo identifications cards that could be used to vote so long as they were unexpired or expired no more than sixty days before voting. Acceptable types of identification included such things as a passport, Texas driver's license, Texas identification card, or a military identification card.

Voters who did not possess any of these could vote a provisional ballot but had to either show an approved photo identification within six days or qualify for a limited exemption (such as the disability certificate, a religious-objection affidavit, or a disaster affidavit) as outlined by the Election Code. The exemptions to this requirement were also very limited as illustrated by the religious-objection affidavit. This affidavit was only acceptable under the following circumstance: If the voter executed a sworn affidavit stating they have a religious objection to being photographed (and have consistently refused photographs for any government purpose), or if the voter executed an affidavit stating they could not obtain identification due to a natural disaster declared by the president or Texas governor within forty-five days of the election that destroyed or prevented access to the voter's identification.

The stricter 2013 photo identification requirement had previously been blocked under preclearance. Texas was not alone in passing legislation that was blocked by preclearance before 2013. Other preclearance states (e.g., Alabama and Mississippi) revised their laws in similar ways.

In 2021, Texas also passed an omnibus voting law (Senate Bill 1, dubbed the "Texas Election Integrity Act") that banned twenty-four-hour voting and drive-through voting (i.e., drive-up voting that occurred in temporary or outdoor polling locations). After the enactment of Senate Bill 1, the Texas Election Code §85.005(a) was amended to require early voting by personal appearance to take place no earlier than 6:00 a.m. and no later than 10:00 p.m. on any given day, thereby eliminating polling locations that were open around-the-clock. Senate Bill 1 also stopped drive-thru voting by mandating that all in-person voting must occur inside a stationary indoor facility. The Texas Election Code (Section 85.062[b]) now specifies that "the polling place may not be located in a movable structure." The revised law also prohibited the use of tents, drive-through canopies, or other mobile structures for curbside general voting.

Texas Senate Bill 1 also set forth tightened identification requirements for voting by mail and gave more powers to partisan poll watchers. Under the revised Texas Election Code §84.002, any application for a mail-in ballot "must include" the applicant's Texas DPS-issued identification number (i.e., driver's license, personal identification card, or election identification certificate) or, if the voter has none, the last four digits of their Social Security number. Texas Election Code §33.056 was added to augment rules pertaining to partisan poll watchers, indicating that that poll watchers are "entitled to observe any activity conducted at the location at which the watcher is serving." Under this section, watchers may "sit or stand near enough to see and hear the election officers" conducting that activity and "a watcher may not be denied free movement where election activity is occurring" within the polling place. Senate Bill 1 made it a Class A misdemeanor for an official to knowingly obstruct a watcher's view or distance them in a way that makes observation ineffective. Between 2012 and 2018, Texas also closed over 750 polling locations. Most of the closed polling sites were reportedly located in predominantly minority communities (McCarthy, 2019). After 2013, Texas has also aggressively gerrymandered electoral maps which have prompted multiple civil-rights lawsuits (Anderson, 2020).

North Carolina's omnibus voting law (House Bill 589) was presented the day after the ruling in *Shelby* was announced. The law introduced a strict photo identification mandate which, like in Texas, required a government-issued photo identification with very limited exemptions. The law also cut the early voting period by a week, eliminated same-day voter registration, ended out-of-precinct ballot counting (i.e., ballots submitted in the wrong precinct would not be counted at all), and eliminated preregistration for underaged voters, among other things.

However, the Fourth Circuit of Appeals, in *North Carolina State Conference of NAACP v. McCrory*, 831 F.3d 204 (4th Cir. 2016) struck down the new legislation as unconstitutional. It found that the law was adopted with racially discriminatory intent in violation of the Fourteenth Amendment Equal Protection Clause as well as Section 2 of the Voting Rights Act. The court noted that the legislature had requested data on racial differences in voting behaviors and then drafted the law to restrict or eliminate five methods disproportionately used by Black voters. In invalidating the law, the federal Fourth Circuit stated that the law targeted Black voters "with almost surgical precision" while providing "only meager justifications." Also, the court found no evidence of voter fraud, the prevention of which was the basis for the legislation, commenting that the provisions of the law "impose cures for problems that did not exist." In 2017, the Supreme Court declined to hear the case, leaving the Fourth Circuit ruling undisturbed. The decision was lauded as a major victory for voting rights advocates.

Georgia has also revised its election laws in numerous ways post-*Shelby*. In 2017, Georgia enacted its "exact match" program. This program required that when a voter registers to vote, the name on the voter registration must "exactly match" the person's name on file with Georgia's Department of Driver Services or by the Social Security Administration. In 2021, Georgia passed Senate Bill 202. Senate Bill 202 added new identification requirements for mail-in ballots like those required by Texas in 2021. Senate Bill 202 also limited how ballot drop boxes could be used. While every county is required to have at least one drop box for absentee ballots, additional drop boxes were limited to one per 100,000 registered voters or one per early voting site, whichever is fewer. Additionally, Senate Bill 202 specified that all drop boxes must be located inside a county elections office or inside an early voting location, and they are only available during the days and hours of advance (early) voting at that site (they are closed and locked after hours and after the early voting period). The law also mandates that drop boxes be under constant surveillance, and it allows outdoor drop boxes only in emergency circumstances (e.g., during a public health emergency). Senate Bill 202 barred officials from mailing unsolicited absentee applications as well.

On the other hand, several provisions of Georgia Senate Bill 202 improve the integrity of the operation of polling places and expand voter access to the ballet box. Relating to the integrity of the polling place, the bill made it a misdemeanor offense for any non-poll worker to give or offer food, drinks, or gifts to voters within 150 feet of a polling place or within 25 feet of any voter standing in line. While some voting rights advocates latched onto this provision as a draconian measure, this aspect of the law was meant to prevent a practice called "line warming." Legislators supporting this ban argued that handing out water or snacks could be construed as electioneering or influencing voters. However, voting rights advocates argued that the practice was meant to ensure people are not dissuaded from voting due to long lines and to help prevent voter discomfort while waiting. As such, the practice was defended as a non-partisan act meant merely to help encourage voter participation. The law does allow official polling station staff to set up unattended self-service water stations for voters.

Relating to improved voter access to the ballot box, the legislation extended in-person early voting in most Georgia counties. It guaranteed three weeks of early voting before general elections, with mandatory voting hours on two Saturdays (9:00 a.m. to 5:00 p.m.) and an option for counties to offer voting on two Sundays (the second and/or third Sunday before Election Day) as well. Previously, Georgia only required one Saturday, and many counties offered no Sunday voting. Yet, like Texas, Georgia has also closed hundreds of polling stations. Over 200 polling stations have been shuttered in Georgia since 2013 (McCarthy, 2019).

Florida revised its election law statutes in ways far too numerous to comprehensively detail here. It also passed a new omnibus election law in 2021 (Senate Bill 90). Voting rights groups characterized the new legislation as an "omnibus voter suppression" and a "sweeping voter suppression law" (Sweren-Becker, 2021). In Senate Bill 90, Florida tightened up its voter photo identification rules, specifically as they relate to mail-in ballots. Voters must provide a Florida driver license number, Florida ID card number, or the last four of their Social Security number with a mail-ballot request made in person or over the phone. No changes were made to the identification card requirements for voting on Election Day. Florida Statutes § 101.043(1) already required voters to present two types of identification to vote, namely, a photo identification card plus one of twelve types of identification enumerated in the statute.

Like Georgia, Florida also limited the use of drop-off boxes. Drop boxes are only permitted at the main elections office, permanent branch offices of the supervisor of elections, and early voting sites (including any site that would qualify as an early voting location). Florida also curtailed the practice of ballot harvesting. Ballot harvesting involves a third party collecting absentee ballots in bulk and delivering the ballots to the applicable precinct. The legislation made it a first-degree misdemeanor offense for any person to possess more than two completed ballots, unless the ballots are from family members. Like Georgia, Florida's Senate Bill 2021 also prohibits the practice of line warming. In 2022, Florida was also the first state to create an elections law enforcement agency (see Question 24). Critics of this law enforcement agency claim that the agency chills and suppresses voting in the state.

There are, of course, other states and other examples beyond those referenced here that have been excluded for purposes of brevity and the avoidance of recounting repetitive actions by other states. There are also more aspects of the laws in each state that are not delineated here. And while the restriction on the number of ballot boxes or the requirement of mandating a photo identification card might seem minor, these laws tend to narrow access to the ballot box. As such, the laws are considered restrictive and are a subtle means of suppressing the vote.

Further Reading

Anderson, Carol. *One Person, No Vote: How Voter Suppression Is Destroying Our Democracy*. Bloomsbury Publishing, 2020.

Berman, Ari. *Give Us the Ballot: The Modern Struggle for Voting Rights in America*. Farrar, Straus and Giroux, 2015.

Brennan Center for Justice. "Effects of Shelby County v. Holder on the Voting Rights Act." June 21, 2023. https://www.brennancenter.org/our-work/research-reports/effects-shelby-county-v-holder-voting-rights-act

Brower, Mac. "Georgia's S.B. 202 Unpacked." Democracy Docket, March 24, 2023. https://www.democracydocket.com/analysis/georgias-s-b-202-unpacked/

Hasen, Richard L. *The Voting Wars: From Florida 2000 to the Next Election Meltdown.* Yale University Press, 2012 (Updated edition, 2015).

Leadership Conference Education Fund. "Democracy Diverted: Poll Place Closures and Right to Vote." September 2019. https://civilrightsdocs.info/pdf/reports/Democracy-Diverted.pdf

May, Gary. *Bending toward Justice: The Voting Rights Act and the Transformation of American Democracy.* Basic Books, 2013 (Updated edition, 2014).

McCarthy, Tom. "More than 1,000 US Polling Sites Closed since Supreme Court Ruling, Report Finds." *The Guardian*, September 11, 2019. https://www.theguardian.com/us-news/2019/sep/11/us-polling-sites-closed-report-supreme-court-ruling

Minnite, Lorraine C. *Keeping Down the Black Vote: Race and the Demobilization of American Voters.* The New Press, 2015.

Singh, Jasleen, and Sara Carter. "States Have Added Nearly 100 Restrictive Laws since SCOTUS Gutted the VRA 10 Years Ago." Brennan Center for Justice, June 23, 2023. available at https://www.brennancenter.org/our-work/analysis-opinion/states-have-added-nearly-100-restrictive-laws-scotus-gutted-voting-rights

Sweren-Becker, Eliza. "Florida Enacts Sweeping Voter Suppression Law." Brennan Center for Justice, April 30, 2021. https://www.brennancenter.org/our-work/analysis-opinion/florida-enacts-sweeping-voter-suppression-law

Tokaji, Daniel P. *The Supreme Court and the Voting Rights Act.* University Press of Kansas, 2016.

Q8: How often has voter fraud taken place in modern national elections, and does the level of fraud justify preventive measures that burden the right to vote?

Answer: No evidence of widespread or systematic voter fraud that would have changed the results of a national election has been uncovered in American national elections held in the last half century through the 2022 elections despite intense efforts to find such evidence. Although isolated incidents of fraud have occurred and have been documented in court cases, academic studies, and government reports, there also has not been a single judicial opinion (on the state or federal level) that has determined that fraud of a significant magnitude to change the outcome of an election has occurred. In over sixty federal- and state-level cases filed regarding the 2020 presidential election, there were no findings of fraud to the magnitude alleged. Numerous academic studies have also focused on voter fraud in the last quarter century and determined that while voter fraud does occur, it is extraordinarily rare.

While government efforts to safeguard the electoral process are of obvious and compelling importance, so too is the obligation to ensure that every lawful vote is counted. Due diligence must be exercised to ensure the complete and unfettered accessibility of the ballot box. As such, policymakers must be considerate of the possibility that any changes to voting process might inadvertently restrict access to the ballot box to lawful voters and must weigh this harm against the need to police against electoral misconduct. To date, the narrative of widespread ballot fraud has been a significant motivating factor for new voting legislation in many Republican-led states (Carter, et al., 2024), and if it is in fact the chief impetus for policymakers, then the existence of electoral fraud should be well established in judicial opinions, academic studies, and governmental reports to justify and legitimize the legislation.

The Facts: As discussed in Question 4, serious and criminal voter fraud has been present in US elections historically. However, in the last half-century (and through the 2020 presidential election), the United States has minimized fraud in its electoral process. As a result, voter fraud has played an increasingly diminished role in American politics in the last few decades. For example, a 2014 study by Loyola Law School Professor Justin Levitt found only thirty-one incidents of voter fraud out of hundreds of millions of votes cast from 2000 to 2014 (Anderson, 2020, xvi). The question is not whether cases of fraud have occurred throughout US history (they have), or whether isolated cases of fraud exist today (they do), but rather whether the level of fraud is sufficient to justify curtailing the voting rights of a majority of Americans.

Long before the 2020 election, many Republicans voiced concerns that election fraud was a widespread and a systematic problem. In 2005, for instance, the Senate Republican Policy Committee stated that "voter fraud continues to plague our nation's federal elections, diluting and cancelling out the lawful votes of the vast majority of Americans" (Keyssar, 2009, 280). Consistent with the concern over the possibility of fraud in the electoral process, Attorney General John Ashcroft made "election fraud and corruption offenses" one of his top priorities upon assuming office at the Department of Justice (Keyssar, 2009, 280). However, over the next five years, and despite an expenditure of a great amount of resources, only 120 indictments were filed, yielding only eight-six convictions in jurisdictions scattered around the nation (Keyssar, 2009, 280). According to author Alexander Keyssar, most of the charges in that five-year period that were brought involved individuals who were mistaken about their eligibility, such as former felons who thought their civil rights were restored and that they were therefore entitled to vote (Keyssar, 2009, 282). No evidence materialized of any large-scale organized efforts to affect the outcomes of federal elections through fraudulent voting during this intense federal scrutiny on the issue.

At the time of the Ashcroft inquiry, the topic received considerable sensational news coverage but without very much substance, as determined by the end of his investigations. Many of the early reported cases were eventually explained away due to routine and uncontroversial reasons unrelated to fraud. For instance, a frequently repeated news story reported that 132 dead people had voted in Detroit, but as Michigan's secretary of state eventually admitted, those absentee ballots had been mailed to those 132 people when those individuals were still very much alive. They died subsequently, in the weeks before Election Day, and the vast majority of those 132 individuals had not even gotten around to filling out their ballots (Keyssar, 2009, 282).

The US Supreme Court has also addressed the issue of the possibility of electoral fraud in the years before 2020. For instance, Justice John Paul Stevens raised the issue of voting fraud in the opinion he authored in *Crawford v. Marion County Election Board*, 553 U.S. 181 (2008). This case involved a challenge to Indiana's voter identification law and whether the strict requirement of a government-issued photographic identification card to vote was a violation of the Fourteenth Amendment's Equal Protection Clause. In Justice John Paul Stevens's opinion in upholding the law, he maintained that "*risk* of voter fraud" was "real" and cited as an example a case of election fraud that had occurred over a century before in New York. Justice Stevens was undoubtedly correct that fraud occurred in New York's election of 1868 and a "risk" of fraud was a legitimate concern, but the finding of electoral fraud in 1868, or the concern over the possibility of fraud, does not address the issue of fraud in fact being perpetrated nor the overall magnitude of the fraud (and whether it is of a magnitude to change an election result).

Although some examples of voter fraud from history (referenced in Question 4) were serious and well-documented instances, none resulted in claims by US presidents for drastic changes to the electoral process—that is, until 2020. Even Richard Nixon, in his razor-thin defeat to John Kennedy, did not demand restrictions to election laws. As Nixon reportedly told journalist Earl Mazo in 1973, "no one steals the presidency of the United States" (Boller, 1984, 300). Nixon "went on to explain how disruptive, as well as impractical, the demand for recount could be and how damaging for the United States abroad" (Boller, 1984, 300).

President Donald Trump has, however, articulated a different perspective on the issue of possible fraud than that expressed by Richard Nixon. Trump implied there would be rampant fraud in the 2016 presidential election before that election even occurred (an election he ultimately won). After his defeat in 2020 to Joe Biden, Trump began trumpeting what critics referred to as "the big lie." Among his claims regarding the 2020 election was that ballot box stuffing was occurring. Because Democratic voters disproportionately cast mail ballots in many states, the late counting of these ballots in swing states shifted lead margins in high-profile races. This factored into conspiratorial thinking about the possibility of fraud in the election. Trump claimed that mail ballots were rife with fraud (Kamal, 2023). Cities like Philadelphia, Detroit, and Atlanta, all Democratic strongholds, drew the ire of Trump in his claims of stuffed ballots and a stolen election (Kamal, 2023). Trump's position was viewed with irony by critics given his recorded phone conversation with Georgia Secretary of State Brad Raffensperger wherein Trump appeared to pressure Raffensperger to "find 11,780 votes," which would have changed the overall results in Georgia from the winner of the state (Joseph Biden) to the loser (Donald Trump) (Shear and Saul, 2021).

President Trump embarked on a months-long attempt to overthrow the electoral results in certain states before Biden's inauguration in 2021, and he continued to repeat claims of a stolen election during the years between his presidencies, from 2021 to 2024. However, claims of electoral fraud were subsequently examined in courts around the country and found to be almost entirely without merit. More than sixty different lawsuits by Trump were all also rejected on the state and federal levels (Campaign Legal Center, 2025; Caruso and Couloumbis, 2022).

An extensive study of these court cases was carried out by eight prominent conservative scholars, including judges and US Senators. They concluded in their July 2022 report, "Lost, Not Stolen: The Conservative Case That Trump Lost and Biden Won the 2020 Presidential Election,":

> Of the 64 cases brought by Trump and his supporters, twenty were dismissed before a hearing on the merits, fourteen were voluntarily dismissed by Trump and his supporters before a hearing on the merits, and 30 cases included a hearing on the merits. Only in one Pennsylvania case involving far too few votes to overturn the results did Trump and his supporters prevail. (Danforth et al., 2022, 3)

For example, in *Law v Whitmer*, 136 Nev. 800, 477 P.3d 1124 (2020), the Supreme Court of Nevada found that the plaintiffs failed to prove that illegal or improper votes were counted so as to raise a doubt as to the legitimacy of the outcome and failed to prove that the outcome of the election was manipulated or altered, among other findings. In a federal district court opinion entitled *Bower v. Ducey*, 506 F. Supp. 3d 699 (D. Ariz. 2020), the presiding federal judge in that case concluded that the plaintiff's claims of fraud in Arizona were based on "anonymous witnesses, hearsay, and irrelevant analysis of unrelated elections." The 2022 "Lost Not Stolen" report concludes: "Even now, twenty months after the election, a period in which Trump's supporters have been energetically scouring every nook and cranny for proof that the election was stolen, they come up empty. Claims are made, trumpeted in sympathetic media, and accepted as truthful by many patriotic Americans. But on objective examination they have fallen short, every time" (Danforth, et al., 2022, 72).

Several other studies and reports also illustrate the lack of widespread fraud in the 2020 election. An Associated Press review in six key states (i.e., Arizona, Georgia, Michigan, Nevada, Pennsylvania, and Wisconsin) found fewer than 475 potential voter fraud cases out of over twenty-five million votes cast, a "minuscule number" that would not have come close to affecting the election outcome (Cassidy, 2021). Many of those cases involved attempts to vote twice or votes cast on behalf of deceased individuals and were often caught by checks already in place (i.e., no need for further restrictive laws that might adversely impact a wide pool of valid voters).

Another study by political scientists Andrew Eggers, Haritz Garro, and Justin Grimmer, published in late 2021, specifically examined statistical claims of fraud in the 2020 election. Their article's title conveys its conclusion: "No Evidence for Systematic Voter Fraud in 2020 Election" (Eggers, et al., 2021). The authors analyzed multiple allegations ranging from suspicious patterns in absentee ballot counts to theories about defective voting machines. In each allegation, the researchers found that either mundane explanation could explain the allegations or there just were outright errors in the allegations' logic (Eggers, et al., 2021). In one instance, one claim posited that late-counted absentee votes were unnaturally counted in favor of one candidate. However, the researchers showed this was an expected result of well-understood geography and partisan preferences toward mail-in ballots (not fraud) among Democratic voters (Eggers, et al., 2021). The authors also examined data from a controversial paper that had purported to find fraudulent absentee voting in

Pennsylvania, and debunked the paper, demonstrating that the patterns were consistent with legitimate turnout in Pennsylvania.

Even the conservative Heritage Foundation voter fraud database fails to substantiate Trump's claims of a stolen presidential election. The database showed only isolated cases of fraud and not on a magnitude that would have changed the result of a presidential election. By 2020, for example, the Heritage Foundation database listed only approximately 1,200 proven cases of any kind of voter fraud over a period of nearly twenty years (and out of hundreds of millions of votes cast). By 2023, that number was modestly higher (around 1,800 cases going back to 1982). This amounted to a fraud rate of about roughly six cases of fraud per ten million votes, which is an infinitesimal fraction of less than 1 percent of 1 percent.

Notably, the Brookings Institution, in a commentary entitled "Widespread Election Fraud Claims by Republicans Don't Match the Evidence," analyzes the Heritage Foundation voter fraud data and finds that it does not document voter fraud significant enough to change the outcome of a general election and that, in fact, the proven voter fraud is "miniscule" (Averill, et al., 2023). For example, it notes that in Arizona, the database documented "just four cases in the [2020] general election" of over 6 million votes cast (Averill, et al., 2023). Brookings noted that, among this small number of cases, the fraud did not even benefit only Democratic candidates. Brookings also noted that the Heritage database included zero cases of proven voter fraud in the 2020 Georgia general election (Averill, et al., 2023). Regarding fraud accusations related to absentee mail-in ballots (a method of voting Trump attacked in an August 2025 press conference), an analysis by researchers at UCLA Voting Rights Project found just 207 individual cases of absentee ballot fraud in a database of elections spanning decades and involving millions of votes (Barreto, et al., 2020).

This scholarship also aligns with assessments by state and federal officials prior to the second Trump administration. Specifically, the US Department of Justice, the Federal Bureau of Investigation, and the Cybersecurity and Infrastructure Security Agency in the first Trump administration all stated they found no evidence of outcome-altering fraud in 2020. The administration's Election Infrastructure Coordinating Counsel, Election Infrastructure Sector Coordinating Executive Committees, and the National Association of Secretaries of State, among others, issued a joint press statement on November 12, 2020, stating that the 2020 election was the "most secure in American history" emphasizing in bolded letters "There is no evidence that any voting system deleted or lost votes, changed votes, or was in any way compromised"

(Cybersecurity & Infrastructure Security Agency, 2020). Numerous state-level audits and recounts also verified the accuracy of results.

These findings have led one political scientist to quip, "The problem is not voter fraud. The problem is the fraud about voter fraud" (College of Social & Behavioral Science, University of Utah, 2024). Such specious claims of fraud and exceedingly minimal instances of actual voter fraud should give policymakers pause before passing restrictive laws that will make it more difficult for Americans to cast their ballots. While elections need to be conducted in a fashion to minimize fraud as much as reasonably possible, using fraud as justification for enacting voter laws that unduly limit access to the ballot box and increase the chances of voter disenfranchisement is equally problematic. This is especially the case when the fraud is on a scale most scholars consider to be "infinitesimal," and at a level that could not be seriously believed to impact the overall election results.

Further Reading

Anderson, Carol. *One Person, No Vote: How Voter Suppression Is Destroying Our Democracy*. Bloomsbury Publishing, 2020.

Averill, Owen, Annabel Hazrati, and Elaine Kamarck. "Widespread Election Fraud Claims by Republicans Don't Match the Evidence." Brookings Institute, November 22, 2023. https://www.brookings.edu/articles/widespread-election-fraud-claims-by-republicans-dont-match-the-evidence/

Baltz, Samuel, Fernanda González, Kevin Guo, Jacob Jaffe, and Charles Stewart III. "Audits of the 2020 American Election Show an Accurate Vote Count." *Proceedings of the National Academy of Sciences, 122*, no. 20 (2025), e2419633122.

Barreto, Matt, Chad Dunn, Michael Latner, Tye Rush, Gabriel Sanchez, and Sonni Waknin. "Debunking the Myth of Voter Fraud in Mail Ballots." UCLA Voting Rights Project, April 14, 2020. https://latino.ucla.edu/wp-content/uploads/2021/08/LPPI-VRP-Voter-Fraud-res.pdf

Beall, Pat. "Analysis of Ballot Fraud Catalog Reveals No Threat." *USA Today*, October 21, 2020.

Block, Ken. *Disproven: My Unbiased Search for Voter Fraud for the Trump Campaign, the Data That Shows Why He Lost, and How We Can Improve Our Elections*. Post Hill Press, 2024.

Boller, Paul F., Jr. *Presidential Campaigns*. Oxford University Press, 1984.

Campaign Legal Center: Advancing Democracy Through Law. "Results of Lawsuits Regarding the 2020 Elections." 2025. https://campaignlegal.org/results-lawsuits-regarding-2020-elections

Carter, Sara, Andrew Garber, Catherine Silvestri, and Connie Wu. "How Voting Laws Have Changed in Battleground States since 2020." Brennan Center for Justice, August 15, 2024. https://www.brennancenter.org/our-work/research-reports/how-voting-laws-have-changed-battleground-states-2020

Caruso, Stephen, and Angela Couloumbis. "Pa. Supreme Court Upholds No-Excuse Mail Voting Ahead of Midterms." *SpotlightPA*, August 2, 2022. https://www.spotlightpa.org/news/2022/08/pa-mail-voting-law-uphelp-state-supreme-court/

Cassidy, Christina A. "Far Too Little Vote Fraud to Tip Election to Trump, AP Finds." December 14, 2021. https://apnews.com/article/voter-fraud-election-2020-joe-biden-donald-trump-7fcb6f134e528fee8237c7601db3328f

Cohen, George M. "The Discipline of Rudy Giuliani and the Real Fraud of the 2020 Election." *Catholic University Law Review, 73*, no. 3 (2024), 325–59.

College of Social & Behavioral Science, University of Utah. "Exposing Myths about Ballot Collection on Native American Reservations." August 14, 2024. https://attheu.utah.edu/research/exposing-myths-about-ballot-collection-on-indian-reservations/

Coster, Helen, Alexandra Ulmer, and Tim Reid. "US Election Experts Worry about Republican Poll Watchers in Swing States." Reuters, October 24, 2024. https://www.reuters.com/world/us/be-aggressive-republican-poll-watchers-battleground-states-worry-us-election-2024-10-24/

Cybersecurity & Infrastructure Security Agency. "Joint Statement from Elections Infrastructure Government Coordinating Council & the Election Infrastructure Sector Coordinating Executive Committees." November 12, 2020. https://www.cisa.gov/news-events/news/joint-statement-elections-infrastructure-government-coordinating-council-election-infrastructure

Danforth, John, Benjamin Ginsberg, Thomas B. Griffith, David Hoppe, J. Michael Luttig, Michael W. McConnell, Theodore B. Olson, and Gordon H. Smith. "Lost, Not Stolen: The Conservative Case That Trump Lost and Biden Won the 2020 Presidential Election." July 2022. https://lostnotstolen.org/wp-content/uploads/2022/07/Lost-Not-Stolen-The-Conservative-Case-that-Trump-Lost-and-Biden-Won-the-2020-Presidential-Election-July-2022.pdf

Eggers, Andrew C., Haritz Garro, and Justin Grimmer. "No Evidence for Systematic Voter Fraud: A Guide to Statistical Claims about the 2020 Election." *Proceedings of the National Academy of Sciences, 118*, no. 45 (2021), e2103619118.

Franke, Joe. "Election Administration Concerns Meet Claims of a Fraudulent Election: A Comprehensive Analysis of the 2020 Presidential Election and Its Aftermath in Wisconsin." *Marquette Law Review, 106*, no. 3 (2023), 683–732.

Fridkin, Kim L., and Patrick J. Kenney. "'A Rigged Election': How Views about Election Integrity Altered the Campaign." In *Choices in a Chaotic Campaign: Understanding Citizens' Decisions in the 2020 Election*, ed. D. B. Sparks and J. V. Cavari, Cambridge University Press, 2024, pp. 122–46.

Garrett, Major, and David Becker. *The Big Truth: Upholding Democracy in the Age of "The Big Lie"*. Diversion Books, 2022.

Grofman, Bernard, and Jonathan Cervas. "Statistical Fallacies in Claims about 'Massive and Widespread Fraud' in the 2020 Presidential Election: Examining Claims Based on Aggregate Election Results." *Statistics and Public Policy*, *11*, no. 1 (2024), 1–16.

Hasen, Richard L. "Identifying and Minimizing the Risk of Election Subversion and Stolen Elections in the Contemporary United States." *Harvard Law Review Forum*, *135* (2022), 265–86.

Heritage Foundation. "Election Fraud Map: A Sampling of Proven Instances of Election Fraud." July 28, 2025. https://electionfraud.heritage.org/

Kamal, Sameea. "California Republicans Buy into 'Ballot Harvesting.'" *CAL Matters*, October 18, 2023. https://calmatters.org/politics/2023/10/california-election-voting-republicans/

Keyssar, Alexander. *The Right to Vote: The Contested History of Democracy in the United States*. Revised edition. Basic Books, 2009.

Persily, Nathaniel, and Charles Stewart III. "The Miracle and Tragedy of the 2020 U.S. Election." *Journal of Democracy*, *32*, no. 2 (2021), 159–73.

Shear, Michael D., and Stephanie Saul. "Trump, in Taped Call, Pressured Georgia Official to 'Find' Votes to Overturn Election." *The New York Times*, January 4, 2021.

Tumulty, Karen. "Voter Fraud Hysteria Isn't New. Just Ask My Ancestors." *The Washington Post*, October 8, 2024. https://www.washingtonpost.com/opinions/2024/10/07/immigrants-texas-vote-fraud-ken-paxton/

Wang, Haiyan, and Jan-Willem van Prooijen. "Stolen Elections: How Conspiracy Beliefs during the 2020 American Presidential Elections Changed over Time." *Applied Cognitive Psychology*, *37*, no. 2 (2023), 277–89.

2

Links between Institutional Structures and Process and Voter Disenfranchisement

Beyond the exclusion of groups or unreasonable restrictions at the ballot box, disenfranchisement of voters can occur indirectly through institutional structures and processes. For example, some critics have alleged the Electoral College weighs votes differently depending on the geographical location of the voter. The weight of a single vote in a small state is worth disproportionately more than a single vote cast in a large state. The practice of gerrymandering also distorts the votes of individuals by arranging districts in such a way that many votes simply do not matter because the voter has been placed within a district dominated by a super majority. The result is that even though individuals can still cast ballots, the impact of their votes is systematically weakened and undermined given how the districts are composed. Voter suppression or disenfranchisement, then, can be subtly embedded in the very design and operation of the government.

Despite voting inequalities built into the government's structure, Congress has attempted to continue to improve voter access after passing the Voting Rights Act of 1965. The National Voter Registration Act of 1993 (NVRA) and the Help America Vote Act of 2002 (HAVA) were two major pieces of federal legislation meant to reduce voter disenfranchisement and modernize the electoral process. NVRA was designed to expand access by requiring states to provide voter registration opportunities when citizens applied for a driver's license. As roughly 87 percent of Americans drove at the time NVRA was enacted, the legislation was seen as a great way to vastly improve voter registrations across most major groups. By allowing citizens to register to vote when applying for a driver's license, the NVRA simplified the registration process and made the act of registration more convenient. Congress also successfully improved voting infrastructure with the passage of The Help America Vote Act (HAVA) in 2002. HAVA provided funds to replace outdated voting machines, which were needed to eliminate the disparity in resources between poorer and wealthier voting precincts. Among other things, HAVA mandated that all states use provisional ballots for voters whose eligibility might be in question.

Q9: Does gerrymandering and redistricting diminish equal or proportional representation or disenfranchise voters?

Answer: While the general practice of gerrymandering does not suppress individual votes per se or disenfranchise an individual from the right to vote, it does operate to dilute the value of a vote and make some votes meaningless because of the way districts are configured. In this sense, a voter can be disenfranchised by living in a grossly gerrymandered district or jurisdiction. While redistricting efforts are needed to add or reduce congressional seats after each national census, the practice of gerrymandering allows the incumbent party to redraw the map to provide maximum electability.

The Facts: The practice of gerrymandering refers to the manipulation of electoral district boundaries to advantage a particular party or group. Redistricting itself typically occurs following each census to ensure equally populated districts and appropriate representation for each district based upon an updated population count. In conducting those redistricting efforts, politicians often draw up electoral maps with the intent to "put a thumb on the scale" and predetermine election outcomes by ensuring the reconfigured district overwhelming supports the incumbent party (i.e., the politicians redrawing the electoral district maps).

As explained by Carol Anderson, "partisan gerrymandering ... seeks to ensconce in power, regardless of the vote count, a particular party's candidate while eliminating the competition (and constituents) form having any real say in the development and implementation of laws and public policy" (Anderson, 2020, 98). In *One Person, One Vote: A Surprising History of Gerrymandering in America*, author Nick Seabrook called gerrymandering "a concerted effort to make the votes of certain groups of people matter more than the votes of others" (Seabrook, 2022, 4). In further defining gerrymandering, Seabrook wrote that "to gerrymander is to distort, to corrupt, to turn institutions that should be working on behalf of the people's interests into perversions that serve only the powerful, the moneyed, or the politically connected. Whenever political machinations over gerrymandering are afoot, no matter who wins, it's always the voter who loses" (Seabrook, 2022, 5). President Benjamin Harrison was blunter and more direct, calling the practice "political robbery" of the people's right to vote (Anderson, 2020, 98).

The practice of gerrymandering has been a major feature in American electoral politics since 1810, when Massachusetts governor Elbridge Gerry created a district in the shape of salamander to maximize and concentrate his supporters and minimize his opponents (Anderson, 2020, 98). The obvious bias of the new electoral map resulted in sardonic references to this form of self-serving redistricting as "gerrymandering," a combination of the governor's surname and the word "salamander." In the years since Elbridge Gerry, politicians have continued to devise deviously planned redistricting, with little regard to grouping geographically related areas (i.e., the eastern half of a county, a north-south-east-or-west quadrant, or even land adjacent or contingent to other parts of the same district). Like Elbridge Gerry's 1810 salamander district, unchecked gerrymandering has led to districts that resemble "contorted yoga positions or Rorshach tests" (Anderson, 2020, 105). Some of the almost laughable gerrymandered districts bear names and resemblances like "the North Carolina Gimpy Leg, the Texas Glock, The Georgia Flat-Cat Road Kill that became the Squirrel Not Yet Hit by a Car, and the Texas 27th Bottle Opener" (Anderson, 2020, 105). In Ohio, gerrymandered districts took the appearance of strange animals and reptiles and were named "the Quail," "the Richland Roarer" (described as "Half Hoss, half Alligator"), "the Sioto Sea-Horse," and the "water-whelp" (a type of fish) (Seabrook, 2022, 69–71). Today in Ohio, the Ninth Congressional District is called "the Snake by Lake" as it entails a long thin line running approximately 100 miles along the banks of Lake Erie, stretching from Cleveland all the way to Toledo (Tebben, 2021).

In autumn 2025, Americans witnessed high-profile gerrymandering sessions blatantly occurring in Texas with the sole and admitted goal being to increase the total Republican seats in Congress. The timing of the redistricting in Texas was unconventional as well, occurring mid-way through the ten-year census period. The mid-cycle partisan re-districting in Texas led voters in California to do the same (to offset the number of votes added by Texas). This tit-for-tat approach to redistricting is now being reviewed by the courts, a destiny and result that has come to be expected in almost every contentious political issue in America today.

Further, presently, gerrymandered districts are being composed with the use of high-powered computer programs able to calculate voting patterns, trends, registration of voters, and other factors, to ensure that the gerrymandered district is practically insulated from opposition votes (Anderson, 2020, 96–117; Seabrook, 2022, 7–9). Those engaged in gerrymandering employ two classic techniques, namely, "packing" and "cracking" (Tebben, 2021). Packing means concentrating as many like-minded voters (e.g., of one party or community) into as few districts as possible, thereby "wasting" their votes in lopsided supermajorities. Cracking means splitting a group of voters across many districts so that they fall short of a majority in each, also diluting their voting power (Li, 2025; Rosseau, 2019). By packing opponents into a handful of districts or cracking them into many, gerrymanderers can all but guarantee a preferred party wins the lion's share of seats even with a minority of the vote. These tactics, enabled by troves of voter data and computer algorithms, have made modern gerrymanders "surgical" in precision. In North Carolina, for example, because of aggressive gerrymandering by Republicans, the redistricted map "sort voters with such careful precision that Republicans are virtually assured of winning 10 of the state's 14 congressional races and could win as many as 11—a wildly skewed result for a perennial battleground state that regularly elects Democrats to statewide offices" (Li, 2025).

This means that those voters of counter-political views who vote in these districts are casting votes that are practically worthless. As explained by one author, partisan gerrymandering embraces "party affiliation and seeks to ensconce in power, regardless of the vote count, a particular party's candidates while eliminating the competition (and constituents) from having any real say in the development and implementation of laws and public policy" (Anderson, 2020, 98). It also means the incumbents of the same party can remain in these districts almost indefinitely. During oral arguments in a redistricting case from 2006 (*Gill v. Whitford*), Justice Ginsburg cut to the chase when she asked what had happened to the "precious right to vote"? A few moments later, Justice Sotomayor inquired further, stating, "It's okay to stake the decks so … even though it [one party] gets a minority of votes [statewide] … it still gets a majority of the states?" Sotomayor went on to ask, "Could you tell me what the value is to democracy from political gerrymandering? How—how does that help our system of government?"

Under the practice of partisan gerrymandering, there is no incentive to vote if you know your voice is basically worthless in an overwhelming stacked district. As such, more voters just stay home. According to author Carol Anderson, "gerrymandering has a horrific effect on voter behavior. Those in competitive districts are more likely to vote; those in safe, uncompetitive districts stay home more often on Election Day" (Anderson, 2020, 115). Further, partisan gerrymandering "dampens turnout in the subsequent election cycle, especially among black [voters]" (Anderson, 2020, 115).

The effect of gerrymandering also means that there are fewer competitive districts and more and more so-called safe districts. As an illustration, in

2016, 97 percent of incumbents won reelection in elections for House of Representative seats (Anderson, 2020, 116). Another example of this can be seen by looking at the State of California. Before the gerrymandering reform in California, between 2002 and 2010, of the 265 congressional seats up for election, only one saw a seat change to the differing party (Anderson, 2020, 116). This prompted then-governor Arnold Schwarzenegger to quip that "the former Soviet Politburo had more turnover" than pre-reform California (Anderson, 2020, 116).

Partisan gerrymandering should be distinguished from racial gerrymandering. Racial gerrymandering would be an unconstitutional practice by the state under the Fourteenth Amendment's Equal Protection Clause. Conversely, partisan gerrymandering does not involve a "suspect classification" (i.e., a decision made because of race) or the need for the Supreme Court to employ its "strict scrutiny" standard. In fact, the Supreme Court has repeatedly declined to hear several partisan gerrymandering cases, saying that the issue is a "political question" to be resolved by other branches of the government and for which there are no clearly defined judicial standards which could be employed.

Before 1962, the Supreme Court had held that challenges to redistricting or gerrymandering cases presented nonjusticiable political questions that were best addressed by the other branches of government, and not the courts. In the famous case *Baker v. Carr*, 369 U.S. 186 (1962), the Supreme Court held that several factors should be considered in deciding whether the case should be dismissed as a political question, including: if the issue has been left to a coequal branch of government; if there is no discernible manageable judicial standards to decide an issue; and if the Court's decision would demonstrate a lack of respect for a co-equal branch.

The *Baker v. Carr* case stemmed from a legal challenge to long-standing districting in Tennessee wherein countryside rural districts played a disproportionately large role in the election of representatives to both the Tennessee legislature and the Tennessee delegation to Congress. Cities like Memphis and Nashville were exploding in population, while that of the rural countryside was atrophying. The Tennessee apportionment law at the time did not take into account the huge disparity in voting power between urban centers and rural parts of the state. As such, the Tennessee law basically stripped "citizens in major population centers of the real weight of their vote" (Anderson, 2020, 101). The result was that one-third of the population in Tennessee living in the rural areas were selecting two-thirds of Tennessee's "elected" representatives (Anderson, 2020, 100). Tennessee had attempted to avoid judicial intervention by claiming that the issue was one of state law and a political choice by the state and not subject to judicial review by federal courts.

The Supreme Court disagreed with Tennessee and held that such cases were reviewable by the courts (phrased in legal jargon, the case was "justiciable") and the case should not be dismissed as a political question. The famous line emanating from the decision was "one person, one vote." Because of the ruling, there was an (at least temporary) acknowledgment that redistricting cases were reviewable under a general notion of whether votes were proportional in some basic way. Thus, in the years that followed, the Court's ruling opened the door to numerous challenges of legislative districts that did not conform to the "one person, one vote" standard. While the Court invalidated maps on equal protection grounds when the discriminatory intention was clear, the Court failed to nullify a single redistricting plan that was the product of partisan gerrymandering. In the 2019 case *Rucho v. Common Cause*, 588 U.S. 684, 718 (2019), the Supreme Court held that there were no judicially discernible and manageable standards by which courts could adjudicate claims of unconstitutional partisan gerrymandering. This, of course, was a departure from the "one person, one vote" standard in the *Baker v. Carr* decision.

Writing for the majority in a highly fractured decision in *Rucho*, Chief Justice John Roberts stated that federal courts are "not equipped to apportion political power as a matter of fairness" and it was "unclear what fairness looks like in this context." Roberts conceded that excessive partisan gerrymandering "reasonably seem[s] unjust" and stressed that the Court did "not condone" the practice of gerrymandering. He indicated that "the Framers gave Congress the power to do something about partisan gerrymandering in the Elections Clause." As a direct result of the *Rucho* opinion, claims of unconstitutional partisan gerrymandering are now not subject to federal court review because they present nonjusticiable political questions. That is, until the Court decides to revisit its decision.

Further Reading

Anderson, Carol. *One Person, No Vote: How Voter Suppression Is Destroying Our Democracy*. Bloomsbury Publishing, 2020.

Baker v. Carr. 369 U.S. 186 (1962).

Cain, Bruce E. *The Reapportionment Puzzle*. University of California Press, 1984.

Cox, Gary W., and Jonathan N. Katz. *Elbridge Gerry's Salamander: The Electoral Consequences of the Reapportionment Revolution*. Cambridge University Press, 2002.

Fraga Bernard, L. "Redistricting and the Causal Impact of Race on Voter Turnout." *The Journal of Politics, 78*, no. 1 (2016), 19–34.

Issacharoff, Samuel, Pamela S. Karlan, and Richard H. Pildes. *The Law of Democracy: Legal Structure of the Political Process*. 5th edition. Foundation Press, 2016.

Li, Michael. "Gerrymandering Explained." Brennan Center for Justice, August 10, 2021, updated August 9, 2025. https://www.brennancenter.org/our-work/research-reports/gerrymandering-explained

McDonald, Michael D. *Reapportionment and Redistricting in the West*. Lexington Books, 2008.

McGann, Anthony J., Charles Anthony Smith, Michael Latner, and Alex Keena. *Gerrymandering in America: The House of Representatives, the Supreme Court, and the Future of Popular Sovereignty*. Cambridge University Press, 2016.

Nagle, John Copeland. *The Gerrymanderers*. University of Michigan Press, 2000.

Oral Arguments. *Gill v. Whitford*, No. 16–1161. October 3, 2017, p. 24. https://www.supremecourt.gov/oral_arguments/argument_transcripts/2017/16-1161_mjn0.pdf

Persily, Nathaniel, ed. *The Realist's Guide to Redistricting: Avoiding the Legal Pitfalls*. 2nd edition. Cambridge University Press, 2010.

Rosseau, Ryan. "Rucho v. Common Cause Leaves the Map Wide Open for Gerrymandering." Thomson Reuters, 2019. https://legal.thomsonreuters.com/en/insights/articles/rucho-v-common-cause-approves-partisan-gerrymandering

Rucho v. Common Cause, 588 U.S. 684, 718 (2019).

Seabrook, Nick. *One Person, One Vote: A Surprising History of Gerrymandering in America*. Pantheon Books, 2022.

Stephanopoulos, Nicholas O., Ruth Greenwood, and Emily Rong Zhang, eds. *Partisan Gerrymandering and the Constitution*. Cambridge University Press, 2019.

Tebben, Susan. "With Gerrymandering Comes Strong Opinions. But What Is It?" *Ohio Capital Journal*, September 20, 2021. https://ohiocapitaljournal.com/2021/09/20/with-gerrymandering-comes-strong-opinions-but-what-is-it/

Winburn, Jonathan. *The Realities of Redistricting: Following the Rules and Limiting Gerrymandering in State Legislative Redistricting*. Lexington Books, 2008.

Q10: Does the operation of the Electoral College disenfranchise voters in presidential elections?

Answer: Yes. The Electoral College potentially disenfranchises American voters at least from the perspective that the weight of a person's vote in larger populated states might be drastically weaker compared to weight of votes from individuals from smaller states. A vote in Florida or Texas or California does not have the same overall weight as a vote in Wyoming or Montana or Idaho, and smaller states play an outsized role in the election of the president through the operational design of the Electoral College. Further, candidates could lose the popular vote, but win the Electoral College vote, and thereby win the presidency. In this sense, one might argue that voters are disenfranchised.

But as a matter of constitutional law, the Electoral College remains the "supreme law of the land" and is firmly embedded in the Constitution as a core electoral feature for presidential elections. As such, the role or use of the Electoral College can only be changed via constitutional amendment. Absent a constitutional amendment to change the Electoral College, it might be possible (but still constitutionally unclear) for states to bypass the Electoral College through the proposed National Popular Interstate Compact. However, this compact has not been ratified by a sufficient number of states to be operational. Additionally, should the National Popular Interstate Compact ever get to the point of reaching the threshold needed to operationalize the compact, it would likely be immediately challenged in the federal courts as being unconstitutional. Thus, absent a declaration by the Supreme Court on the compact's validity after its passage, the possible constitutionality of the proposed National Popular Interstate Compact will remain unclear.

The Facts: The Electoral College is firmly rooted in United States Constitution and is the constitutionally authorized method of selecting the President of the United States. The Electoral College comprises 538 state-appointed electors (one for each member of the House and Senate, plus three for DC). Article 2, Section 1 of the Constitution gives states the authority to decide how they will select these electors. Voters in each state cast ballots for a slate of electors. In most states the statewide popular-vote winner gets all of that state's electoral votes. (Maine and Nebraska allocate one elector per congressional district and two at-large to the statewide winner.) Electors meet in their states in December to cast official votes, which are sent to Congress and counted in a joint session in early January. A majority of 270 electoral votes is required to win. If no candidate reaches 270, the House chooses the president by state delegations (one vote per state), and the Senate chooses the vice president (one vote per senator).

In two elections for president in the twenty-first century (in 2000 and 2016), the candidate who received the greatest number of the popular vote ended up losing the Electoral College vote and thereby losing the presidency. This has prompted some to argue that the Electoral College operates in an undemocratic fashion and distorts the overall weight of individuals voting for president depending on where the vote is cast (i.e., the state wherein the voter resides). For example, in "A Constitutional Anachronism: Why the Electoral College Should Be Abolished or Its Operation Re-configured" (Beckman, 2022), published in *Cumberland Law Review*, the author argued that the Electoral College system fundamentally undermines the democratic principle of equality in voting and leads to the indirect disenfranchisement of hundreds of thousands of voters (as was the case in the election of 2000) or millions of voters (as was the case in the 2016 election).

In theory, according to the Supreme Court, despite anomalous practices like gerrymandering, American political equality in voting rests on the principle of "one person, one vote" as articulated in *Baker v. Carr*, 369 U.S. 186 (1962). Yet, with the Electoral College, each state's voting power is weighed differently, seemingly therefore at odds with the "one person one vote" principle. Because electoral votes are allocated differently to each state (with each state's total being its number of Senators plus Representatives), small states enjoy an outsized influence per voter compared to large states. Every state, no matter how small, is guaranteed at least three electoral votes. This means states with very low populations end up with far fewer people per elector. This leads to the clear structural imbalance wherein "one vote does not equal one vote" between different states in presidential elections (Beckman, 2022, 197).

Wyoming and California serve as good examples to illustrate the disparity in voting power between big and small states in the Electoral College. Wyoming, one of the least populated states, has three electoral votes for its roughly half-million residents, whereas California, the most populous state, has fifty-four electoral votes (based on the 2020 census) for its tens of millions of residents. When one calculates the population-to-electoral vote ratio, the disparity is striking. A single voter's ballot in Wyoming carries the weight of about 3.6 votes in California (Beckman, 2022). In other words, an individual Wyoming voter has well over three times the influence in the Electoral College as an individual California voter. Or phrased yet another way, because a Wyoming vote is worth almost four times that of a California vote, three California votes are negated or disenfranchised.

The fact that smaller states like Wyoming or Delaware are overrepresented in their voting power, while larger states like California, Texas, Florida, and New York are underrepresented is a clear example of indirect voter disenfranchisement. Critics of the Electoral College system indicate that no citizen's vote should be based solely on state lines. As Chief Justice Earl Warren once wrote in *Reynolds v. Sims*, 377 U.S. 533, 562–3 (1964), land or acreage does not vote, rather people vote, and "legislators represent people, not trees or acres."

Yet that is exactly what the Electoral College mechanism ensures, under the direction of the Constitution.

Beyond the allocation of electoral votes among states by different weights, the "winner-takes-all" rule used by most states also magnifies voter inequality and potentially distorts electoral outcomes. Under the winner-takes-all approach (also known as "unit rule" or the "general-ticket system"), the presidential candidate who wins the popular vote in a state receives all of that state's electoral votes regardless of how narrow the margin happened to be. This state-level rule (which is a choice made by the states, not a constitutional mandate) effectively disenfranchises the losing side's voters in each state and skews the election results far away from the principle of proportional representation of voters' will. If 49.9 percent of a state's voters choose one candidate and 50.1 percent choose another, 100 percent of the state's electoral votes go to the slight winner, and 49.9 percent of those voters are left with zero representation in the Electoral College tally (Beckman, 2022). The votes of the minority (perhaps up to 49.9 percent of the total votes in a state) no longer count toward the overall national vote count to select a winner, as the electoral votes cast for the state are all that matter in the election. The statewide winner-take-all rule, in practice, "ensures that votes are not equally treated" and often creates "variations of 1,000-to-1 and more in the weight of a vote" between different states or different scenarios (Beckman, 2022). Amplifying the electors-per-state problem described earlier, the winner-takes-all approach turns small differences into total shutouts and makes close votes in small states more consequential than landslides in large states. This, in a way, effectively disenfranchises hundreds of thousands of voters.

A comparison of New Mexico and Utah in the 2000 election provides an example of how the winner-takes-all rule can produce extreme disparities and distort the vote. Each of these states had five electoral votes. In New Mexico, Al Gore won the popular vote by a razor-thin margin of 365 votes, winning all five of New Mexico's electors. In Utah, George W. Bush won the state by 312,043 votes and likewise received all five of Utah's electors. Each candidate ended up with the same number of electoral votes despite the disparity in the two contests with the popular vote. This is the winner-take-all approach, in which the magnitude of victory does not matter. Given that Gore's slim margin in New Mexico (365 votes) yielded the same electoral payoff as Bush's 312,000 vote margin in victory in Utah, one person's vote in New Mexico could be said to be worth 855 people's votes in Utah in securing the same number of electoral votes. Such an outcome illustrates how practices related to the Electoral College can skew and distort the translation of individual votes, or worse, disenfranchise or discount ballots as a result of the way the system operates.

Another example illustrating the problem can be seen in the 2000 presidential election in Florida. Florida's then-twenty-five electoral votes were awarded to George W. Bush based on a 537-vote lead in that state. Gore's shortfall of 537 votes in Florida was less than one thousandth percent of his nationwide lead of over 537,179 more votes nationwide. Yet, due to winner-take-all in Florida, those few hundred votes in one state carried the day and Bush received all of Florida's elector votes and thus the presidency. A shortfall of 537 votes in Florida wiped out the 537,179-vote lead nationwide.

The winner-takes-all rule not only creates disparities in voting weight, but it also has the effect of suppressing political competition and voter motivation in many states. If you belong to the political minority in a solidly "red" (Republican) or "blue" (Democratic) state, you have little incentive to vote because the outcome in your state is a foregone conclusion, and your vote will not affect any electoral votes. Conversely, if you are part of the majority in a safe state, your vote adds to a surplus that does not translate into additional electoral influence. In either case, vast numbers of votes in non-competitive states are irrelevant to the presidential outcome. Republican Dean Murray, a supporter of reform, encapsulated the problem well when he stated that "a vote should be a vote regardless of where it was cast. A voter in Ohio should not be more important than a voter in Kansas ... every voter should be heard, and every vote should count equally" (Beckman, 2022, 197).

Despite this effect, and beyond the fact that the Electoral College is constitutionally required, it is worth noting that there are also a few advantages to the Electoral College system. First, if the nationwide popular vote was all the mattered in the selection of a president, candidates might focus all their efforts on the large population centers and urban areas and disregard or ignore more rural areas of the country who have their own distinct electoral issues and voter values. The Electoral College forces candidates to campaign and consider regional issues outside of just the large concentration of voters on the East and West Coasts. The Electoral College thereby ensures candidates do not completely ignore smaller states in the interior of the country. Politicians, for example, do not automatically ignore the issues of farmers in Iowa or Kansas because of the more sparsely populated location of these voters. Second, if there are claims of voting fraud or irregularities someplace in the country that might require a recount, the Electoral College ensures that such a recount would only need to be done in those states reporting problems and not nationwide. Any post-election recount or investigation would then be more localized in nature as well. From this perspective, one could argue that the Electoral College provides a safeguard to potential post-election chaos if a recount or investigation is required in whichever state is reporting or encountering a problem.

There are two additional benefits to the Electoral College in lieu of relying just on the national vote count. One, to ultimate win the office, a candidate must build a coalition of supporters from different regions around the United States and not just rely on the support of the voters in large urban population centers. Second, the Electoral College may reduce the cost of campaigns in the sense that certain states can be ignored. That is, if certain states are solidly aligned with one political party or another, the Electoral College system in essence allows candidates to utilize their resources and energies on the true battleground locations around the country and not on piling up the vote in areas already in a party's favor or where the candidate has little chance of taking the state. Thus, it makes campaigning less taxing on political candidates. Finally, even though the Electoral College occasionally produces results in conflict with the nationwide popular vote, that has only happened in a handful of instances in the country's rich two hundred and fifty plus-year existence, and only twice in the first eight presidential elections in the twenty-first century.

One proposed solution for bypassing the Electoral College without having to secure a constitutional amendment is the National Popular Vote Interstate Compact (NPVIC). The NPVIC would substitute the national popular vote as the criterion used to determine a winner without formally amending the Constitution to eliminate the Electoral College. Under the NPVIC, states agree to award all their electoral votes to the winner of the nationwide popular vote, rather than the winner of the vote in their own state. As Article I of the Constitution allows each state to determine the "time, place, and manner" of elections, states have the authority to determine how the state's allocation of electors in the Electoral College are determined. Thus, under the proposed NPVIC, every voter's ballot would carry the same weight toward the outcome, regardless of the state wherein the voter is located, because only the national total would matter.

But the NPVIC is not currently operational as it takes effect only once a critical number of states have joined. More specifically, the NPVIC only becomes operational when the participating states together hold at least 270 electoral votes (the minimum needed to elect a president) (Beckman, 2022, 211). As of 2025, only seventeen states and Washington, DC, have agreed to the NPVIC, equaling 209 electoral votes. This is only 77 percent of the total 270 electoral votes needed. The compact would need states representing at least sixty-one more electoral votes to agree to the NPVIC before it can take effect.

The benefit of the NPVIC is that it bypasses the arduous constitutional amendment requirements by using the states' existing constitutional power to determine how to allocate their electors. Instead of needing approval from two-thirds of Congress and three-fourths of the states (as a constitutional amendment would require), the NPVIC only needs a coalition of states representing the majority needed for the Electoral College (i.e., 270 electoral votes). This would allow the national popular vote to be dispositive without formally abolishing the Electoral College. Beyond not having a sufficient number of states who have agreed to the NPVIC, the second drawback/problem with the NPVIC is that its enactment would most likely be challenged in the federal courts. It is also unclear what would happen if a state that once votes in favor of the NPVIC later attempts to rescind its consent to the NPVIC when new politicians from a different party and point of view come into office. As such, the constitutionality of multiple aspects of the NPVIC will be in doubt until the Supreme Court has had the chance to review the constitutional legitimacy of the NPVIC.

Further Reading

Beckman, James A. "A Constitutional Anachronism: Why the Electoral College Should Be Abolished or Its Operation Re-configured." *Cumberland Law* Review, *52*, no. 1 (2022), 163–214.

Best, Judith. *The Case against Direct Election of the President: A Defense of the Electoral College*. Cornell University Press, 1971.

Davidson, Joe. "National Popular Vote Plan Challenges Undemocratic Electoral College." *Washington Post*, September 13, 2024. https://www.washingtonpost.com/politics/2024/09/13/national-popular-vote-plan-electoral-college

Edwards, George C. *Why the Electoral College Is Bad for America*. 3rd edition. Yale University Press, 2019.

Hardaway, Robert M. *The Electoral College and the Constitution: The Case for Preserving Federalism*. Praeger, 1994.

Koza, John R., Barry Fadem, Mark Grueskin, Michael Mandell, Robert Richie, and Joseph Zimmerman. *Every Vote Equal: A State Based Plan for Electing the President by National Popular Vote*. 4th edition. National Popular Vote Press, 2013.

Longley, Lawrence D., and Neal R. Peirce. *The Electoral College Primer 2000*. Yale University Press, 1999.

Neale, Thomas H. "The Electoral College: How It Works in Contemporary Presidential Elections." Congressional Research Service (CRS), RL32611 (2017).

Petrocelli, William. "Voters in Wyoming Have 3.6 Times the Voting Power That I Have. It's Time to End the Electoral College." HUFFPOST, November 10, 2016. https://www.huffpost.com/entry/its-time-to-end-the-electoral-college_b_12891764

Ross, Tara. *Enlightened Democracy: The Case for the Electoral College*. World Ahead Publishing, 2012.

Q11: Has the federal government enacted legislation making it easier to register to vote and/or preventing states from voter registration purges?

Answer: Yes. After the Voting Rights Act of 1965, the next major piece of federal legislation was the National Voter Registration Act of 1993 (NVRA), often referred to as "the Motor Voter Law." This legislation vastly simplifies voter registration, making it much easier by offering an array of different methods, including registration by mail and registering to vote when applying for a driver's license. The law also puts specific rules in place that states must follow before purging voting registration lists and prohibits states from removing previously registered voters within ninety days of a federal election. The NVRA also limits how states may impose residency requirements. States cannot require more than thirty days of residency as a condition for voter registration. Also, the NVRA requires states to accept a uniform federal voter registration form on which applicants swear (under oath) that they are US citizens, without requiring additional documents. As such, the law has served as a check on state governments that wish to impose additional criteria on voters (at least in elections for federal officials), such as proof of citizenship.

The Facts: As discussed earlier in this book, the Voting Rights Act drastically changed election practices in the southern United States and made voting more inclusive. Practices like literacy tests and poll taxes were made illegal. This expanded the group of people who were eligible to vote, and theoretically, made it more likely that people would vote. Yet, despite this milestone legislation, considered to be one of the greatest legislative acts of the twentieth century, voter registration still languished across the country from the 1960s through the early 1990s.

The reason for the stagnant registration rates was, in part, a problem of disparity between income brackets and wealth. According to author Carol Anderson, "the top income brackets achieved more than 80 percent voter registration rates, however from 1972 to 1992, voter registration among the lowest income quintile saw a nearly 18 percent drop—from 61.2 percent in 1972 to 43.5 percent in 1992" (Anderson, 2020, 73). Further, beyond the income disparity impact on registration (or rather on the ability of individuals from differing economic brackets to get clear information on registration rules), there was also a patchwork of sometimes-confusing, and sometimes-onerous, registration requirements in place from state to state.

The overall lack of general voter participation in the presidential elections of 1988 and 1992 was additional impetus for Congress to pass the Motor Vehicle Law. Foundering registration rates alarmed members of Congress. In 1988, voting in the presidential election had reached its lowest point in over forty years (Crocker, 2013, 2). Roughly half (44 percent) of eligible American voters declined to vote in the 1992 presidential election (Rogers, 2009, 1). Proponents in Congress for the new federal legislation "believed that simplifying and improving the voter registration process would eliminate a major barrier to low participation in the future" (Rogers, 2009, 1).

The official name of the legislation was The National Voter Registration Act (NVRA), but it quickly became known as the "the Motor Voter Law." This was an apt name because under the act one could register to vote while applying for a driver's license. The act was signed into law by President Clinton on May 20, 1993, and came into effect on January 1, 1995. The preamble to the legislation declares the right to vote to be a "fundamental right," and "that it is the duty of the Federal, State, and local government to promote the exercise of that right" (Anderson, 2020, 73). According to the language of the legislation, this duty and obligation of the federal and state governments to "promote the exercise of that right," include giving appropriate consideration to "discriminatory and unfair registration laws and procedures" that "disproportionately harm voter participation by various groups, including racial minorities" (Anderson, 2020, 73).

The most well-known feature of the NVRA is that each state's department of motor vehicles (DMV) must provide voter registration as part of the application in receiving a driver's license. Under the NVRA, registering to vote occurs automatically when filling out the necessary paperwork for the state driver's license application. Under the law, applicants are given the choice to opt out of the voter registration, but little data is available to suggest that very many people opt out of the automatic registration. When a driver submits a change of address form to the DMV, the NVRA requires states to treat this as a change of address for voter registration purposes as well.

The second major feature of the NVRA is that it requires each state to allow any eligible voter to register by mail for federal elections. This makes registration easier as well. Under the provisions of the NVRA, states must create a mail-in registration form that may be sent to eligible voters in the state. Second, the NVRA specifies that states must "accept and use" this mail-in form to register the voter. Prior to this legislation, in many states, prospective voters would have to travel to a specific governmental office to register to vote. The NVRA also expanded the list of government offices that could handle voter registration applications.

When the act was passed, it was assumed that the lion share of new registration would come by way of applying for a driver's license since the Department of Transportation estimated that approximately 87 percent of the voting age population obtains driver's licenses (Federal Election Commission, 1997, 13). While voter registration through state DMV offices did account for the greatest number of new registrations at 33.10 percent, registrations by mail accounted for nearly as many overall registrations at 29.74 percent (Federal Election Commission, 1997, 13).

The NVRA also contained enforcement provisions to ensure compliance. First, the law made it a federal offense to interfere with or intimidate during registration efforts. Second, the NVRA criminalized knowingly submitting false registration information. The former criminal offense was to deter those who might attempt to thwart good faith eligible voters from registering, while the latter offense was meant to combat potential fraud. Finally, the law included important enforcement mechanisms. The NVRA authorized the Department of Justice to bring lawsuits against state governments for non-compliance and enabled individuals to sue non-conforming states as well. This enforcement power is similar to that included in the Voters Rights Act.

The NVRA provides standards for states to follow relating to voter list maintenance, including basic rules and what conditions must be met before states can purge voter registration lists. (See Question 19 for more detail on this topic.) The NVRA also provides a national standard deadline for a state's ability to purge voter registrations directly preceding in an upcoming election. The law makes clear that states are prohibited from conducting any large-scale purges in the last ninety days before a federal election (either a primary election or a general election). This ninety-day period is sometimes described as the NVRA imposed "quiet period." The "quiet period" only applies to large-scale purges, meaning that states cannot systematically remove ineligible voters as part of a mass purge. (See Question 20 for information on why states might remove voters from voter registrations lists.)

As to the act of registration itself (as opposed to voter turnout once registered), the NVRA required the collection of voter registration information as part of the driver's license application process, but the law does not specify when a voter must register before an election. This is an issue of state law under the state's power to regulate "time, place, and manner" of elections under Article I, Section 4 of the Constitution. Because of this, registration procedures and deadlines vary by state, and a state's deadlines may be different for online, by mail, or in-person registration. Almost half of the states (and the District of Columbia) offer same-day registration for the day of the general election in November. Other states require registration before Election Day, with some deadlines as early as October 6. However, the NVRA does specify that states cannot require individuals to reside in-state for more than thirty days as a condition for voter registration.

The NVRA has been deemed a success, as it is responsible for the gradual increase in registrations over the course of several years. The Congressional Research Service reported that from 1992 (the year preceding NVRA enactment) to 2012 (date of the report to Congress), the national voter registration rate as a percentage of the total voting age population increased by approximately seven percentage points (Crocker, 2013). This equates to tens of millions of new registrations attributable to the NVRA.

Yet, the large increase in registrations has not translated into a corresponding increase in voter turnout. Shortly after the NVRA's passage, some scholars suggested that the new law had the potential to increase voter turnout by as much as ten percentage points (Highton and Wolfinger, 2001). Yet, voter turnout in the 1996 and 2000 presidential elections and the 1998 midterm elections, after the NVRA went into effect, was lower than the two most comparable national elections, which took place in 1992 and 1994 (Kernell et al., 2012, 501). So while the ease of registration to vote removed a major barrier to voting, the increase in registration rates has not served as the expected cure for the problem of low voter turnout during actual elections.

Nevertheless, the law has served as an effective check on state governments that wish to impose additional criteria on those submitting their federal registration forms, such as a state attempting to mandate that applicants must provide proof of citizenship to vote in federal elections. An example of this can be seen in Kansas's enactment of legislation called the Secure and Fair Elections (SAFE) Act. SAFE was initially enacted in 2011 and was one of the most stringent voting laws in the country. As originally enacted, SAFE required several sweeping changes to Kansas election law, including requiring proof of citizenship to vote, requiring a government-issued photo identification for in-person voting, and requiring a photo identification for mail-in ballots. It also required documentary proof of citizenship for new voter registrations, which could entail presentation of a birth certificate, passport, or naturalization document. Under SAFE, applicants who submitted a registration without proof of citizenship were placed in a "suspense" list and were required to provide the required document within ninety days, or the registration would be canceled. This documentary proof-of-citizenship requirement was not only the strictest in the nation, but also unique at the time (only Arizona had a similar rule).

Almost immediately, Kansas's proof-of-citizenship mandate ran into conflict with the NVRA. The NVRA requires states to accept a uniform federal voter registration form on which applicants swear (under oath) that they are US citizens, without requiring any additional documents. Seeking to enforce the new Kansas law, Kansas (joined by Arizona) petitioned the US Election Assistance Commission (EAC) to add state-specific instructions on the federal form requiring proof of citizenship for Kansas registrations. The EAC denied the request, and Kansas and Arizona sued the EAC. In November 2014, the US Court of Appeals for the Tenth Circuit ruled that the EAC could not be compelled to include Kansas's proof-of-citizenship requirement on the federal form and require voters to provide that documentation in voting in federal elections. That is, states cannot require documentary proof-of-citizenship from those voters using the federal registration form and for purposes of voting in any federal election but would be free to still include the documentation as it relates only to state-, county-, or municipal-level elections in Kansas. The US Supreme Court declined to hear Kansas's appeal in June 2015, leaving the Tenth Circuit's decision intact. This meant that, at least for federal elections, under the NVRA, Kansas could not extend its documentation rule to individuals using the federal registration form for purposes of voting in any federal election. The ruling was a significant early defeat for the SAFE Act's reach and also illustrated the power and scope of the NVRA.

Further Reading

Alvarez, R. Michael, and Thad E. Hall. *Point, Click, and Vote: The Future of Internet Voting*. Brookings Institution Press, 2004.

Anderson, Carol. *One Person, No Vote: How Voter Suppression Is Destroying Our Democracy*. Bloomsbury Publishing, 2020.

Crocker, Royce. "The National Voter Registration Act of 1993: History, Implementation, and Effects." Congressional Research Service, September 18 (2013), 7–5700.

Federal Elections Commission. "The Impact of the National Voter Registration Act of 1993 on the Administration of Elections for Federal Office 1995–1996: A Report to the 105th Congress." Washington, DC (1997).

Herron, Michael C., and Daniel A. Smith. *From Registration to Recounts: The Election Ecosystem of the United States.* Cambridge University Press, 2012.

Highton, Benjamin, and Raymond E. Wolfinger. "The Political Implications of Higher Voter Turnout." *British Journal of Political Science, 31*, no. 1 (January 2001), 179–223.

Kernell, Samuel, Gary C. Jacobson, and Thad Kousser. *The Logic of American Politics*, 5th edition. Sage/Congressional Quarterly, 2012.

Keyssar, Alexander. *The Right to Vote: The Contested History of Democracy in the United States.* Revised edition. Basic Books, 2009.

Lomax, Tamika L. *Motor Voter and the Transformation of American Registration Policy.* University Press of America, 2002.

National Voter Registration Act of 1993 (NVRA), P.L. 103–31, 107 Stat.77, 42 U.S.C. §1973gg et seq.

Rogers, Estelle H. "Issue Brief: The National Voter Registration Act: Fifteen Years On." American Constitutional Society for Law and Policy, November (2009).

Tokaji, Daniel P. *Election Law in a Nutshell.* West Academic Publishing, 2013.

Q12: Has election infrastructure been modernized and improved to help protect against voter disenfranchisement?

Answer: Yes. In 2002, Congress enacted the Help America Vote Act of 2002 (HAVA), which not only poured billions of dollars into the state governments to help modernize and update antiquated equipment but also amended the National Voters Registration Act with additional standards meant to further insulate elections from fraud. For the first time federally, HAVA also required that first-time voters present proof of the voter's identification (e.g., as part of the mail-in registration application or when they vote in person for the first time). Under the law, for federal elections, if a person registers to vote by mail and does not include this proof of voter identification, then the voter must provide that documentation when they vote in person in a federal election. This would lead to the further development and proliferation of voter identification laws adopted and/or debated in states around the country in the years since HAVA enactment.

The Facts: Not since the contested 1876 election of Rutherford B. Hayes and Samuel Tilden did a presidential election exhibit as many problems as the

2000 election between Al Gore and George W. Bush. Various types of voting machines were being utilized between the different states and even different counties within a state. Some election sites utilized the old punch card system (replete with "hanging chads," resulting from holes not being fully punched out), while others had lever-operated voting machines, and others had computerized voting booths that recorded votes electronically (with printed paper back-ups). Nowhere was the dysfunction more evident than in the state of Florida. As Florida began its recount of votes during the 2000 presidential election, the media displayed images as to how antiquated and diverse some of the ballot-counting machines were among different voting precincts within a single state. Further, until the US Supreme Court put a stop to the Florida recount, George W. Bush only had a 537-vote lead over Al Gore. Those 537 votes (and perhaps less) were the only difference between Al Gore and George W. Bush being elected president. Whoever won the state of Florida collected the then-twenty-five electoral votes and would secure the presidency. So every vote truly counted.

After the chaotic and close election of 2000, and with the intense media focus, members of both political parties (as well as the American people) clamored for improvements and modernization to voting across the entire country. A Gallup Organization Poll from November 2001 found that 42 percent of those surveyed said that the 2000 election revealed either a "constitutional crisis or a major problem" (Curry, et al., 2003, 549). The result was the enactment of HAVA in 2002. HAVA passed in both chambers of Congress by wide numbers (357–49 in the House of Representations; 92–2 with several abstentions in the Senate) (Underhill, 2022). President George W. Bush signed the legislation into law on October 29, 2002.

According to the US Department of Justice (DOJ), HAVA accomplished multiple goals. The first was the creation of a federal election assistance agency, the US EAC. The second was by "providing funds to states to improve election administration and replace outdated voting systems" (Department of Justice, n.d.). Describing HAVA as "providing funds to states" almost seems to downplay the injection of funds to the states vis-à-vis HAVA that did occur. According to the EAC, "Since 2003, the EAC has administered more than $4.35 billion in HAVA formula funding to the states and territories, including Election Security and CARES funding totaling $1.4 billion from 2018 to 2024" (EAC, 2025). This was a significant investment in the modernization of electoral equipment, totaling billions of dollars from 2003 through 2024.

The HAVA funding is still ongoing. As reported by Wendy Underhill:

> In 2018, 380 million was appropriated for the general improvements grant program, with encouragement that it be used for election security. In 2020, two outlays totaling $825 million were provided to help run elections during a pandemic, and in 2022, $75 million was appropriated … [and] all presidents in the 21st century have signed off on funds to support federal elections (including George W. Bush, Barack Obama, Donald Trump, and Joe Biden). (Underhill, 2022)

Underhill's article quotes an EAC member who opined that even after close to twenty-five years, "much of HAVA is still unrealized" (Underhill, 2022).

Finally, the third accomplishment listed by the DOJ as a main achievement of HAVA was the creation of "minimum standards for states to follow in several key areas of election administration" (Department of Justice, n.d.). These minimum standards covered a variety of different areas, including the allowance of "second chance voting" in certain cases of clear ballot error, the mandate of the creation of statewide voter registration databases to ensure the uniform collection of data across the states, and providing for the uniform usage of "provision ballots" to allow a voter to still record their voting preferences if challenged at the time of voting and wish to have their vote preserved. Additionally, for federal elections, if a person registers by mail and does not include proof of identification, then that voter must present that proof of identification at the time that they do vote in person. HAVA also enabled the greater dissemination of voter information and assistance, the training of poll workers, and EAC negotiated grants to states to continue with the mission and spirit of HAVA.

The nation's huge investment of cash to modernize election equipment and processes has narrowed the discrepancies between richer and poorer voting precincts within a particular state as well as between states. Gone are the lever-pulling machines and punch cards with hanging chads. Many votes are now cast on paper and then optically scanned into computer systems. In some places, new computerized voting machines were brought online through baseline security criteria and functionality developed by the EAC. A requirement for the new machines was that they could show voters their selections at the end of the completed ballot, and allow casting of an alternate ballot if an error occurred in recording the vote. This is called "second chance voting," first introduced via HAVA and made possible because of modern voting equipment.

Before the year 2000, in many states, voter registration lists were kept separately by counties, meaning that there was no integration of information across the state and no means of identifying faulty or fraudulent votes. Many counties still had antiquated paper lists of registered voters. As explained in a report by the House of Representatives, Section 303(a) of HAVA required each state to "implement a single, uniform, official, centralized, interactive computerized statewide voter registration list that contains the name and registration information, including a unique identifier, of every legally registered voter in the State to serve as the official voter registration list for the conduct of all elections for Federal office in the State" (House of Representatives, 2002). As such, HAVA requires new voter registrants to provide either their driver's license number or the last four digits of their Social Security number. State governments, in turn, must verify their voter database with other official records to ensure accuracy (e.g., the state's Department of Motor Vehicles or the Social Security Administration). Congress also mandated in HAVA that states regularly update their registration lists and correct inaccuracies.

Proponents of the law have affirmed that the HAVA provisions operate to reduce registration errors (Brennan Center for Justice, 2002; Underhill, 2022). However, statewide voter registration databases have not always been implemented without controversy. For example, Georgia's Exact Match Program and Florida's "No Match, No Vote" Law required that registrations be put on hold if there were the slightest mismatch between records (such as shortened name, a minor typo, or a hyphenated last name). Kansas's Interstate Voter Registration Cross-Check Program sought to prevent voters from registering or casting ballots in more than one state but produced a high rate of false positives due to loose matching standards. State use of the Electronic Registration Information Center, a nonprofit organization, to verify records and comply with HAVA has also been controversial.

As referenced briefly, for federal elections held after January 1, 2004, HAVA requires that states must offer voters the chance to cast a provisional ballot. A provisional ballot might be cast if there was a problem during the voting process. The provisional ballot is meant to allow individuals to cast a ballot and then subsequently address whatever problem they encountered. This is referred to as "curing" a ballot. The problems a voter might face include their name not appearing on the state's voter registration list, the lack of a requisite voter identification documentation or card, or their eligibility to vote otherwise being challenged (e.g., felons attempting to vote in states that preclude that practice). If the voter can fix the problem in the time dictated by state, the vote would be counted after the fact.

The mandate of states having to offer a provisional ballot to any voter whose eligibility is in question is contained in Title III (Section 302) of HAVA. These provisional ballots are often referred to as "fail safe ballots," as election officials keep these ballots separate, examine them, and then later count any ballots that should have been allowed on election day. HAVA also mandates that election locations must have posters and instructions on how to cast a provisional ballot at that election site. States must also provide a way for voters to track the status of their provisional ballot (e.g., on a website or via calling a toll-free telephone number).

Lastly, for the first time, HAVA introduced a requirement that new first-time voters must provide proof of voter identification when registering by mail. For these new voters, if this information is not provided as part of the mail-in registration, it must be presented when voting for the first time in a federal election. Additionally, under HAVA, states are free to adopt stricter voter identification laws beyond the basics required by the federal statute and applicable for federal elections. Types of acceptable voter identification, both under HAVA and stricter state voter identification laws and approaches, are explored in more detail in Question 13.

Further Reading

Brennan Center for Justice. "The Help America Vote Act." 2002. https://www.brennancenter.org/sites/default/files/legacy/d/HAVA%20Fact%20Sheet.pdf

Curry, James A., Richard B. Riley, and Richard M. Battistoni. *Constitutional Government: The American Experiment.* 5th edition. Kendall/Hunt Publishing, 2003.

Department of Justice, Civil Rights Division. "The Help America Vote Act of 2002." Accessed May 25, 2025. https://www.justice.gov/crt/help-america-vote-act-2002

Election Assistance Commission (EAC). "HAVA Grant Programs." July 22, 2025. https://www.eac.gov/grants/hava-grant-programs

Help America Vote Act of 2002 (HAVA), Pub. L. No. 107–252, 116 Stat. 1666 (2002), 52 U.S.C. §§ 20901–21145.

House of Representatives. Conference Report on H.R. 3295-Helf America Vote Act of 2002. 107th Congress (2001–2002), October 8, 2002. https://www.congress.gov/bill/107th-congress/house-bill/3295

Underhill, Wendy. "The Help America Vote Act: 20 Years Later." National Conference of State Legislatures, June 1, 2022. https://www.ncsl.org/state-legislatures-news/details/the-help-america-vote-act-20-years-later

Q13: What actions regarding voter identification have state governments taken in response to the 2002 passage of the Help America Vote Act?

Answer: As a matter of federal law, the Help America Vote Act (HAVA) required for the first time that new voters provide proof of identification when voting or as part of the registration application to vote. In 2025, HAVA is still the only *federal* law requiring that voters supply proof of identity either at the point of in-person voting or by supplying a photo identification or last four digits of the voter's social security number in the registration application. In the legislative history and text of HAVA, Congress also indicated that state governments were free to pass more rigorous voter identification requirements "so long as [they] are not inconsistent with" the terms of HAVA. Since HAVA was enacted, on the state level, calls and proposals relating to proof of voter identification have proliferated and have resulted in numerous states adopting various voter identification requirements beyond the HAVA baseline requirements. Whether this proliferation was a direct result of HAVA or just the natural progression of state laws on the topic is debatable. In fact, there were a handful of states that required proof of voter identification before HAVA. However, the number of states requiring this proof after 2002 doubled and then tripled.

The Facts: Section 303(b) of HAVA requires that when casting a ballot for the first time, a voter present either a photo identification or a copy of a current utility bill, bank statement, government check, paycheck, or other government document showing the name and address of the voter. The only exception to this requirement is if the prospective voter provides proof of identity during mail-in voter registration. That is, a prospective voter can avoid having to provide proof of identity on the day of voting if they submit a copy of these documents with the registration form or by providing a driver's license or Social Security Number that matches the government's records for that person (EAC, 2008, 1).

As a starting point, it should be recognized that HAVA played a role in helping to usher in more frequently utilized and/or more rigorous voter identification laws. The voter identification requirement in HAVA was the first time, and is still the only time, in which federal law dictates that proof of identity must be provided for first-time voters who registered to vote by mail. While approximately eleven states already required that voters provide proof of identity before HAVA was even promulgated, the number of states requiring this proof greatly increased after HAVA's enactment. Beyond those eleven states with preexisting rules on this subject, one could argue that a federal law requiring proof of identity nationwide for first-time voters eased the mindset of the American population into the idea that proof of identity was a normal and reasonable thing to require to vote. In other words, it could be argued that HAVA normalized the notion of requiring voters to provide proof of identity when voting, and that such a requirement was not a radical concept or proposal.

The text of HAVA itself left open the possibility that states could enact their own voter identification laws (including even more strict and rigorous laws) so long as the new state laws were not otherwise incompatible with the provisions of the National Voters Registration Act and/or HAVA. As the United States Election Committee (EAC) explained in its authoritative guide on the implementation of HAVA (published six years after the law went into effect): "Congress left it up to the States to decide whether to implement the law as the only ID requirement or to expand on it and require more from voters" (EAC, 2008, 1). And, as suggested, the states decided to expand on it, and quite rapidly.

How quickly did states move on the HAVA prompt that states could also provide their own standards? The numbers are illustrative. According to the EAC, in just the first two years after HAVA enactment, by 2004, the number of states requiring some sort of proof of voter identity jumped from eleven to nineteen (EAC, 2008, 1). By 2006, the number jumped even higher still, with a total of twenty-four states (almost 50 percent of the country) requiring all voters to provide identification at the polls (EAC, 2008, 1). By 2024, the number leaped again, with a total of thirty-six states (over a three time increase from the number of states in 2002) promulgating laws that require voters to present some form of identification when voting in person at the polls (National Conference of State Legislatures, 2025). Of these thirty-six states, approximately twenty-three require a government-issued photo identification at the polls (e.g., a state-issued driver's license, military ID card, US passport, etc.). The remaining thirteen states will accept non-photo identification documentation that shows the voter's name and correct address, such as voter registration cards, bank statements, utility bills, and the like (National Conference of State Legislatures, 2025). In 2023, Wyoming and Texas revised its laws to allow valid concealed carry permits as an acceptable type of government-issued photographic identification needed to vote (National Conference of State Legislatures, 2025).

Some states, such as Florida, require a combination of identifications. Florida Statutes § 101.043(1) requires voters to present two types of identification to vote, namely, a photo identification card (not necessarily a government-issued one) plus one of twelve types of identification enumerated in the statute: a

Florida driver license; a Florida identification card issued by the Department of Highway Safety and Motor Vehicles; a US passport; a debit or credit card; military identification; student identification; retirement center identification; neighborhood association identification; public assistance identification; a veteran health identification card issued by the US Department of Veterans Affairs; a license to carry a concealed weapon or firearm issued pursuant to Florida statute 790.06; or an employee identification card issued by any branch, department, agency, or entity of the federal government, the state, a county, or a municipality. The Florida statute also requires that the photo identification contains the voter's signature on the card. (This would exclude student photo identification cards and the like.) If the card lacks a signature, an additional identification that provides the elector's signature is required. This makes it highly likely that the voter would still need to produce a Florida driver's license as the requisite photo identification along with another type of identification card from the list.

Further Reading

Election Assistance Commission (EAC). "Case Studies on the Impact of the Help America Vote Act's Identification Requirements for First-Time Voters." May 2008. https://www.eac.gov/sites/default/files/eac_assets/1/15/case%20study%20on%20impact%20of%20HAVA%20id%20requirements%20for%20first%20time%20voters%20public%20meeting%20may%2022%202008.pdf

Florida Statutes Section § 101.043(1).

Help America Vote Act of 2002 (HAVA). Pub. L. No. 107–252, 116 Stat. 1666 (2002), 52 U.S.C. §§ 20901–21145.

National Conference of State Legislatures. *Voter ID Laws.* April 16, 2025. https://www.ncsl.org/elections-and-campaigns/voter-id#:~:text=Thirty,Voter%20Verification%20Without%20ID%20Documents

3

Disenfranchised Groups Based upon Status

Disenfranchisement in America has occurred for a variety of reasons. Large segments of the population were historically disenfranchised based upon their own immutable characteristics (e.g., race or gender). As discussed in Chapter 1, Black Americans were explicitly disenfranchised until after the ratification of the Fifteenth Amendment, and women were explicitly disenfranchised until the ratification of the Nineteenth Amendment. In modern America, other groups might be disenfranchised based on an individual's criminal conduct (i.e., felony disenfranchisement) or based upon a person's condition of homelessness. Other groups subject to potential disenfranchisement include members of the military (and their immediate families), college-aged students, and those adjudicated to be mentally incompetent.

In many states, felony conviction results in a complete and explicit ban on voting, so that the felon would be completely barred from voting in that state. The disenfranchisement of other groups, however, comes about by way of logistical obstacles faced by members of those groups. College-aged voters may encounter obstacles when navigating residency requirements or dealing with restrictive identification laws that might not recognize a college identification card. Homeless individuals face similar obstacles and might be disenfranchised because of their lack of a permanent residential address, lack the necessary identification documentation to vote, or inability to travel to distant polling locations. They may even be purged from registration lists if they do not receive mail asking them to confirm their registration status. Mental incompetency laws can occasionally operate to disenfranchise people simply because they require a live-in guardian or full-time caretaker. These examples demonstrate that voter suppression is not always the result of explicit and intentional denial of the ballot but may also be caused by obstacles or unique concerns applicable to specific groups.

Q14: Does felony disenfranchisement adversely impact particular demographic groups?

Answer: Yes. One of the most significant collateral consequences of felony convictions in the United States (on the state or federal level) is the loss of voting rights. This is sometimes referred to as felony disenfranchisement. In many states, once convicted of a felony, an individual is permanently barred from future voting, unless the person can petition the government for a "restoration of civil liberties" (a state-specific procedure). In other states the right to vote can be restored.

Felony disenfranchisement has hit Black communities the hardest. In 2016, one in thirteen African Americans had lost their right to vote because of a felony conviction, compared with one in fifty-six of every non-Black vote (Anderson, 2020, 93; The Sentencing Project, 2016). In Michelle Alexander's book entitled *The New Jim Crow: Mass Incarceration in the Age of Colorblindness*, the author postulated that the disenfranchisement of Black voters under felony disenfranchisement rules was a continuation of hundreds of years of disenfranchising Black voters: "an extraordinary percentage of Black men in the United States are legally barred from voting today, just as they have been throughout most of American history" (Alexander, 2012, 1).

The Facts: A common misconception is that this felony disenfranchisement rules apply only to "active felonies" (i.e., wherein the offender is still incarcerated). In fact, the majority of disenfranchised individuals are not in prison. (Also, several states allow prisoners to vote while still incarcerated.) National data reveals that three out of four people disenfranchised due to felonies have finished their sentences and/or are on probation and parole (Uggen, et al., 2024).

The war on drugs that began in the 1980s resulted in Black Americans being disproportionately represented in the criminal justice system. Since 1980, the felony disenfranchisement rate in the United States has grown by 500 percent (Anderson, 2020, 93). Because Black Americans have been incarcerated at such higher rates than other groups, the felony disenfranchisement rule/policy has had a clear impact on Black voters in the United States (The Sentencing Project, 2024).

Data illustrates the point. In 2024, it was estimated that approximately 4.4 million Americans were unable to vote because of a current or past felony conviction (The Sentencing Project, 2024). These disenfranchised individuals amount to roughly 2 percent of possible voters in the United States. Because of higher incarceration and convictions for Black Americans, approximately 5 percent of all Black Americans were disenfranchised due to a felony conviction (Sentencing Project, 2024). Practically, this means that roughly one in nineteen Black adults in the United States cannot vote because of a felony record (Sentencing Project, 2024). In many instances, convictions include a very old criminal record and/or a conviction for a nonviolent, low-echelon drug offense, prosecuted more frequently in Black communities than other communities in the 1980s. Additionally, of the 4.4 million individuals disenfranchised (regardless of race), approximately 2.8 million individuals have completed their criminal sentences but remain disenfranchised due to restrictive state laws (Sentencing Project, 2024; Uggen, et al., 2024).

Approximately 1.9 percent of white adults were disenfranchised in 2022. This meant that only one in fifty-two white adults were unable to vote compared with the one in nineteen Black adults (Sentencing Project, 2024). A researcher in 2000 discovered that one in sixteen Black adults nationwide was disenfranchised compared to one in sixty non-Black adults (Sentencing Project, 2024). Up to one in seven Black adults could not vote due to past convictions in several southern states (Sentencing Project, 2024). According to the Sentencing Project's "Locked Out 2024" report, Florida led the country in 2024 with the highest absolute numbers of disenfranchised citizens, with over 961,000 people disenfranchised due to felony convictions (Sentencing Project, 2024). About 730,000 of those individuals have completed their sentences but remain disenfranchised because of the inability to pay required fines, fees, or restitution, which are sometimes unclear. This has prompted one author to declare Florida to be "the national champion of voter disenfranchisement" and an "electorally dark place" because of this practice (Anderson, 2020, 94).

The origins of felony disenfranchisement laws date back to Reconstruction (Holloway, 2014). The failure of voters to pay back taxes or poll taxes arrears in some southern states amounted to a felony, and once a person was convicted of a felony, they lost their eligibility to vote. Some have argued that modern felony disenfranchisement is a vestige of that era, no different from literacy tests, poll taxes, and like, as a means for states to circumvent the Fifteenth Amendment (Holloway, 2014).

Over time, some exceptions to the rule began to appear. At the onset, there were "lifer" states that would never allow a convicted of felon the chance to vote. These states had laws specifying that a convicted felon could never vote in the state, no matter how long ago the conviction was or under what circumstances. Florida, Kentucky, Iowa, and Virginia were all lifer states. Of those four states,

Florida was considered the most draconian. As stated by author Carol Anderson, "the majority [of the disenfranchised felons] are in Florida. The Sunshine State is actually an electorally dark place of 1.7 million citizens because 'Florida is the national champion of voter disenfranchisement'" (Anderson, 2020, 93–4). But Florida is also a prime illustration of how public support for the rule can erode over time.

In the late 1990s, many states began to eliminate or make more lenient their felony disenfranchisement rule, including Florida in 2018. From 1997 through 2023, twenty-six states and the District of Columbia expanded voting rights for those with prior felony convictions. This led to over two million people regaining the right to vote (Porter and McLeod, 2023). The number of disenfranchised individuals fell from approximately 6.1 million in 2016 to 4.6 million in 2022, a 24 percent decrease in those previously disenfranchised in just a six-year period (Porter and McLeod, 2023). In 2024, the number further dropped to just over 4.1 million or a 31 percent decrease since 2016 (Uggen, et al., 2024).

For many years, Florida led the country in the disenfranchisement of felons (Morse, 2021). On average, the state barred over one million people a year from voting (Uggen, et al., 2020; Uggen, et al., 2024). Then in 2018, much to the celebration of many in Florida at the time, voters in Florida overwhelmingly voted to amend their state constitution (Morse, 2021). Amendment 4 was intended to end the state's lifetime felony disenfranchisement rule. However, the very next year, in 2019, the Florida Legislature passed Senate Bill 7066, which restricted the voting rights of people who had not paid court-ordered monetary sanctions. This effectively re-disenfranchised the majority of those individuals whose rights were initially restored by Amendment 4 (Morse, 2021; Uggen, et al., 2020; Uggen, et al., 2024). According to The Sentencing Project, by 2024, Florida once again became the "nation's disenfranchisement leader in absolute numbers, with over 961,000 people currently banned from voting, often because they cannot afford to pay court-ordered monetary sanctions" (Uggen, et al., 2024).

Florida's position has been criticized as being akin to a modern-day poll tax since many of the former felons are reported to be low-income and disproportionately people of color and who cannot pay the often thousands of dollars of court fees to restore their right to vote (Holloway, 2014; Lerner, 2023). Further, the state of Florida lacks a central database that lets former felons look up whether they have any old outstanding court costs (including interest on old costs) or unpaid restitution. Thus, even those individuals who might believe that they have satisfied all the court-imposed penalties, and made good faith efforts to do so, may still decide to simply stay home because they cannot verify these details through the State and do not wish to risk incarceration by attempting to vote under uncertain circumstances. In fact, several individuals were arrested and prosecuted in Florida for fraudulently voting when they thought they were permitted to vote but were later told that there were still outstanding fees of which they claimed they were not aware. One reported case involved a 69-year-old woman who was awoken at approximately 3 a.m. in the morning to find Florida law enforcement standing outside her door to serve an arrest warrant on her illegally voting, despite the fact that the woman believed her fees had been paid and she had been issued a voter identification card by her county supervisor of elections. Over a dozen individuals were prosecuted under these circumstances between 2022 and 2024 in Florida.

In addition to Florida, the states of Tennessee, Virginia, and Iowa also stand out as historically harsh states as it relates to each state's adherence to the felony disenfranchisement rule. Tennessee's application of the rule reportedly precluded 470,000 citizens, or 9.3 percent of the adult population from voting in 2022 (Lerner, 2023). This was the highest reported rate of disenfranchisement for both Black and Latino voters of all fifty states (Lerner, 2023). The numbers in Florida and Tennessee combined amounted to more than 6 percent of the adult population in those states, or one of every seventeen adults (Uggen, et al. 2024).

Tennessee's restrictions are considered onerous because the state makes the pathway to regaining the right to vote very difficult. While it is theoretically possible to achieve the "restoration of civil liberties" in Tennessee, like Florida, the state makes it very difficult for people to successfully meet all of its requirements. Unlike Florida, Tennessee prohibits people on probation and parole from voting, meaning that a person's sometimes-long parole period must be satisfied as a requisite first step. Then, like Florida, Tennessee requires that those seeking the restoration of rights repay all restitution and court costs (as well as any applicable child support). For the few individuals who have fulfilled all of these state-imposed obligations, the right to vote was still not restored. In July 2023 Tennessee enacted a law that prohibits any individual from seeking to regain their right to vote unless they also successfully received a pardon from the governor or have had a court restore their full rights of citizenship (Lerner, 2023).

In Virginia, the state constitution itself prohibits the restoration of civil liberties (including the right to vote) for felons unless the restoration is ordered by the state's governor (Lerner, 2023). While Virginia's former governor (Ralph Northam) issued an executive order restoring the right to vote for approximately

69,000 individuals in 2021, the state's current governor (Glenn Youngkin) rescinded Northam's executive order for anyone not covered under the 2021 executive order and for future individuals convicted of felonies.

Like Virginia, Iowa's constitution also expressly prohibits people who have committed felonies from voting unless pardoned by the governor. Iowa governor Kim Reynolds issued an executive order restoring voting rights to all people who have completed their sentences (excluding homicide convictions), but the next governor of Iowa could rescind the order, just as was done in Virginia. Because of this possibility, Reynolds herself urged a state constitutional amendment to make the restoration permanent, but the Republican-led legislature blocked that effort, and any future Iowa governor could rescind her executive order.

At the other end of the spectrum, there are states that never had a felony disenfranchisement rule or that have abolished it. In Maine, Vermont, and the District of Columbia, there is no revocation of the right to vote for felons. In these three jurisdictions, a person can even vote while incarcerated by voting via an absentee ballot (National Conference of State Legislatures, 2024). Because of reforms in recent years, twenty-three states now immediately restore an individual's right to vote upon release from prison. In the years 2019–20 alone, Nevada, Colorado, Louisiana, and New Jersey all passed laws to automatically restore voting rights once a person leaves prison.

While the trend has been the liberalization and/or elimination of the felony disenfranchisement rule, whether and to what extent a felony disenfranchises a voter varies by state, and some states still harshly cling to the rule. As of this writing, state rules can be summarized as falling within four categories. First, one in ten states have rules that specify that felons lose their voting rights indefinitely or require a governor's pardon for voting rights to be restored and face an additional waiting period after completion of sentence (including parole and probation) or require additional action before voting rights can be restored. Second, in fifteen states, felons lose their voting rights during incarceration, and for a period of time after, typically while on parole and/or probation, after which time voting rights are automatically restored after any outstanding fines, fees, or restitution is paid. Third, in twenty-three states, felons lose their voting rights while incarcerated but receive automatic restoration upon release (except that in one of these states, Maryland, convictions for buying or selling votes can only be restored through pardon despite the automatic restoration for other crimes). Fourth, in the District of Columbia, Maine, and Vermont, felons never lose their right to vote, even while they are incarcerated (National Conference of State Legislatures, 2024). Last updated in September 2024 (but still available in June

2025), the Civil Rights Division of the US Department of Justice makes available a helpful and easy to follow state-by-state guide, entitled "Guide to State Voting Rules That Apply After a Criminal Conviction," which explains what steps a former felon must take depending on the person's state of residency (Civil Rights Division, 2024).

While progress has clearly been made in decreasing the number of individuals denied the right to vote due to the felony disenfranchisement rule, millions of Americans are still barred from voting because of the rule in 2026. And while the trend is the liberalization or abolishment of the felony disenfranchisement rule, roughly 1.7 percent of the adult American voting population are still disenfranchised under the rule, a majority of whom are non-white individuals (Uggen, et al., 2024).

Further Reading

Alexander, Michelle. *The New Jim Crow: Mass Incarceration in the Age of Colorblindness.* The New Press, 2012.

Anderson, Carol. *One Person, No Vote: How Voter Suppression Is Destroying Our Democracy.* Bloomsbury Publishing, 2020.

Aviram, Hadar, Allyson Bragg, and Chelsea Lewis. "Felon Disenfranchisement." *Annual Review of Law & Social Science, 13* (2017), 295–311.

Civil Rights Division, United States Department of Justice. "Guide to State Voting Rules That Apply after a Criminal Conviction." September 2024. https://www.justice.gov/crt/voting-rights-policy-and-guidance

Holloway, Pippa. *Living in Infamy: Felon Disfranchisement and the History of American Citizenship.* Oxford University Press, 2014.

Lauerman, James E. "Evaluating Congress's Constitutional Basis to Abolish Felony Disenfranchisement." *Washington Law Review, 98,* no. 1 (2023), 253–91.

Lerner, Kira. "The States Where It's Impossible to Vote If You Have a Felony Conviction." *The Guardian,* September 7, 2023. https://www.theguardian.com/us-news/2023/sep/07/states-felony-conviction-voting-rights

Meredith, Marc, and Michael Morse. "The Politics of the Restoration of Ex-Felon Voting Rights: The Case of Iowa." *Quarterly Journal of Political Science, 10,* no. 1 (2015), 41–100.

Morse, Michael. "The Future of Felon Disenfranchisement Reform: Evidence from the Campaign to Restore Voting Rights in Florida." *California Law Review, 109* (2021), 1143–92.

National Conference of State Legislatures. "Restoration of Voting Rights for Felons." October 18, 2024. https://www.ncsl.org/elections-and-campaigns/felon-voting-rights

Porter, Nicole, and Morgan McLeod. "Expanding the Vote: State Felony Disenfranchisement Reform, 1997–2023." The Sentencing Project, October 18, 2023. https://www.sentencingproject.org/reports/expanding-the-vote-state-felony-disenfranchisement-reform-1997-2023/

The Sentencing Project. "6 Million Lost Voters: State-Level Estimates of Felony Disenfranchisement." 2016. https://www.sentencingproject.org/app/uploads/2022/08/6-Million-Lost-Voters.pdf

The Sentencing Project. "Mass Incarceration Trends." May 21, 2024. https://www.sentencingproject.org/reports/mass-incarceration-trends/

Uggen, Christopher, Ryan Larson, Sarah Shannon, and Arleth Pulido-Nava. "Locked Out 2020: Estimates of People Denied Voting Rights Due to a Felony Conviction." The Sentencing Project, October 30, 2020. https://www.sentencingproject.org/reports/locked-out-2020-estimates-of-people-denied-voting-rights-due-to-a-felony-conviction/

Uggen, Christopher, Ryan Larson, Sarah Shannon, Robert Stewart, and Molly Hauf. "Locked Out 2024: Four Million Denied Voting Rights Due to a Felony Conviction." The Sentencing Project, October 10, 2024. https://www.sentencingproject.org/reports/locked-out-2024-four-million-denied-voting-rights-due-to-a-felony-conviction/

Q15: Could a person be disenfranchised because of a judicial determination of "mental incompetency" or being classified by the state as an "idiot"?

Answer: Depending on the potential voter's legal residence and place of voting, a person might be at risk of being disenfranchised. Historically, many (if not all) states barred those with "mental incapacity" or "intellectual disability" from voting. Many state constitutions (e.g., Ohio, Mississippi, Kentucky, Iowa) used terms like "idiots" or "insane people" in their state constitutions. And while the trend is to allow people with mental diseases or disorders to vote so long as the person has not been judicially adjudicated to be mentally incapacitated, there are a handful of states that still cling to the notion that a person should be disenfranchised because of a mental illness. States removing voters from voter registration lists due to mental disorders did, however, account for approximately 1 percent of all removals nationwide from 2018 to 2020, according to Election Assistance Commission (Election Assistance Commission, 2021).

The Facts: Laws regarding mental incompetence to vote (like other topics in this book) are impacted and molded by historical practice. In the United States, the old rule was that someone deemed to be seriously incapacitated or under the grips of severe dementia should not vote. Many states have, as a matter of state constitutional laws, denied the right to vote to those individuals deemed mentally unbalanced.

Ohio, for example, in 1851 added a provision that remains in its constitution specifying that "no idiot or insane person shall be entitled to the privileges of an elector" (Article V, section 6). Iowa, Mississippi, New Jersey, Nevada, and Kentucky historically employed the same language of "idiots" and "insane persons" in their constitutional disenfranchisement provisions as well (Puente, 2024). States like Iowa, New Jersey, and Nevada have replaced these terms with alternate phrases, for example, indicating that the person must be "adjudged [to be] mentally incompetent" (Puente, 2024). Besides removing potentially offensive language, the change in terminology also make clear that a court must have determined incompetency in order for disenfranchisement to occur.

According to a summary published with the American Bar Association, thirty-five states have constitutional provisions that prohibit mentally incapacitated individuals from voting (Bourque, 2022). Thirteen state constitutions lack these clauses (Bourque, 2022). The thirteen states that are silent in their constitutions as to the issue of mental competency to vote include Illinois, Pennsylvania, North Carolina, North Carolina, Michigan, New Hampshire, and Vermont, among others (Vasilogambros, 2018). Many states have found ways around archaic constitutional language through court orders (interpreting the provisions in modern light) or state statutes (Bourque, 2022). The procedure in many states is to obtain a court order in order to disenfranchise a prospective voter with a mental illness. A court order to appoint a guardian over the ill person would also suffice.

No provision in the federal Constitution explicitly forbids states from denying the right to vote because of a mental condition (as the Fifteenth Amendment does, for example, by forbidding states to disenfranchise on the basis of race). That said, the Fourteenth Amendment, ratified in 1868, does provide some constitutionally less absolute protection in this regard. As a matter of federal constitutional law, and as the Supreme Court has affirmed as early as 1886 in the case *Yick Wo v. Hopkins*, 118 U.S. 356 (1886), voting is a "fundamental political right, because [its] preservative of all [other] rights." The Fourteenth Amendment to the US Constitution guarantees citizens both the "due process of law" and the "equal protection of the laws." Under the Court's Fourteenth Amendment jurisprudence, a state's deprivation of a "fundamental right" is analyzed by the Court's most exacting level of review called "strict scrutiny." This level of review is so strict that one Supreme Court justice once quipped that government laws are often struck down as unconstitutional because "strict scrutiny is strict in theory, but fatal in fact."

Under a strict scrutiny analysis, for a state law to pass constitutional muster if challenged, the state must show that the law in question is narrowly tailored to serve a compelling government interest (Judson, 2004, 858). Few question that the integrity of elections satisfies a compelling government interest. As such, the constitutionality of state laws hinges on whether the state laws are truly "narrowly tailored" (or narrowly drafted) and designed in a way to be minimally harmful and not overbroad. The US Department of Justice has warned that state disenfranchisement cannot be based on unjustified assumptions about mental health (Bazelon Center for Mental Health Law, 2025). For example, a statute providing that everyone who had once seen a psychiatrist is prohibited to vote would be unconstitutional for failure to meet the strict scrutiny test because it is not "narrowly tailored" to meet the "compelling governmental interest." Not everyone who has seen a psychiatrist is incapable of making competent voting choices.

States have attempted various approaches to the issue of "mentally impaired" individuals and the issue of voting. The federal government has provided some guidance to states on the topic through its National Voter Registration Act of 1993. That federal law explicitly permits states to remove voters from voter registration rolls if a court has previously determined an individual to be previously "adjudged mentally incapacitated, [and] where such removals are allowed by state law" (52 U.S. Code § 20507[a][3][B]).

State approaches fall into different categories. About thirty states disqualify a voter only if a court has found them mentally incapable of voting. Of those thirty states, approximately twenty states have a presumption in favor of the individual to vote, which presumption can be rebutted by a judge who determines that the person is incompetent and unable to understand the act of voting. The case of *Wood v. Coconio County (In re: Wood)*, 551 P.3d 1163 (Ariz. Ct. App. 2024), illustrates this approach. In this case, an Arizona Court of Appeals panel in 2024 struck down state guardianship laws that had automatically stripped an incapacitated person of the right to vote without an individualized assessment. Annette Wood, a 63-year-old under a general guardianship in Coconino County, was barred from voting by Arizona's Constitution because of her mental status. Wood appealed, arguing that the disenfranchisement violated her due process rights under the Fourteenth Amendment. The Court of Appeals agreed and held that the guardianship statutes violated due process by terminating a person's voting rights with no independent assessment by the court. The trial judge believed that the old law, as it stood, was unfair as it placed the burden on the citizen to prove her competence to vote, rather than having the burden rest with the state. The judge believed, rather, that a state must prove the lack of competency by clear and convincing evidence before the right to vote could be deprived.

Another approach used by a shrinking number of states is that disenfranchisement is automatic for any individual subject to full guardianship even without a court's explicit ruling that the person cannot understand the act of voting. About seven states adhere to this approach as of 2024, including places like Mississippi, Kentucky, and Iowa (Puente, 2024). These states define "mentally incapacitated" or "incompetent" by virtue of a need for a full-time guardian. Maine also fell into this group until a Maine court overturned this law in 2001, and voters rejected the automatic bar as well in 2023 (Hogan, 2023).

Massachusetts and Connecticut take a unique third approach. In these two states, an individual wishing to vote who is under guardianship may only vote if the individual or their guardian petitions a court or files paperwork with the state evincing that the person has the capacity and desire to vote. The onus is on the voter or guardian to affirmatively elect to vote and prove to the government their interest and competency.

Opponents of the blanket disenfranchisement of individuals subject to mental guardianship arrangements claim that mental disorders are no different from a broken leg or arm, or cancer, and federal laws like the Americans with Disabilities Act (ADA) and the Voting Accessibility for the Elderly and Handicapped Act allow other people with disabilities to vote. While the ADA enables thousands of disabled people to vote who otherwise would not have been able to vote (because of disabilities ranging from blindnesses to mobility issues), the ADA does not cover and does not explicitly prohibit states from deeming a person ineligible to vote due to a mental incapacity. The bottom line for these advocates is that "under federal law, a person cannot be barred from voting because of [mental] 'incompetence' except in very limited circumstances. [And] as a rule, if a person is competent enough to go the polls and vote, or to complete an absentee ballot, federal law requires that the person be allowed to vote" (Bazelon Center for Mental Health Law, 2025).

Opponents of allowing people who have mental incompetencies to vote argue that people who are mentally incompetent (i.e., those with full-time guardians) are more susceptible to voter fraud schemes and undue influence by guardians or relatives. While the scenario might sound farfetched, abuse could occur in a variety of ways. For instance, according to one source, "Alzheimer's patients … could be given a ballot while awake but only partially alert, and their caretaker or family member could cast it for them. Or a staff member at an assisted living facility could fill out or influence the ballots for dozens of people with severe cognitive issues" (Vasilogambros, 2018). Stanford law professor (and expert in voting rights) Pamela Karlan has worried that "some people's cognitive abilities are so impaired, they shouldn't vote. They have no idea what's going on" (Vasilogambros, 2018).

Further Reading

Bazelon Center for Mental Health Law. *Voting Rights Guides and Resources*. Accessed July 8, 2025. https://www.bazelon.org/our-work/voting/

Bourque, Catherine. "Updates to State Voting Laws for Individuals with Limited Capacity." American Bar Association, February 2, 2022. https://www.americanbar.org/groups/law_aging/publications/bifocal/vol-43/vol43-issue3/voting-laws-limited-capacity/

Brescia, Nicholas F. "Modernizing State Voting Laws That Disenfranchise the Mentally Disabled with the Aid of Past Suffrage Movements." *St. Louis University Law Journal, 54*, no. 3 (2010), 943.

Civil Rights Division, US Department of Justice. "About the National Voter Registration Act." April 5, 2023. https://www.justice.gov/crt/about-national-voter-registration-act

Doraisamy, Naomi. "Out of Mind, Out of Sight: Voting Restrictions Based on Mental Competency." *Idaho Law Review, 56*, no. 2 (2020), 135.

Election Assistance Commission (EAC). "Election Administration and Voting Survey 2020." 2021. https://www.eac.gov/sites/default/files/document_library/files/2020_EAVS_Report_Final_508c.pdf

Hogan, Samantha. "Maine's Constitution Says People in Guardianships with Mental Illness Cannot Vote. Voters Can Change That in November." *The Maine Monitor*, October 8, 2023. https://themainemonitor.org/maines-constitution-says-people-in-guardianships-with-mental-illness-cannot-vote-voters-can-change-that-in-november/

Judson, Janis. "Strict Scrutiny." In *Affirmative Action: An Encyclopedia*, Vol. *II*, ed. James Beckman, Greenwood Publishing, 2004, pp. 857–9.

Lewis, Frank W. "Why Does the Word 'Idiot' Appear in the Ohio Constitution?" *Signal Cleveland*, January 18, 2024. https://signalcleveland.org/why-does-the-word-idiot-appear-in-the-ohio-state-constitution/

Puente, Victor. "Good Question: What Does Amendment 1 Mean by 'Idiots and Insane Persons'?" *WKYT*, October 18, 2024. https://www.wkyt.com/2024/10/18/good-question-what-does-amendment-1-mean-by-idiots-insane-persons/

Schiffler, Courtney. "Voting Rights for People with Diminished Mental Capacity." *Mitchell Hamline Law Review, 48*, no. 2 (2022), 657.

Vasilogambros, Matt. "Thousands Lose Right to Vote under 'Incompetence' Laws." *Stateline*, March 21, 2018. https://stateline.org/2018/03/21/thousands-lose-right-to-vote-under-incompetence-laws/

Wingen, Matt. "Voting Rights under Guardianship." *American Bar Association*, October 16, 2024. https://www.americanbar.org/groups/law_aging/publications/bifocal/vol46/vol46issue1/votingrightsandguardianship/

Wood v. Coconino County (In re: Wood), 551 P.3d 1163 (Ariz. Ct. App. 2024).

Yates, Tiffany. "A First Amendment Analysis of Voting Rights of the Mentally Incapacitated: Why Are You Calling Me an Idiot, Why Can't I Vote?" *First Amendment Law Review, 15*, no. 1 (2016), 121.

Q16: Are college students at greater risk of disenfranchisement?

Answer: College students are not explicitly disenfranchised any differently from other groups. However, many college students, particularly out-of-state students, do encounter logistical challenges and have greater difficulty meeting a state's requirements for voting. These difficulties may result in de facto disenfranchisement. Challenges may include meeting a state's voter identification requirements, residency requirements, and registration rules, among other things. The various legal and procedural barriers, taken together, create an environment in which college students often face additional steps or extra scrutiny, compared to the general population, when attempting to vote.

The Facts: In 1971, the Twenty-Sixth Amendment was ratified. The amendment lowered the voting age to 18. Since that time, there has not been widespread recognition of the subtle disenfranchisement of college student voters. In practice, college and university students (especially out-of-state students) often face legal and logistical challenges that amount to de facto disenfranchisement. These legal and logistical challenges have increased significantly since 2016.

One major obstacle for college voters post-2016 are newer state laws that impose stringent voter identification requirements and exclude or limit student identification cards as acceptable proof of voter identification at the polling place. Approximately eleven states have not allowed college identification cards for the purposes of voting. Seven states (Arizona, Idaho, North Dakota, Ohio, South Carolina, Tennessee, and Texas) expressly prohibit the use of any form of student identification as voter identification (Fair Election Center's Campus Vote Project, 2025). Other states (e.g., Florida) make college identification cards difficult, if not impossible, to use. For example, in Florida Statutes Section § 101.043(1), pertaining to identifications needed to vote, while college identification cards are listed as acceptable as one type of possible identification, the college identification card must have both a photograph and a signature on the card. Very few student identification cards have such signatures.

A handful of other states (e.g., Alaska, Delaware, and Missouri) effectively disallow the usage of college identification cards by omitting them from the state's list of approved/acceptable types of photo identifications. Iowa and Utah will allow the use of a college or university identification card, but only if the person also produces proof of current residence (Castillo, 2024; Voting Rights Law, 2023). In these states (except for Iowa), students must provide an alternative form of identification (e.g., in-state driver's license, passport), which is problematic for an out-of-state student (with an out-of-state driver's license), many of whom also do not possess passports. Students physically present and enrolled in one of these states will be precluded from voting unless they attempt to submit an absentee ballot with their original state of residency.

While at first glance, twenty of the thirty-seven states requiring an identification card to vote do accept a college student identification card, the specific requirements as to what must be on the presented college identification card vary widely. Some states like Florida, as noted, require that the college identification card be signed. Wisconsin requires that the identification card contains the student's name, photo, signature, card issuance date, and a listed expiration date (within two years). The voting student must also concurrently present proof of current enrollment (e.g., an official college issued list of enrolled classes for the semester or a fee statement) (Castillo, 2024). Some states (e.g., Georgia and Indiana) only accept college identification cards from a public university or college in the state (i.e., no private college identification cards). Similarly, Wyoming only accepts college identification cards from the University of Wyoming or one of Wyoming's community colleges (Castillo, 2024).

In addition to the potential problems imposed by identification card rules in certain states, some states have residency and registration rules that adversely impact out-of-state students. Perhaps one of the more prominent illustrations of this involved the state of New Hampshire. In 2018, New Hampshire passed House Bill 1264 into law (which went into effect in 2019) which amended the definition of residency to include anyone who votes in New Hampshire. Phrased another way, anyone voting in New Hampshire would be considered a legal resident of New Hampshire for all other purposes (e.g., legally obligated to obtain a New Hampshire driver's license, pay any applicable state taxes, registering his or her vehicle[s] in New Hampshire, etc.). As such, in order to vote, an out-of-state student in New Hampshire would have to obtain a new in-state license, possibly spend hundreds of dollars registering his or her vehicle (and pay state property tax on the vehicle), and other costs. Proponents of the law said that affected students were not disenfranchised as they could cast an absentee ballot back in their home state. However, many individuals prefer to vote in person because of problems with absentee ballots (e.g., higher rate of rejections than in-person voting) and are unable to travel sometimes long distances home to vote in person (and take time away from school to do so).

Another barrier to voting for college students in certain states is a lack of a convenient voting location or confusing information as to how and where (and perhaps when) students are supposed to vote. For instance, in Florida, the state refused to allow early voting sites on college campuses. Then, in 2014, Florida's then-secretary of state banned county election officials from trying to set up early polling locations on campuses. This had the result of denying a close and convenient polling location to over 800,000 Florida college students. This ban was then challenged in federal court, and in 2018, a federal judge struck down the ban, finding a "stark pattern of discrimination" against college-aged voters, "unexplainable on grounds other than age," and a state policy that created a "secondary class of voters" who could not easily vote early (Bousquet, 2018). Florida quickly bypassed the ruling the following year by enacting a law in 2019 requiring that early voting locations in Florida have a certain amount of accessible parking. This requirement largely precluded Florida campuses as early voting locations because many campuses in Florida did not have the requisite parking. Since many students must therefore vote off campus, they face transportation barriers, as many do not have cars (especially during their freshman and sophomore years).

College students may also find that it is sometimes unclear where they are to vote. Some campuses are gerrymandered, meaning students from the same university but living in different dorms on campus might be assigned different polling locations. Students often change dorm addresses from year to year, which might change their polling location. Students living off campus may also change their temporary address over time. It is not unforeseeable that a student might not keep on top of changing his or her official registration address during their years of college or university study. There have been instances of college students being bounced back and forth from one polling precinct to another, with each polling place denying the students the right to cast a vote (beyond a provisional ballot).

Because of these potential obstacles to voting in person, students might opt to vote via absentee ballot in their home state instead. This decision is also not without complications. Voting by absentee ballot can be cumbersome, and the rejection rate for ballots is higher with absentee votes. In 2024, four states (Missouri, Mississippi, Oklahoma, and South Dakota) required absentee voters to get their ballot notarized and/or witnessed for the ballot to be counted as valid. Students reported not receiving their requested ballots in the mail with sufficient time to complete them and send them back to their home state. A University of Virginia student from Missouri had her absentee ballot returned to her stamped "may need to be notarized," which prompted the student to rush to find a notary and get the absentee ballot back again in time (Galper and Bond, 2024).

Another University of Virginia student from Louisiana reported that she never received an absentee ballot after requesting one, and when she contacted the state, she was told that she should have "emailed the registrar her request by sending a copy of her student ID and forms of the Louisiana state registrar" (Galper and Bond, 2024). But to make matters worse, after sending Louisiana the requested forms, the student reported that she still failed to receive an absentee ballot, and finally instead opted to vote in person in Virginia (Galper and Bond, 2024). Fortunately for this student, Virginia allows a Virginia college-issued student identification card as appropriate voter identification, allowing this student to vote. Otherwise, the student would have lost her right to vote in the 2024 election. New rules enacted in Texas in 2021 also caused a "surge in rejected mail ballot applications, as students and other voters failed to meet stricter identification matching requirements for absentee forms" (Galper and Bond, 2024). Texas (like Louisiana) now requires that students send a copy of their state issued identification (e.g., Texas Driver's license) to the state registrar to be considered for an absentee ballot.

On paper there does not appear to be any explicit suppression of college-aged voters. In fact, voter turnout among the 18- to 29-year-old group increased by 11 percent from 2016 to 2020 (Smith and Pothier, 2024). However, voter suppression may occur in indirect ways, as "unfriendly" voting practices pertaining to students creates a situation where groups of students are disenfranchised in practice, even though state laws appear neutral.

Further Reading

Bousquet, Steve. "Judge: Florida's Early Voting-on-Campus Ban Shows 'Stark Pattern of Discrimination.'" *Tampa Bay Times*, July 14, 2018. https://www.tampabay.com/florida-politics/buzz/2018/07/24/judge-faults-state-and-approves-early-voting-on-college-university-campuses/

Castillo, Evan. "Can I Use My College Student ID to Vote?" *BC: Best Colleges*, August 15, 2024. https://www.bestcolleges.com/news/states-vote-using-college-student-id/

Fair Election Center's Campus Vote Project. "Student ID as Voter ID." June 2025. https://campusvoteproject.org/student-id-as-voter-id/

Frost, Jennifer. *Let Us Vote!: Youth Voting Rights and the 26th Amendment*. New York University Press, 2022.

Galper, Bennett, and Jackie Bond. "Out-of-State Students Endured Obstacles in Obtaining Absentee Ballots." *Cavalier Daily* (University of Virginia), November 13, 2024. https://www.cavalierdaily.com/article/2024/11/out-of-state-students-endured-a-series-of-obstacles-in-obtaining-absentee-ballots

Smith, Erin Geiger, and Leina Pothier. "The New Battle over Youth Disenfranchisement." *The State Court Report*, March 11, 2024. https://statecourtreport.org/our-work/analysis-opinion/new-battle-over-youth-disenfranchisement

Voting Rights Law. "Voting with Student ID in 2023: The State of the Law & Pending Legislation." March 20, 2023. https://votingrightslab.org/wp-content/uploads/2023/12/VRL-Fact-Sheet_-The-State-of-Student-ID-Law-March-2023.pdf

Q17: Are the voting rights of military members and their families impacted by virtue of military service?

Answer: No, but obstacles relating to the handling of military absentee ballots do exist. While military families often face unique obstacles because of frequent deployments and permanent change of station (PSC) assignments every couple of years, federal law particular to the military makes voting in federal elections via absentee ballots routine. Under the Uniformed and Overseas Citizens Absentee Voting Act (UOCAVA) of 1986, and subsequent amendments to the law, such as the 2009 Military and Overseas Voter Empowerment Act (MOVE), all states are required to allow all uniformed service members and their dependents to register and vote by absentee ballot using their last state of residency. Military members and their dependents do face several unique obstacles and difficulties, particularly as state laws enacted after the 2020 election have sought to restrict the liberal use of absentee ballots, but nothing that should be characterized as the wholesale disenfranchisement of the vote.

The Facts: The issue of military service adversely impacting the ability of a service member to vote dates as far back as at least the American Civil War. The 1864 presidential election took place during the war, and President Abraham Lincoln was anxious that the over two million citizens who served in the Union Armies would be unable to vote because almost all of them were stationed far away from their state of residence. Not allowing Union soldiers to vote would have resulted in the potential disfranchisement of between two and two and a half million voters. President Lincoln was able to encourage military voting through absentee voting. Further, if a northern state refused to accept an absentee ballot, Lincoln had instituted a liberal leave policy, allowing the soldier to travel home to cast his vote and then return to camp. All told, approximately 40,267 Union soldiers voted, far fewer than expected. These voters strongly supported Lincoln, who won 75.8 percent of the ballots (American Battlefield Trust, 2024). The main federal laws aimed at preventing disenfranchisement of military members (and dependents) today, such as UOCAVA and MOVE, rely chiefly on the same use of absentee ballots as in 1864.

Today, for military voters, the Federal Voting Assistance Program (FVAP) recommends that military members (and dependents) start the voting registration application through the use of the Federal Post Card Application (FPCA). The FPCA doubles both as a voter registration request and a request for an absentee ballot. The major drawback is that the FVAP recommends military voters send in a new FPCA every year, and especially when the service member experiences a change in military assignment (often called a PCS, meaning "permanent change of station").

In 1986, Congress enacted UOCAVA (amended by MOVE in 2009). This law mandates that all states must accommodate the use of absentee ballots by military voters and their dependents in federal elections. The absentee ballot goes to the service members' last legal domicile or legal residency, regardless of where the person is currently stationed or their family is living. Family members of service members enjoy the same protection by virtue of the Military Spouses Residency Relief Act. UOCAVA mandates that all states must accept a military member (or dependent's) absentee ballot, so long as the ballot otherwise complies with the state's rules on the handling of absentee ballots. (Some state rules can be idiosyncratic, creating problems for voters, as we will see.) MOVE mandates that states send out blank ballots at least forty-five days before an election and offer service members the ability to send their ballot back via some electronic means (e-mail, fax, online portal uploads, etc.), in addition to sending the ballots back by regular mail.

A vast majority of service members and dependents polled expressed satisfaction with having their votes counted. Approximately 74 percent of active-duty service members and 66 percent of military dependents were pleased with the process. Over 83 percent of active duty and 73 percent of active-duty spouse respondents stated they would need an absentee ballot "almost every time" or "every time" to vote in every election (federal, state, local) during their time in the military because of the far-flung military assignments. Over 72 percent of active duty and spouse respondents required an absentee ballot because they were not registered to vote in the same place they resided. Finally, over 92 percent of active-duty service member respondents felt they received their absentee ballot with enough time to return it before the election (Institute for Veterans and Military Families, 2018). This last point is relevant when considering one of the chief arguments from critics in how military members are treated, namely, that ballots arrive too slow or too late for service members to effectively vote (Smith and Bell, 2024).

After the 2020 election, numerous states put restrictions on the liberal use of absentee ballots. Since most military voters and dependents vote via absentee ballot and rely on the proper processing and counting of these ballots, these new voting restrictions or deadlines for absentee ballots (enacted in twenty-eight states since 2020) are the biggest threat related to disenfranchisement of the military vote. Sarah Streyder, the executive director of Secure Families Initiative (a group for military spouses dedicated to mobilizing and protecting the military vote), has expressed the worry that onerous state absentee ballot rules will have the effect of disenfranchising the military voter community:

> 2020 taught us that our voters are like a canary in the coal mine in some ways … we are some of the most vulnerable voters to some of these policies … the states that have decreased the time service members have to register and return their ballots are making it even more difficult for military voters to get their ballots counted. (Padilla, 2024)

Since 2020, at least twenty-eight states promulgated new more onerous restrictions of registration deadlines or ballot turnaround deadlines. Ohio and Tennessee, for example, decided to shorten the deadline for ballots to arrive to be counted. Arizona shortened its "cure" period for remedying problems that might exist on ballots. West Virginia changed its law to require the cancellation of the registration of absentee voters if the service member (or a dependent) obtained an out-of-state driver's license (Padilla, 2024).

As a Brennan Center for Justice report stated, service members may not notice these changes to state law until it is too late and they have been inadvertently disenfranchised (Smith and Bell, 2024). Various surveys have indicated that many service members are barely able to get their ballots back to their home state in time and they have difficulty tracking their ballot once submitted (Institute for Veterans and Military Families, 2018). Approximately 70 percent received no confirmation that their ballot/vote was received and counted, and 71 percent could not say with any certainty the status of their ballot/vote (Institute for Veterans and Military Families, 2018).

To make matters worse, the Federal Voting Assistance Program reported that in 2022, 15 percent of active-duty military voters surveyed never received their requested absentee ballot or got it too late to use it (Federal Voter Assistance Program, 2022). For example, a military spouse at an Air Force base in Florida never received an absentee ballot from Texas despite multiple requests, lamenting "it's not going to count because we didn't get to vote" (Lamothe and Sonne, 2020). A Marine gunnery sergeant said his ballot "didn't arrive until Election Day" (Lamothe and Sonne, 2020). Approximately half of all service members claim not to have voted, citing obstacles like problems with registering to vote or obtaining an absentee ballot as the reason (Kheel, 2024).

The Federal Voting Assistance Program noted that in 2020 the military community vote trailed the general public, with turnout at 27 percent compared to about 46 percent for the general population (Clarke, 2024). Some have claimed that this gap is a consequence of lack of confidence in the military absentee ballot being handled properly, or that military ballots arrived too late to count or just weren't counted (Clarke, 2024). Khiet Ho, a Marine Corps spouse and lead researcher at Secure Families Initiative, a military family organization that in part works to expand military voting, wrote that "we know that when there is a lack of confidence in voting, there is less likelihood to vote" (Kheel, 2024). As another military voting advocate (Jaimie Boyle) stated, military voters may decide it is just not worth the trouble if their "vote" is just going to "get lost in the shuffle" (Kheel, 2024). And at the end of the day, dissuading a person from voting has the same ultimate effect of disenfranchisement by more overt means.

Further Reading

American Battlefield Trust. "The Election of 1864 and the Soldiers' Vote." October 24, 2024. https://www.battlefields.org/learn/articles/election-1864-and-soldiers-vote

Clarke, Joseph. "Researchers Set Out to Tackle Voting Challenges of Military Members." United States Department of Defense News, 2024. https://www.fvap.gov/info/reports-surveys/StateoftheMilitaryVoterhttps://www.defense.gov/News/News-Stories/Article/Article/3673840/researchers-set-out-to-tackle-voting-challenges-of-military-members/

Federal Voter Assistance Voter Program. "State of the Military Voter." 2022. https://www.fvap.gov/info/reports-surveys/StateoftheMilitaryVoter

Gardner, Amy, Jacqueline Alemany, and Dan Lamothe. "GOP Lawsuits Targeting Overseas Voting Draw Ire of Military Personnel." *The Washington Post*, October 15, 2024. https://houlahan.house.gov/news/documentsingle.aspx?DocumentID=4305

Huefner, Steven F. "Lessons from Improvements in Military and Overseas Voting." *University of Richmond Law Review*, *47*, no. 3 (2013), 833.

Inbody, Donald S. "Inbody, Voting by Overseas Citizens and Military Personnel." *Election Law Journal*, *14*, no. 1 (2015), 54.

Inbody, Donald S. *The Soldier Vote: War, Politics, and the Ballot in America*. Palgrave Macmillan, 2015.

Institute for Veterans and Military Families. "Military Families: Perceptions, Challenges, and Barriers to Voting Participation and Absentee Voting." MOAA: Military Family Initiative, September 2018, 1–203. https://ivmf.syracuse.edu/wp-content/uploads/2019/10/MOAA_Voting-Participation-and-Absentee-Voting-Report-Sept-2018-Full-Report.pdf

Kheel, Rebecca. "GOP Lawsuits Threaten to Disenfranchise Military Voters, Advocates Warn." Military.com, October 16, 2024. https://www.military.com/daily-news/2024/10/16/military-voters-advocates-worry-votes-wont-count-amid-gop-election-challenges.html

Lamothe, Dan, and Paul Sonne. "As Election Day Arrives, a Fight about Military Ballots Takes Center Stage." *The Washington Post*, November 2, 2020. https://www.washingtonpost.com/national-security/as-election-day-arrives-a-fight-about-military-ballots-takes-center-stage/2020/11/02/73257ff6-1d37-11eb-9ec3-3a81e23c4b5e_story.html?_pml=1

Padilla, Mariel. "If You're in the Military, Voting This Year Could Be Tricky." July 12, 2024. *19thnews.org*, last Accessed July 12, 2025. Available at https://19thnews.org/2024/07/military-voting-challenges-election-2024/?itm_source=parsely-api

Smith, Erin Geiger, and John Bell. "Facts and Myths about the Uniformed and Overseas Citizens Absentee Voting Act." Brennan Center for Justice, October 18, 2024.

https://www.brennancenter.org/our-work/research-reports/facts-and-myths-about-uniformed-and-overseas-citizens-absentee-voting-act

Stilwell, Blake. "How Absentee Voting for US Troops Won the Civil War and Ended Slavery." Miitary.com, April 22, 2020. https://www.military.com/military-life/how-absentee-voting-us-troops-won-civil-war-and-ended-slavery.html

Q18: Are unhoused individuals at greater risk of disenfranchisement?

Answer: Yes. While homeless individuals in the United States are not explicitly barred from voting, they do face unique barriers that effectively disenfranchise them. Proving residency for voter registration is difficult, especially in states with strict residency requirements. The absence of a permanent address also complicates compliance with photo identification laws in those states that require an address to accompany the photograph and name. Unhoused individuals often lack reliable access to mail, which is essential for receiving voter registration materials and warnings about potential voter roll purges. The inability to receive consistent mail may also lead to confusion about polling locations.

The Facts: Homeless individuals have the unqualified right to vote just as any other voter in America. The lack of a permanent residence does not invalidate this right. Yet, the homeless population has an abysmal voting rate in federal elections, averaging approximately 10 percent compared with a 54 percent turnout among the general voting population (Grether, 2024; National Low Income Housing Coalition, 2024).

Wealth or property ownership (or the lack thereof) is not explicitly conditions for voting. States eliminated the land ownership requirement for voting well over two hundred years ago, and the Twenty-fourth Amendment, ratified in 1964, prohibited the use of poll taxes in federal elections. Additionally, in the last quarter century, multiple federal cases have struck down state laws that have attempted to limit the right of the homeless to vote based upon either a lack a permanent residence or because the person's "residency" was not of sufficient duration.

One example of this can be seen in the Supreme Court case of *Dunn v. Blumstein*, 405 U.S. 330 (1972). In this case, the Court struck down a Tennessee law requiring that voters reside in Tennessee for a full year (and in the county where the person would be voting for at least three months) before even *registering* to vote. James Blumstein, a new resident and professor who was denied registration under this law, challenged the law as unconstitutional. Blumstein claimed that his right to vote and his right to travel were improperly restricted by the law. Tennessee argued that the waiting period was needed to prevent voter fraud and ensure an informed electorate as to region-specific issues.

The Court in *Dunn* noted that the law penalized recent movers (new residents) by denying them the ballot. In so doing, Tennessee was impeding its citizens freedom of interstate travel as well as the right to vote. The Court ultimately held that such lengthy residency rules violated the Equal Protection Clause (and the strict scrutiny analysis) because the Court found no Fourteenth Amendment compelling interest—specifically, that Tennessee has not established a sufficient relationship between its interest in an informed electorate and the fixed durational residence requirements. The one-year period was also found to not be a "narrowly tailored" measure by the state. The Court held that "a period of 30 days appears to be ample to complete whatever administrative tasks are needed to prevent fraud and insure the purity of the ballot box." Phrased another way, the state's interest in preventing voter fraud was achievable by far much less restrictive means (i.e., a thirty-day period), and the law should have been far more "narrowly tailored" to achieve those goals. The NVRA supports only a thirty-day residency period.

Another relevant federal case (*Pitts v. Black*, 608 F. Supp. 696 [S.D.N.Y. 1984]) addressed the issue of "residency" specifically as it related to the homeless. In that case, a federal district court held that the homeless could not be disenfranchised by virtue of lacking a permanent home address. New York had claimed that "residency," for purpose of voting, meant that only those individuals who had a fixed, permanent, home address were qualified to vote. The court in *Pitts*, similar to the Supreme Court in the *Dunn* case, rejected this argument. The court held that New York's restrictions were unreasonably restrictive and violated the Fourteenth Amendment's Equal Protection Clause. The court issued an injunction preventing New York from refusing to allow homeless individuals to vote solely because they lacked a "non-traditional" residency. In the same year as the *Pitts* decision, another federal court (in *Committee for Dignity and Fairness for the Homeless v. Tartaglione*, 1984 U.S. Dist. LEXIS 23612 [E.D. Pa. Sept. 14, 1984]) approved a consent decree allowing homeless voters in Philadelphia to register using shelter addresses if the shelter would accept mail on their behalf.

These three cases collectively stand for the proposition that a person's status as homeless is not a valid legal ground to deny an individual the right to vote. And while state governments retain authority to set reasonable rules regarding the logistics of voting, including rules pertaining to registration (e.g., what proof of identification is needed, when someone must be registered to vote before an election, whether convicted felons can register to vote, etc.), a state cannot violate the Equal Protection Clause by placing unreasonable and inequitable restrictions on voters.

Federal statutory law reinforces this as well. The National Voter Registration Act (NVRA) of 1993 provides that state governments cannot require more than thirty days living in residency in the jurisdiction in question for purposes of voter registrations. The NVRA also requires state election officials to accept a descriptive location instead of a conventional street address on the voter registration form. As such, under the NVRA, it would not be unacceptable for the person registering to vote to indicate his or her residence to a specific park bench next to the tennis court in a city park (assuming those details to be true). As explained by a National Conference of State Legislatures report, it would not be unusual for homeless voters to register by "using the address of shelters, bus stations, corners or parks or by identifying on a map where they sleep to ensure they are sent the correct ballot. It may also be possible to indicate a campground or RV park as a 'home base' for purposes of voter registration" (National Conference of State Legislatures, 2025).

While state requirements for registration are by no means consistent and/or uniform, there has been a movement toward inclusion of the homeless population, as opposed to away from it. Another major federal statute, the Help America Vote Act of 2002 (HAVA), also improved access to the ballot to the homeless population. If a homeless voter's identification is in doubt, or if his or her name is missing from the voter registration list, HAVA allows the person to still cast a vote (a provisional ballot), with the hope that the error can be identified and corrected after the election.

While some states may allow the listing of unconventional residences, the state may also require that the voter provide proof that they reside at the address claimed. This involves documentation like a utility bill, bank statement, credit card statement, or a driver's license, among others. Homeless people often have difficulty producing the basic documentation needed for registration or voting. Additionally, even if the non-traditional address is accepted, subsequent verification mailings, or notice of a possible registration purge, would likely be returned as undeliverable.

Another potential problem for homeless voters is photo identification. Most homeless individuals lack government issued driver's licenses. Some states offer free identification cards. However, even with those free state cards, one typically needs some secondary poof of address or identity. Even obtaining a copy of a birth certificate (a basic form of secondary documentation to prove identity) requires a fee for a certified copy, transportation to and from the place issuing the birth certificate, or other costs. One positive step that some states have taken to cure this problem is to allow a person to sign an affidavit under pains and penalties of perjury in lieu of a photographic identification card. Courts in Texas, North Carolina, and Wisconsin, in adjudicating strict voting identification challenge cases, have required states to offer free identification cards or alternatives like affidavits.

Voter registration purges present yet another obstacle. Homeless individuals may habitually spend a great amount of time at a park, a street corner, or the intersection of two roads, and this location may be listed on the person's initial registration form. But obviously, these voters will lack the ability to receive mail at those locations. As such, when a state attempts to purge its voters rolls, per the NVRA, the first step is notification in writing to the affected individual. When that written notification never reaches the homeless person, or that individual never sends the required postcard back, the voter will be purged/cancelled after two election cycles of inactivity. And even if the voter appears at the very next election, poll workers will be more exacting in the documentation expected of the homeless voter. In many cases, this results in the person being purged from voter databases. Under the NVRA, homeless voters can register by mail using a shelter address, but few homeless individuals are aware of this possibility (Grether, 2024).

The lack of a personal vehicle and/or money to pay for transit to a voting facility, or even to obtain a free state identification card, is another impediment (Grether, 2024). In *Crawford v. Marion County Election Board*, 553 U.S. 181 (2008), Justice John Paul Stevens, writing for the majority in the case, acknowledged that homeless people would face difficulties in trying to obtain a free state identification card. Justice David Souter, writing in dissent in *Crawford*, also stressed the undue costs on the homeless population. Justice Souter wrote that, regardless of the card being provided free of charge by the state, the homeless nevertheless would not be able to bear the cost for travel as well as for fees for underlying documents. According to Souter, imposing these additional financial burdens on the poor and homeless was akin to a poll tax.

If an unhoused individual surmounted all of these obstacles and actually made it to the polls, the voter might further suffer from the scrutiny of overzealous or partisan poll watchers. The homeless voter may be targeted because their identification card does not list a traditional house and street address or list the name of a local shelter. Georgia, for example, revised its election statutes in 2024 to empower its poll watchers to flag and challenge voters with "nonresidential" addresses. Official Georgia Code Annotated Section 21-2-230(b) now provides that if a voter's registration address is nonresidential (e.g., P.O. box, business, shelter, dormitory, etc.), a poll watcher or any eligible elector may cite that fact as probable cause to challenge the voter's eligibility. Further, election officials in Georgia must "immediately consider such challenge" and uphold it if probable cause exists.

Further Reading

Grether, Maggie. "The Hidden Barriers to Voting While Unhoused." *The Nation*, October 23, 2024. https://www.thenation.com/article/politics/voting-barriers-suppression-unhoused-homelessness/

National Conference of State Legislatures. "Voting for People with Nontraditional Residences." January 7, 2025. https://www.ncsl.org/elections-and-campaigns/voting-for-people-with-nontraditional-residences

National Low Income Housing Coalition. "15-2 Voting While Experiencing Homelessness: Making Unhoused Voices Heard in Our Democracy." September 3, 2024. https://nlihc.org/resource/15-2-voting-while-experiencing-homelessness-making-unhoused-voices-heard-our-democracy

Sequeira, Robbie. "Homeless People Already Struggle to Vote. This Law Could Make It Harder." *Stateline*, October 25, 2024. https://stateline.org/2024/10/25/homeless-people-already-struggle-to-vote-this-law-could-make-it-harder/

4

Voter Registration and Voting Registration Poll Purges

A citizen cannot vote without first properly registering to vote. There are set rules concerning registration that vary between states such as what sort of documentation must be provided to register and how long a voter registration lasts. States are tasked by law with maintaining accurate voter registration lists. While list maintenance is a legitimate administrative need, overly aggressive purges or flawed data-matching systems risk sweeping eligible voters off the rolls. Further, voter registration purges may be improperly conducted (i.e., taking place too close to an upcoming election or based upon impermissible reasons). Problems with voter registration purges are made more challenging when states have relied on faulty databases such as Kansas's Interstate Crosscheck Program or Georgia's Exact Match program. Eligible voters may be removed without notice (if the state mailing card is misplaced or not delivered) and will likely be challenged at the polls for failing to appear on the most current voting registration list.

One well-known example of a failed voter registration update is Florida's "felon purge" in the 2000 election. Thousands of eligible voters were wrongfully flagged and removed from the voting rolls due to the lax scrutiny of felon names and the mismatch of those names with lawful voters with the same name. The system also failed to account for clemency and pardon records, among other things. These failures led to numerous false positives and the disenfranchisement of lawful voters.

Q19: What are the legal requirements of state voter registration purges?

Answer: After 1993, as discussed in Question 11, some basic restrictions on voter registration purges were put into place by Congress through the passage of the National Voter Registration Act (NVRA). While the focus of the NVRA was on the registration of new voters, Section 8 contains rules on how to keep individuals registered, how voter registration lists should be maintained by states, and what steps a state must take to remove a person from the state's voter registration list. Prior to 1993, there were no uniform standards. Massive voter registration purges were conducted before 1993 based upon unclear standards or for questionable reasons. After 1993, basic baseline rules are in place to guide states.

The Facts: Section 8 of the NVRA contains procedures that states must adhere to regarding voter list maintenance. The basic underlying expectation of Section 8 is that state governments are expected to keep a "uniform, nondiscriminatory list-maintenance program" and not purge voters for ideological reasons or for reasons that are arbitrary and capricious in nature.

As to how soon before an election that purges of voter rolls may occur, the NVRA makes clear that states are prohibited from conducting any large-scale purge in the last ninety days before a federal election (either a primary election or a general election). This ninety-day period is sometimes described as the NVRA imposed "quiet period." This "quiet period" only applies to large-scale purges, meaning that states cannot systematically remove ineligible voters as part of a mass purge, but the NVRA does not prohibit all removals. Removals for individual cases may occur (and are allowed) at any time in certain circumstances, such as the removal of a person who dies, someone who requests cancellation of registration, or a person who has recently been convicted of a disenfranchising felony.

Beyond the ninety-day "quiet period" rule, there are great variances among states as to when and how they conduct purges of their voter registration lists/databases. The main factors typically considered by states include change of status (voter registration in a different state, permanently moving out of state, felony convictions, mental incapacitation, and, of course, death). Another justification by state governments for purges is the removal of voters who failed to vote in a previous election (i.e., voter inactivity).

As a rule, the voter inactivity criterion is expressly forbidden by the NVRA in subpart (b)(2) of Section 20507, entitled "Requirements with respect to administration of voter registration." This provision indicates that a state "shall not result in the removal of the name of any person from the official list of voters registered to vote in an election for Federal office by reason of the person's failure to vote." However, the law also provides an exception to that rule, through which a state can remove an individual from its list of eligible voters if certain conditions are met. First, the voter in question has not responded (in person or in writing) to a notice sent by the applicable registrar about the intention of the state to remove the voter from the registration rolls. Second, the voter in question has not voted or appeared to vote in two or more consecutive general elections for federal offices.

Regardless of the reason for the state's intention to remove voters from its voter rolls, under the terms of the NVRA, before removal, states need to send a notification to the voter of the intended purge. The state may continue with the purge only if no follow-up inquiry occurs. "Then, and only then, is the process of purging supposed to begin" (Anderson, 2020, 24).

However, the notification step, the chance for the voter to "correct the record" and contest the purge, has been problematic. First, in many states, the state's notification takes the form of "mailing a postcard crammed with fine print" (Anderson, 2020, 76). A small postcard jammed with legal fine print might get only a cursory review when someone is reviewing their mail, potentially overlooking its importance. Also, demographic discrepancies present themselves in response rates to state notices:

> White voters are 21 percent more likely then Black or Hispanic voters to respond to their official requests; homeowners are 32 percent more likely to respond than renters (and whites in cities tend to homeowners in cities, while Black Americans and Hispanics are renters whose residences may more frequently change); and the young are 74 percent that the old to respond. (Palast, 2016)

As a writer for *The Atlantic* indicated, "not only common sense but statistical surveys show that most people who receive such governmental postcards don't return them—either because they don't understand the legalese they bear, or because they mean to and forget, or because they just lose the card" (Epps, 2018). In one case reviewed by the Supreme Court, Justice Stephen Breyer (in a dissent in *Husted v. A. Philip Randolph Institute*, 138 S. Ct. 1833 (2018)) cited figures showing that in 2012 in Ohio, the state sent roughly 1.5 million postcards but only received about 235,000 replies, a response rate of approximately 15 percent.

According to author Carol Anderson, "Ohio has been in the forefront" of voter registration purges, and "no state has been more aggressive or consistent in attacking the heart of the NVRA" than Ohio (Anderson, 2020, 75). Based on state provided data, from 2011 to 2016, Ohio "wiped out two million people from the state's list of registered voters ... 1.2 million of those have been eliminated solely because they voted infrequently" (Anderson, 2020, 75). Further, Ohio passed its guiding state election law statute to provide what it characterized as a "supplemental process" to the NVRA. Under this process, Ohio would send out NVRA confirmation notices to voters who had not voted in two years and then would remove those individuals who *neither* responded *nor* voted in the next two general elections.

Ohio's law was challenged and reviewed by the United States Supreme Court in 2018 in the *Husted v. A. Philip Randolph Institute* case referenced earlier. In that case, the Supreme Court upheld the Ohio voter list maintenance procedure as valid. Opponents to Ohio's law argued that the law violated Section 8 of the NVRA. The Supreme Court held that Ohio's law "follows subsection (d) [and the NVRA] to the letter" and, as such, "does not violate the Failure to Vote Clause or any other part of the NVRA." In the Court's opinion, it was also noted that the NVRA's ban on removal "by reason of ... failure to vote" was interpreted in light of the amendments to the 2002 Help America Vote Act (HAVA). The amendments to HAVA clarify that the NVRA does not forbid using nonvoting as a factor to remove a person from the state's registration lists. Rather the NVRA only forbids removal *solely* for nonvoting. Because Ohio election law utilized nonvoting in combination with statutory notice and a wait period, the Court found the practice in compliance with Section 8 of the NVRA. This significant ruling on the NVRA affirms a state's ability to use voters' inactivity as a major factor for possible purging, so long as the NVRA safeguards (e.g., notice, waiting period, and failure to vote two additional times after receiving notification) are in place.

To be sure, other states have developed other criteria for voter registration purges that have not yet been challenged and upheld in the courts. The result is large groups of otherwise qualified voters removed from state registration rolls. Anderson reports the impact in just the last twenty years (2000–20) as follows: "Virginia: 41,637 purges; Florida: 182,000 purges; Indiana: 481,235 purged; Georgia: 591,549 purged; Ohio: two million purged" (Anderson, 2020, 72).

Further Reading

Anderson, Carol. *One Person, No Vote: How Voter Suppression Is Destroying Our Democracy*. Bloomsbury Publishing, 2020.

Epps, Garrett. "Politics: The Supreme Court Blesses Voter Purges." *The Atlantic*, June 12, 2018. https://www.theatlantic.com/politics/archive/2018/06/the-supreme-court-blesses-voter-purges/562589/

Hardy, Lydia. "Voter Suppression Post- Shelby: Impacts and Issues of Voter Purge and Voter ID Laws." *Mercer Law Review*, *71*, no. 3 (2020), 857–78.

Husted V. A. Philip Randolph Institute, 138 S. Ct. 1833, 201 L. Ed. 2d 141 (2018).

Liptak, Adam. "Supreme Court Weighs Purge of Ohio Voting Rolls." *New York Times*, January 10, 2018. https://www.nytimes.com/2018/01/10/us/politics/supreme-court-ohio-voting-rolls-purge.html

Palast, Greg. "The GOP's Stealth War against Voters: Will an Anti-voter-fraud Program Designed by One of Trump's Advisers Deny Tens of Thousands Their Right to Vote in November?" *Rolling Stones Magazine*, August 24, 2016. https://web.archive.org/web/20170903204215/http:/www.rollingstone.com/politics/features/the-gops-stealth-war-against-voters-w435890

The National Voter Registration Act of 1993 (NVRA). P.L. 103–31, 107 Stat.77, 42 U.S.C. §1973, gg et seq.

Wolf, Richard. "Supreme Court Says States Can Remove Voters Who Skip Elections, Ignore Warnings." *USA Today*, June 11, 2016. https://www.usatoday.com/story/news/politics/2018/06/11/supreme-court-states-purge-voters-who-dont-vote/587316002/

Q20: What are the chief reasons why voters are removed from voter registration lists?

Answer: The top three reasons for the removal from voter registration polls are a change of address to another jurisdiction, inactivity in voting coupled with the voter's failure to respond to confirmation mailings from the state regarding registration, and death of the voter. These three rationales typically account for about 80 percent of all voter removals.

The Facts: Since 2004, the United States Election Assistance Commission (EAC) has conducted a nationwide survey after each general election and reported this data to Congress. During that time, the top three reported reasons for voter removal remained the same in each report, although there was some fluctuation between the top two reasons depending on the specific election year. EAC reported nationwide data from the years 2018 to 2020 and found that almost one-third of all removals (32.1%) were based on a voter being inactive for two consecutive federal elections and not responding to the states attempt to confirm that the voter wishes to no longer vote in that state (EAC, 2021). To remove a voter from voter registration lists when the voter has been inactive for two election years, the state must first send out a confirmation notice by mail to determine if the voter wishes to remain an active registered voter. In most states, if the voter fails to respond to this notice, the state is permitted to remove the voter.

The second most common reason during the same 2018–20 time period for removal from a registration list was the voter's change of address from one jurisdiction to another. This typically entailed a voter moving out of a county or state, resulting in a permanent change of address. A move from one jurisdiction to another accounted for about 28.5 percent of all revocations analyzed by the EAC during this time period. The third major reason as to why voters are removed from voter registration lists is that the voter has died. Purges of voter registration list for this reason represented about 21.4 percent of the removals in the 2018–20 period (EAC, 2021).

Approximately 82 percent of all removals from 2018 to 2020 were for one of the three reasons discussed. Data from 2016 were consistent, with 82 percent of removals attributed to the same for the top three reasons, although the change of address and inactivity percentages flip-flopped. In 2016, about 31 percent of removals were due to moves (compared to 28.5% in 2018–20), 26 percent due to confirmation notice coupled with inactivity (compared with 32.1% in 2018–20), and 25 percent due to death (compared with 21.6% in 2018–20) (EAC, 2017).

The remaining 18 percent of removals were for reasons like a felony conviction, a voter affirmatively cancelling their registration, a voter being removed from registration rolls because of mental incapacity, a voter appearing in a voter registration list from another jurisdiction (duplicate registrations), fixing data errors, or other removals not classified under the main NVRA categories. Each of the remaining reasons constituted only small percentage of voters nationwide. For instance, felony convictions accounted for approximately 1.6 percent of all voter removals nationwide during this period. Removals for erroneous data errors, while small as an overall percentage, can quickly amount to thousands of incorrectly purged voters. For example, Virginia's erroneous removal of approximately 3,400 otherwise qualified voters in 2023 was a database error that resulted in those individuals being "incorrectly flagged as committing repeat felonies" (Schneider and Vozzella, 2024). Most of those voters were added back onto Virginia's Voter Registration list in time for the 2024 presidential election. It was also reported that in Virginia, during Governor Glenn Youngkin's first two- and one-half years in office (from January 2022 to July 2024), "most of the 6,300 voters who were purged by the governor's administration as noncitizens" were removed due to simple "paperwork errors" like failing to check a box (Schneider and Vozzella, 2024). Specifically, "most of the 6,303-name purge stemmed from errors on paperwork at the Department of Motor Vehicles" wherein, "in many cases, legal citizens simply forgot to check a box indicating citizenship" (Schneider and Vozzella, 2024).

States can analyze various government databases to determine whether removal is appropriate. Two examples of such databases include the US Postal Service (change of address forms) and Department of Motor Vehicles records (driver's licenses). Roughly thirty-two states (and the District of Columbia) have used the nonprofit Electronic Registration Information Center system (called ERIC). At least every two months, each of the participating ERIC states submits its voter registration data and motor vehicle licensing data to ERIC (Democracy Docket, 2023).

Further Reading

Democracy Docket. "What Is the Voter Roll Organization ERIC? Explainer: ERIC, The Voter Roll Program." March 29, 2023. https://www.democracydocket.com/analysis/what-is-the-voter-roll-organization-eric/

Election Assistance Committee (EAC). "Election Administration and Voting Survey 2020 Comprehensive Report 2020." 2021. https://www.eac.gov/sites/default/files/document_library/files/2020_EAVS_Report_Final_508c.pdf

Election Assistance Committee (EAC). "EAVS Deep Dive: Registering to Vote." September 20, 2017. https://www.eac.gov/documents/2017/09/20/eavs-deep-dive-registering-vote

Schneider, Gregory S., and Laura Vozzella. "Youngkin Stokes Fear of Vast Noncitizen Voting in Virginia. Records Don't Show It." *Washington Post*, October 9, 2024. https://www.washingtonpost.com/dc-md-va/2024/10/09/youngkin-noncitizen-voters-virginia/

Q21: Did the Interstate Crosscheck Program improve voting access and protect against voter fraud, or did it suppress the vote?

Answer: The Interstate Crosscheck Program was an attempt to eliminate duplicate and fraudulent voter registration by sharing voter registration records across states. Despite its widespread usage, the program was subject to a myriad of mistakes, mismatches, and false positives that removed otherwise eligible voters from voter registration lists. Therefore, it inadvertently hindered voter access, resulting in voter suppression. The problems with the Interstate

Crosscheck Program illustrate how state efforts to clean up the registration rolls by removing duplicates (and initially mandated by HAVA in 2002) could also sweep up eligible voters due to data matching errors or overly broad matching criteria.

The Facts: The Interstate Voter Registration Cross-Check Program (often referred to as "Crosscheck") was created in 2005. It was a data-sharing initiative rather than a law. The original participating states were Kansas, Iowa, Missouri, and Nebraska, and the program expanded to twenty-eight states by 2016. Crosscheck reportedly processed as many as 98 million voter records at its height.

The idea behind the program was to aggregate the voter registration rolls of member states into a single database to detect people registered in multiple states (who could potentially vote more than once). Participating states uploaded their registration files and the Kansas Secretary of State's office ran matches on first name, last name, and full date of birth. Any two records from different states that matched on those fields were flagged as "potential duplicate registrants." Like Georgia's "Exact Match" program discussed elsewhere in this book, the underlying justification of the Crosscheck database was to eliminate fraudulent voter registration and duplicative voting.

However, Crosscheck raised serious concerns about voter suppression and racial bias. Crosscheck did not require matching Social Security numbers, middle names/initials, suffixes (e.g., Jr., Sr.), or other identifiers, thus increasing the risk of misidentifying distinct individuals as one person (Sturgis, 2016). By matching only first and last names and birthdates, the program generated enormous numbers of false positives involving entirely different individuals who happened to share a name and birthday. In 2014 alone, it was reported that Crosscheck flagged over 7 million voter registrations as possible duplicates, yet fewer than four individuals in the entire country were charged with voting twice. Not one of those flags led to a fraud conviction outside the state of Kansas (Palast, 2016). Because the matching criteria were so basic, the system also disproportionately flagged names common among minority communities.

Journalist Greg Palast, who obtained and analyzed Crosscheck files from several states, concluded that the system had a "built-in racial bias" that effectively targeted minority voters (Palast, 2016). Palast found that Crosscheck would list many minority voters as duplicates based on loose name matches, such as treating José Garcia in one state as the same person as Joseph Garcia in another. Common surnames among Black, Hispanic, and Asian Americans meant these groups were hit hardest by the false accusations of double registration. By one estimate, the Crosscheck system ended up flagging one in six Hispanic voters, one in seven Asian American voters, and one in nine Black American voters in participating states as potential double registrants (Palast, 2016). While not necessarily designed with overt bias, the outcome of Crosscheck's methodology was undeniably skewed toward disenfranchising minority communities (Sturgis, 2016).

An official state review of Virginia's use of Crosscheck showed that 75 percent of its flagged "duplicates" had different Social Security digits (i.e., were mismatches) (Virginia State Board of Elections, 2014). Another study, conducted by scholars from Harvard University, Stanford University, the University of Pennsylvania, and Microsoft, reported that the Interstate crosscheck program would mistakenly "eliminate about 200 registrations used to cast legitimate votes for every one registration used to cast a double [i.e., illegal] vote" (Goel, et al., 2017; Ingraham, 2017). That is, 200 legitimate voters would be removed from the state's registration database for every single correct double registration removed. One voter database consultant (who worked for several Fortune 500 companies) dismissed Crosscheck's "childish methodology" and its propensity for being "too error prone" (Anderson, 2020, 87). As this expert further explained, "God forbid, if your name is Garcia, of which there are 858,000 in the United States and your name is Joseph or Jose. You're probably suspected of voting in 27 states" (Anderson, 2020, 87). A study quoted in the *Washington Post* reported that simple name and date-of-birth matching "fails for practically all common American names" and can produce false-positive rates on the order of 75 percent or more (Ingraham, 2017). The *Washington Post* itself reported that Crosscheck's overall false identification rate was roughly 99.9 percent (Ingraham, 2017).

According to author Carol Anderson, because of the Crosscheck database, "342,556 names were immediately identified as suspect because they appeared to be registered in another state" and "those who were already on an 'inactive voters' list were summarily removed, meaning a stunning 41,637 names were 'canceled' from voter rolls most of them just before Election Day" (Anderson, 2020, 86). Per Anderson, "Texas set out to purge 80,000 voters, even though the crosscheck match was considered by Texas to be 'weak'" (Anderson, 2020, 86). In Ohio, crosscheck flagged close to half a million voters as being ineligible (Anderson, 2020, 85). In North Carolina, the Secretary of State alerted the Republican-dominated legislature "that at least 35,750 dual voters were stalking the rolls [and] in Georgia and Washington, Crosscheck seemed to identify a total of more than one-million unscrupulous voters" (Anderson, 2020, 86).

Errors made through the Crosscheck program took on an even greater import in close elections. The presidential election in 2016 was extremely tight, with Hillary Clinton winning the popular vote over Donald Trump, who won the Electoral College. That year, Arizona purged almost 271,000 voters from its database, Michigan removed nearly 450,000 voters, and North Carolina eliminated close to 600,000 (Anderson, 2020, 87). These staggering numbers fueled the narrative of suspected massive voter fraud. However, double voting is actually very rare. The flawed Crosscheck program, through false positives, disenfranchised legitimate voters in the name of preventing perceived (but unsubstantiated) widespread fraud.

Former Kansas officials themselves later conceded that the system was "rife with false positives" (Lowe, 2017). As Anderson has written, "the devastation of Georgia's Exact Match was amplified in nearly thirty states by the Interstate Crosscheck program" before responsible parties could put a stop to that error-prone computer program (Anderson, 2020, 81). Anderson did not mince words when she wrote: "Crosscheck is such a fundamentally flawed database that its 'success' rate is an epic failure for democracy" (Anderson, 2020, 86).

Privacy concerns became central in 2017 when federal auditors found security problems in Crosscheck's database integrity. The Department of Homeland Security temporarily shut the program down after discovering that it had exposed the personal information (including Social Security numbers) of nearly 1,000 Kansas voters (Hegeman, 2019). Prior to this legally mandated suspension, twelve states (Alaska, Arizona, Colorado, Florida, Illinois, Kentucky, Massachusetts, New York, Oregon, Pennsylvania, Virginia, and Washington) had already withdrawn from the free program. Crosscheck was then suspended indefinitely in December 2019 following a lawsuit by the ACLU over poor data security.

Further Reading

Anderson, Carol. *One Person, No Vote: How Voter Suppression Is Destroying Our Democracy*. Bloomsbury Publishing, 2020.

Goel, Sharad, March Meredith, Michael Morse, David Rothschild, and Houshmand Shirani-Mehr. "One Person, One Vote: Estimating the Prevalence of Double Voting in U.S. Presidential Elections." October 24, 2017. https://www.dropbox.com/scl/fi/0w7790bwripeh6knfzyr4/OnePersonOneVote.pdf?rlkey=t5v4ymfn2ktkrjxmj3joi1lsw&e=1&dl=0

Hegeman, Roxana. "Multistate Voter Database Suspended in Lawsuit Settlement." AP News, December 10, 2019. https://apnews.com/general-news-2c82eb782e578bbb81c121ec453fbee8

Ingraham, Christopher. "This Anti-fraud Program Gets It Wrong over 99 Percent of the Time. The GOP Wants to Take It Nationwide." *The Washington Post*, July 20, 2017. https://www.washingtonpost.com/news/wonk/wp/2017/07/20/this-anti-voter-fraud-program-gets-it-wrong-over-99-of-the-time-the-gop-wants-to-take-it-nationwide/?noredirect=on&utm_term=.5eae3d898fbe

Lowe, Peggy. "Kansans Caught in Crosscheck System Singled out for Kobach's Voter Fraud Campaign." NPR: Kansas City, February 7, 2017. https://www.kcur.org/politics-elections-and-government/2017-02-07/kansans-caught-in-crosscheck-system-singled-out-for-kobachs-voter-fraud-campaign

Lowe, Peggy. "Kansas Voter Tracking System Championed by Former SOS Kris Kobach Is 'Dead.'" NPR: Kansas City, December 10, 2019. https://www.kcur.org/politics-elections-and-government/2019-12-10/kansas-voter-tracking-system-championed-by-former-sos-kris-kobach-is-dead

Palast, Greg. "The GOP's Stealth War against Voters: Will an Anti-voter-fraud Program Designed by One of Trump's Advisers Deny Tens of Thousands Their Right to Vote in November?" *Rolling Stones Magazine*, August 24, 2016. https://web.archive.org/web/20170903204215/http:/www.rollingstone.com/politics/features/the-gops-stealth-war-against-voters-w435890

Smith, Sherman. "ACLU: Kansas to Abandon Crosscheck." *The Topeka-Capitol Journal*, December 10, 2019. https://www.cjonline.com/story/news/politics/state/2019/12/10/aclu-of-kansas-announces-deal-to-abandon-crosscheck-for-foreseeable-future/2111244007/

Sturgis, Sue. "Controversial Anti-voter Fraud Program Risks Disenfranchising Voters through Racial Bias, Report Finds." *Facing South*, September 2, 2016. https://www.facingsouth.org/2016/09/controversial-anti-voter-fraud-program-risks-disenfranchising-voters-through-racial-bias

Virginia State Board of Elections. "Annual Report on Voter Registration List Maintenance Activities Report to the House and Senate Committees on Privileges and Election." January 6, 2014. https://web.archive.org/web/20180202071528/https://www.elections.virginia.gov/Files/maintenance-reports/2013SBEListMaintenancereport.pdf

Q22: Do any centralized federal databases currently exist to verify voter registration?

Answer: The now-suspended Interstate Crosscheck Program, despite its widespread usage, was subject to a myriad of mistakes and false positives. States used this data to remove otherwise eligible voters from voter registration lists by the hundreds of thousands while failing to improve the overall integrity of voter registration. Eventually, a much better program was put into place, namely, the Electronic Registration Information Center (ERIC). ERIC was founded in 2012 as a state-governed nonprofit. This program gained widespread acceptance for several years. At its height, ERIC was adopted by thirty-three states and the District of Columbia. Controversy involving perceived bias has since led some Republican-led states to withdraw from participation in ERIC.

The Facts: In its early days, the Electronic Registration Information Center (ERIC) ran concurrently with the Interstate Crosscheck Program (2005–19). Both programs had the same goal of identifying voter fraud, although ERIC attempted to improve on the error-prone Crosscheck database. ERIC's mission was to enable participating state governments to securely share data (including voter registrations, motor vehicle records, US Postal Service change-of-address updates, and Social Security death records) and to identify voters who have moved, filed duplicate registrations, or died, as well as eligible but otherwise unregistered citizens. ERIC provides reports on this data to each participating state. States, in turn, utilize the data to update their voter lists in accordance with federal and state laws and remove voters as each state deems appropriate.

In the first decade after its launch, ERIC was hailed as a bipartisan success in election administration. ERIC purported to have processed documentation for 63 million voters from 2012 to 2025, helped identify nearly 12 million voters who moved from one state to another, identified 1 million duplicate registrations, and located more than 580,000 deceased voters on the rolls. Controversy started after the 2020 election when a right-wing website, *The Gateway Pundit*, published articles claiming ERIC was financed by left-wing financier George Soros and that ERIC's unstated goal was to beef up the number of liberal voters (Fifield, 2023). President Donald Trump attacked the nonprofit as well claiming that ERIC "pumps the rolls" with Democratic voters (Vasilogambros, 2023).

This controversy led to a series of Republican-led states deciding to withdraw from ERIC in 2023. These included Alabama, Florida, Louisiana, Iowa, Missouri, Ohio, West Virginia, Virginia, and Texas. But not all Republican-led states left, and some pushed back against the departures. Georgia's Secretary of State Brad Raffensperger, for example, defended ERIC and criticized those leaving as putting "politics" over actual election integrity. Raffensperger chastised his fellow Republicans saying that they were "reacting to disinformation" and "hurting their own state & others" by abandoning the best tool available for the protection against election fraud (Ballotpedia, 2025). Kentucky's Republican Secretary of State has also been a vocal supporter of ERIC and resisted calls to quit. By 2025, membership in ERIC had stabilized at twenty-five states plus the District of Columbia.

Several withdrawing states have pursued ad hoc agreements with a smaller number of states run by ideologically similar officials. West Virginia, Ohio, Florida, Virginia, and Tennessee have one such arrangement to swap data. After quitting ERIC, Virginia had to pay $28,960 to a private company to replicate a limited amount of the national data (i.e., address and death records) that Virginia had previously received through its membership in ERIC (Fifield, 2023).

Alabama and Missouri officials spent months devising inferior in-house cleaning methods (Fifield, 2023). A consortium of ex-ERIC states led by Alabama launched the Alabama Voter Integrity Database (AVID) in 2023–4 as an alternative to ERIC. AVID has thus far attracted about nine Republican-led states to share data (Wood, 2025).

However, experts have criticized AVID's lack of transparency and technical rigor, noting that it essentially links state databases without the sophisticated matching and security protocols that made ERIC effective (in contrast to the Interstate Crosscheck Program) (Wood, 2025). One elections analyst commented that these break-off states are "largely trying to build the ugly stepchild version of ERIC" (Wood, 2025). AVID and other ad hoc state arrangements have also been criticized for not having the scale and size of ERIC, making it much more difficult for these states to identify voters with common names or catch duplicate registrations (Wood, 2025).

Further Reading

Ballotpedia. "Electronic Registration Information Center (ERIC)." Accessed August 12, 2025. https://ballotpedia.org/Electronic_Registration_Information_Center_(ERIC)

ERIC. Official Website. Accessed August 12, 2025. https://ericstates.org/

Fifield, Jen. "Documents Show Republican-led States Struggling to Clean Voter Rolls after Leaving ERIC." *Votebeat*, December 13, 2023. https://www.votebeat.org/2023/12/13/cleaning-voter-rolls-after-eric-election-security-voter-fraud/

Underhill, Wendy. "More Withdrawals from Voter Data Group ERIC Likely." *National Conference of State Legislatures*, June 20, 2023. https://www.ncsl.org/state-legislatures-news/details/more-withdrawals-from-voter-data-group-eric-likely

Vasilogambros, Matt. "Why Republican-led States Keep Leaving a Group That Verifies Voter Rolls." *Missouri Independent*, May 22, 2023. https://missouriindependent.com/2023/05/22/why-republican-led-states-keep-leaving-a-group-that-verifies-voter-rolls/

Wood, Colin. "Conservative States Are Building Their Own Voter Database." *STATESCOOP*, April 15, 2025. https://statescoop.com/conservative-states-avid-eric-voter-database/

Q23: Have states utilized other database-related matching programs that suppress the vote?

Answer: Yes. Notable examples of state database matching programs include Georgia's "Exact Match" Program and Florida's "No Match, No Vote" program. Advocates of these programs claim that they were designed to disqualify unqualified potential voters and/or to prevent fraud in voting registration applications and that the databases have their origin in a federal congressional mandate first specified by the Help America Vote Act of 2002. However, such programs have resulted in Americans be disqualified from voting for reasons having nothing to do with the issues the programs were expected to identify. As with the Interstate Crosscheck Program, a high probability of false positive results based upon vague voter qualification information exists. These programs also place a burden (and a time limit) on applicants to fix any identity-related problems identified by the state. And, the application of these programs appears to disqualify minority groups disproportionately.

The Facts: The impetus for state-computerized database programs used to verify the accuracy of voter registration lists came with the passage of the Help America Vote Act (HAVA) of 2002. Before 2000, in many states, voter registration rolls were kept separately by counties, often in handwritten ledger books, and there was little to no cross-referencing among counties. With no real integration or crossflow of information across the state, there were no means of identifying duplicative or fraudulent votes. As such, one of the perceived improvements by Congress in HAVA was requiring each state to "implement a single, uniform, official, centralized, interactive computerized statewide voter registration list that contains the name and registration information, including a unique identifier, of every legally registered voter in the State to serve as the official voter registration list for the conduct of all elections for Federal office in the State" (House of Representatives Conference Report, 2002).

As discussed in Questions 12 and 13, for first time new voter mail-in registrations, HAVA requires new voter registrations to provide either their driver's license number or the last four digits of their Social Security number, or other qualifying documentation establishing voter identification. State governments, in turn, must verify their voter lists with other records to ensure accuracy (e.g., DMV records or records from the Social Security Administration). HAVA mandates these checks to reduce registration errors and improve electoral integrity (Brennan Center for Justice, 2002; Underhill, 2022). HAVA has succeeded in achieving drastically improved voting infrastructure and reduced registration errors, but it also opened the door for disenfranchisement resulting from efforts to prevent voter fraud, such as some state-level matching programs used to verify registration list accuracy. Early state programs, such as Georgia's "Exact Match" Program, Florida's "No Match, No Vote" Law, and Kansas's SAFE ACT, appeared to risk disenfranchisement based on a host of relatively minor mismatching issues bearing no relation on whether the individual should be eligible to vote. Grounds for potential disqualification might be a voter's name appearing with their middle initial on a registration list while their driver's license contained their full middle name, a shortened version of their name (e.g., Tim) appearing in one location while their full name (Timothy) appeared on their license, or the simple transposition of two letters in a mistyped version of their name.

Georgia's "Exact Match" program was enacted into law in 2017 and provided that when a voter registered to vote, the name on the voter registration must "exactly match" the person's name on file with Georgia's Department of Driver Services or the Social Security Administration. If the name on the application did not exactly match the name in government databases, the voter registration application was put in a "pending" status, and the individual was notified by correspondence from the state that the application was incomplete and that the individual needed to provide additional documentation. Thus, under Georgia law, the burden was placed on the individual to produce satisfactory evidence to prove his or her identity. Potential voters in the "pending" status had twenty-six months from the date of the application to clear up any problems with the voter's mismatched information. After that time, if the person did not respond or provide additional information, the individual's application would be rejected, and he/she would have to submit a new registration application to vote.

This system was criticized almost from the very start. Data from Georgia's Secretary of State showed that by mid-2018 over 50,000 registrations had been placed on hold by "Exact Match" (Diaz, 2019). Another analysis found that roughly 80 percent of pending registrations were for Black, Latino, or Asian voters (Campaign Legal Center, 2021). In July 2018 about 51,000 registrations were in pending status, and nearly four-fifths were members of minority groups (Campaign Legal Center, 2021). As one author noted, "minority voters are more likely statistically to have names with hyphens or suffixes or other punctuation that can make it more difficult to match their name in databases," and "the evidence indicates that minority residents are more likely to be flagged than are whites" (Valverde, 2018). In effect, tens of thousands of otherwise valid citizens were unable to register because of minor data mismatches (Diaz, 2019).

Georgia first concocted a version of its matching program approximately four years before the Supreme Court (in *Shelby County v. Holder*, 2013) overturned long-standing preclearance requirements of the Voting Rights Act for states with a history of racially discriminatory voting practices. As such, the state was required to obtain approval from the federal government for proposed changes to its election laws and policies. Georgia's system included verification of citizenship. The Department of Justice indicated that thousands of naturalized citizens had been erroneously flagged by the state as "potential non-citizens" and had their registrations stalled (Campaign Legal Center, 2021). Of 7,007 people flagged, more than half were in fact citizens (Evan, 2009). The Department of Justice rejected the program, declaring that the "flawed system frequently subjects a disproportionate number of African-American, Asian, and/or Hispanic voters to additional and, more importantly, erroneous burdens on the right to register to vote" (Mock, 2018). The program eventually passed federal review in 2010 with a few new safeguards in place, but it was suspended during a civil rights lawsuit challenge in 2016, only to be enacted into law with minor changes in 2017. In 2021, the Lawyers' Committee for Civil Rights under Law noted that the program in its various forms had "failed Georgia voters for the past 12 years," disproportionately affecting minority applicants (Diaz, 2019). Author Carol Anderson called it a "monstrous little program" that had a "horrific effect on voter registration, especially for minorities" (Anderson, 2020, 80–1). According to Anderson, Black Americans, who were one-third of all applicants, "accounted for 64 percent of the tens of thousands of voter registrations that Georgia's secretary of state (Brian Kemp) canceled or 'placed in pending status'" (Anderson, 2020, 81). If this were not sufficiently shocking, "Asian-Americans and Latinos were more than six times as likely as white voters to have their applications halted" (Anderson, 2020, 81).

By the time of the gubernatorial election in Georgia in October 2018, the storm clouds had already gathered overhead. In the contest between Brian Kemp and Stacey Abrams, Stacey Abrams identified approximately 53,000 applications that were on hold under the "exact match" law, with a reported disproportionate number belonging to Black voters. This raised alarms on multiple levels. First, the 53,000 votes were within the margin of error for the election. Second, voting rights advocates noted that the policy was effectively suppressing minority votes (Valverde, 2018).

The law was challenged in *Georgia Coalition for the Peoples' Agenda, Inc., et al., v. Brian Kemp* (2018). In that lawsuit, the Lawyers' Committee for Civil Rights Under Law argued that the "exact match" practice was discriminatory and a "voter suppression scheme." The lawsuit complaint included examples of ways in which a no-match could happen based on minor discrepancies in spelling, spacing, or punctuation between voter registrations and other government databases. The program "was fraught with errors—a missing 'e' in the name Carole, a hyphen where one was not supported to be, an errant 'y' instead of an 'i' in Nicki, or any of the other numerous typographical errors that can happen when two large bureaucracies are processing millions of applications" (Anderson, 2020, 81).

Kemp pointed out at the time that "pending" applicants could still vote. As the American Civil Liberties Union (ACLU) of Georgia stated, they could vote "if they provide at the polls a photo ID that 'substantially' reflects the name on the voter registration form" (Valverde, 2018). However, overly zealous partisan poll-watchers might try to disqualify a person because of a minor discrepancy in the documentation. Also, the Georgia law was constructed so that the onus for proof of voter identification was on the applicant to produce additional documentation within a 26-month period that would satisfy the Board of Elections.

While the coalition lawsuit was pending, Georgia's political leadership shifted. After the contentious 2018 gubernatorial election (which Kemp won while controversies over voter suppression swirled), Kemp and Georgia decided to dismantle the exact-match program. In April 2019, newly elected Governor Brian Kemp signed House Bill 316, which "largely ended" the exact match system. The bill amended Georgia's election code to eliminate the strict match protocol for most fields, including abandoning the requirement that every letter or number match exactly. The program's citizenship check continued, however. Under the new post 2019-rules, an applicant is no longer automatically placed in pending status for a name or identification card mismatch. However, if records indicate a person is a noncitizen, the application can still be flagged until the person provides proof of citizenship. At the end of the program, Georgia's exact-match program had only a negligible impact on preventing ineligible registrations (Diaz, 2019), but a significant and well-documented impact on delaying or denying legitimate registrations, particularly among voters of color (Campaign Legal Center, 2021).

Florida has a program that is comparable to Georgia's now-defunct "Exact Match" program. In fact, during several heated exchanges between Brian Kemp and Stacy Abrams, Kemp was often quick to point out that he thought the Georgia system was like Florida's "No Match, No Vote," which he indicated was upheld by Florida courts. Like Georgia, Florida's computerized program had its genesis in the language of the Help American Vote Act of 2002. Florida's "No Match, No Vote" law is codified at Florida Statutes Section 97.053(6). This statutory provision requires that new voter registration applications "may be accepted as valid only after" Florida's Department of Elections verifies the voter's driver's license number, state issued identification card number, or last four digits of the voter's social security number listed on the voter's registration application form.

Unlike Georgia, however, at least initially, the onus is on the state of Florida to reconcile the voter's registration application with databases consulted, instead of immediately placing the burden upon the voter to "prove the state wrong." Election officials are obligated to attempt to resolve mismatches (e.g., double-checking various government databases). After reasonable efforts, if the state cannot verify the information by matching it to an available database, then the law requires the state of Florida to notify the applicant of problems with the application (i.e., no match) and to work with the voter in producing some further proof of identity. That is, election officials must affirmatively reach out to the voter and assist them in resolving the issue. Also unlike Georgia's program, which imposed a twenty-sixth-month deadline, the Florida law does not put a time limit on how quickly a voter must act to rectify the situation. The state does not cancel the registration application after a fixed period. As mandated by HAVA, flagged individuals can cast a provisional ballot.

In the first three weeks of its operation in 2008, the Florida program reviewed approximately 131,000 voter applications, and of that amount, roughly 15 percent (or 20,000 applications) were flagged as "no-matches" and held aside (McClatchy Newspapers, 2008). Many of the discrepancies were of a minor nature (date entry errors, a person using a nickname, transposing a number on their driver's license number or social security number). But unlike with

Georgia's law, where the burden was on the voter to prove that the state was in error, the Florida statute placed the initial burden of resolution on the state, a feature that may have saved the Florida program from the eventual fate of Georgia's.

While Florida's program was challenged in the courts when the law was new in 2008, the law has been upheld since that time, and Florida's exact-match policy has continued with relatively little change to the statute. It remained part of the voter registration verification in 2024. Occasionally, protests and lawsuits do arise. Most recently, in 2024, civil rights groups, purportedly representing tens of thousands of Floridians, have claimed damage by the no-match rule. Their lawsuit alleged that, since 2018, more than 43,000 individuals across twenty-six Florida counties submitted valid voter registration applications but have "never been able to register to vote successfully solely due to the 'exact match' requirement" (Sheridan, 2024). The suit, filed in federal court in Orlando, argued that Florida's law was unconstitutional and disproportionately disenfranchised people of color. The data cited show that while Black American voters comprise about 14 percent of registrants in those counties, they accounted for 31 percent of the applications deemed unverified or denied due to a mismatch. Latino Americans were over-represented among those blocked as well. White applicants (57% of registrants) made up only 7 percent of the unmatched rejections (Sheridan, 2024).

While Florida's law has continued to survive multiple judicial challenges, the state has struggled to demonstrate major benefits from the program in preventing fraud. The no-match protocol has failed to catch significant numbers of impersonators or ineligible individuals and has instead mainly caused delays with registrations for people who eventually prove their identity (McClatchy Newspapers, 2008). In 2008, Florida's own data showed that of the initial batch of flagged registrations, a large number were resolved when people provided correct information or officials found minor errors, indicating that they were in fact legitimate and lawful voters.

Further Reading

Anderson, Carol. *One Person, No Vote: How Voter Suppression Is Destroying Our Democracy*. Bloomsbury Publishing, 2020.

Brennan Center for Justice. "The Help America Vote Act." 2002. https://www.brennancenter.org/sites/default/files/legacy/d/HAVA%20Fact%20Sheet.pdf

Campaign Legal Center. 2021. "Challenging Georgia's Racially Discriminatory 'Exact Match. Policy (Georgia Coalition for the People's Agenda v. Raffensperger)'." April 12, 2021. https://campaignlegal.org/cases-actions/challenging-georgias-racially-discriminatory-exact-match-policy-georgia-coalition

Complaint in *Georgia Coalition for the Peoples' Agenda, Inc., Et. Al., V. Brian Kemp*, 2018. https://lawyerscommittee.org/wp-content/uploads/2018/10/Georgia-exact-match-complaint-.pdf

Diaz, Nick. "Georgia Largely Abandons Its Broken 'Exact Match' Voter Registration Process." Lawyers Committee for Civil Rights under Law, April 5, 2019. https://www.lawyerscommittee.org/georgia-largely-abandons-its-broken-exact-match-voter-registration-process/

Evan, Desiree. "VOTING RIGHTS: DOJ Finds Georgia Voter Screening Inaccurate and Discriminatory." Facing South, June 4, 2009. https://www.facingsouth.org/2009/06/voting-rights-doj-finds-georgia-voter-screening-inaccurate-and-discriminatory.html

Florida Statute 97.053. "Qualification and Registration of Electors." 2025. http://www.leg.state.fl.us/statutes/index.cfm?App_mode=Display_Statute&Search_String=&URL=0000-0099/0097/Sections/0097.053.html

House of Representatives. Conference Report on H.R. 3295-Helf America Vote Act of 2002. 107th Congress (2001–2002), October 8, 2002. https://www.congress.gov/bill/107th-congress/house-bill/3295

McClatchy Newspapers. "US Election: Registration Law Leads to Accusations of Voter Suppression in Florida." *The Guardian*, October 1, 2008. https://www.theguardian.com/world/2008/oct/01/uselections2008.florida

Mock, Brentin. "How Dismantling the Voting Rights Act Helped Georgia Discriminate Again." Bloomberg, October 16, 2018. https://www.bloomberg.com/news/articles/2018-10-15/how-georgia-s-exact-match-program-was-made-possible

Sheridan, Kerry. "Lawsuit Claims 'Exact Match' Voter Policy in Florida Disenfranchises People of Color." NPR/WUSF, September 18, 2024. https://www.wusf.org/politics-issues/2024-09-18/lawsuit-exact-match-voter-policy-florida-disenfranchises-people-of-color

Underhill, Wendy. "The Help America Vote Act: 20 Years Later." National Conference of State Legislatures, June 1, 2022. https://www.ncsl.org/state-legislatures-news/details/the-help-america-vote-act-20-years-later

United States District Court for the Northern District of Florida. "Order Denying Motion for Preliminary Injunction." Case No. 4:07CV-402-SPM/WCS, June 24, 2008. https://www.brennancenter.org/sites/default/files/legacy/Democracy/FloridaNAACPvBrowning-06.24.08.Order.Denying.PI.pdf

Valverde, Miriam. "Georgia's 'Exact Match' Law and the Abrams-Kemp Governor's Election, Explained." *Politico*, October 19, 2018. https://www.politifact.com/article/2018/oct/19/georgias-exact-match-law-and-its-impact-voters-gov/

Q24: Do state election police forces exist to investigate and protect against voter fraud?

Answer: Generally, states do not have law enforcement agencies dedicated to enforcing election laws. However, Florida has created an Office of Election Crimes and Security, and it is possible that other states may adopt Florida's approach in the future. Critics are concerned that such "police forces" might do more harm than good. Those critics argue that an election police force merely duplicates and replaces other law enforcement resources already in place and operating in a satisfactory manner, and that a specialized state election police force might (intentionally or unintentionally) suppress or chill certain legitimate voters.

The Facts: In the aftermath of allegations of voter fraud and repeated unsubstantiated claims of a "stolen election" in the election of 2020, Governor Ron DeSantis began coordinating with the Florida legislature to pass enabling legislation for the creation of a new state law enforcement agency dedicated chiefly to the topic of election fraud. In April 2022, DeSantis signed the passed legislation (Senate Bill 524), creating the first-of-its-kind statewide Office of Election Crimes and Security (OECS). At the time of its creation, the OECS in Florida was claimed to be "one of the nation's only election police units" (Fineout, 2022). DeSantis stated at the signing ceremony for the legislation that "I don't think there's any other place in the country that you should have more confidence that your vote counts than in Florida" (Fineout, 2022).

OECS was charged with investigating complaints relating to voter misconduct or election fraud. On those cases which OECS determines merits further action, OECS then "refers all evidence of potential election crimes to the Florida Department of Law Enforcement (FDLE), the Office of Statewide Prosecution, or the local state attorney for the judicial circuit in which the alleged violation occurred" (Florida Department of State, 2025). At its creation, the OECS, along with the Florida Department of Law Enforcement, received approximately $2.6 million in state funds to begin operating immediately and were authorized twenty-five positions. The staff is a mix of investigators and sworn law enforcement officers (Fineout, 2022).

Opponents of the law immediately decried the creation of OECS, with one election official calling it a "recipe for disaster" (Fineout, 2022). Democratic lawmakers in both the Florida House and Senate unanimously opposed the creation of OECS, arguing that it was an unnecessary agency and an unnecessary use of state funds. Critics also claimed that OECS might be used to intimidate certain voters. Democratic state representative Yvonne Hinson complained that "even the governor has said that Florida's 2020 election was secure. Yet this new election crime task force has been developed to solve a problem that does not exist" (Fineout, 2022). Hinson also called the creation of the new agency a "bullying tactic [that] targets communities of color," elaborating that "[t]his bullying tactic will intimidate and immobilize workers, families, and everyday people" (Fineout, 2022). On the need for such an agency at all, a report published with Brennan Center for Justice opined, "There is no evidence of widespread fraud in Florida's elections (or any state's elections, for that matter). Yet state lawmakers created a highly unusual election police office earlier this year at the request of DeSantis to investigate 'election irregularities'" (Brennan Center for Justice, 2022). Several weeks before DeSantis signed the legislation into law, Michael Waldman at the Brennan Center for Justice warned that "to create law enforcement squads to aggressively search for vanishingly rare fraud doesn't just waste taxpayer money. It's one more way partisans are using the myth of widespread voter fraud to cast doubt on free and fair elections" (Barber, 2022).

Within a few months of its creation, the OECS had initiated criminal proceedings against the first twenty individuals investigated by the OECS, all previously convicted felons who had registered and voted in the 2020 election. As addressed elsewhere in this book, Florida amended its state constitution in 2018 to allow for the restoration of voting rights for felons but excluded any felon who was convicted of murder or of a felony sexual offense. These first OESC prosecutions were of felons who had been previously convicted for either the offense of murder or a felony sexual offense. However, very early on in the trial proceedings, virtually all of the charged individuals had made clear that they were led to believe they were lawfully entitled to vote. Some produced evidence, such as voter registration cards sent to them by the state of Florida, while others were erroneously advised by voting outreach and registration workers that they were allowed to vote based upon Florida's passage of Amendment 4. According to the Brennan Center for Justice,

> Making matters worse, government officials have permitted and, in some instances, outright encouraged people with past convictions to register to vote. And at the same time, the department of state—the office tasked with verifying voter eligibility for those with past convictions—has left ineligible voters on the

rolls for years after it approved their registrations, making them think they are allowed to vote. (Brennan Center for Justice, 2022)

Another problem relates to the changes the Florida legislature enacted in restricting the ability of former felons to vote. Specifically, in 2019, Florida passed legislation specifying that former felons could not vote if any amount of court costs was still outstanding. Curiously though, Florida lacks a centralized database to check if court fees have been paid, so many former felons were confused about whether they could or could not vote and whether a long-forgotten court cost might still be outstanding.

The claim that the charged individuals had reason to believe that they were entitled to vote raised problems with the prosecution of these cases, especially when the individuals produced evidence showing that they had voted in good faith under the belief that they were entitled to vote. According to one of the defense attorneys (Robert Barrar) in one of the charged election fraud cases, "Intent is core to these cases. A prosecutor must prove that a defendant knowingly and willingly registered to vote or knowingly and willingly voted while ineligible. It is not enough for a conviction to show solely that the voter cast their ballot while ineligible" (Cohen, 2022). The chief author of Florida's Amendment 4, Republican Florida legislator Jeff Brandes, also stressed that the "intent" of the voter should be considered. Brandes wrote that "it was our intent that those ineligible would be granted some grace by the state if they registered without intent to commit voter fraud" (Cohen, 2022).

In one highly publicized case, charges were eventually dropped against a 69-year-old woman who reportedly was arrested at approximately 3 a.m. (Soule, 2023). The woman reportedly answered the door in her pajamas and sleepers to find two law enforcement agents ready to take her into custody. The case was dismissed after the defendant was able to produce corroborating evidence that she thought she was entitled to vote (Soule, 2023).

Approximately half of the first twenty individuals prosecuted by the OECS were either convicted—some of lesser offenses (e.g., making a false affirmation on a voter registration form)—or pled guilty to the charged offense (LaGrone, 2024). A few cases were dismissed very early on after being initiated; one case was dismissed within sixty days of the state's filing of charges (Cohen, 2022). Among those who were found guilty or pled guilty, not a single defendant received more than a sentence of probation by the judge, with no jail sentences, despite the fact that many of the defendants were facing five years in prison and a $5,000 fine for one count of making a false affirmation on a voter application (i.e., signing the form indicating that you are eligible to vote) and one count of voting as an unqualified elector.

The first case of the twenty to go to a jury trial did not occur until February 2023. In that case, the defendant was a convicted felon who had voted in 2020 despite not qualifying to have his right to vote restored under Florida law. The defendant alleged to have believed his right to vote was restored. In fact, on the voter registration form, the defendant had openly disclosed his felony record but mistakenly claimed that his right to vote was restored. At the end of the trial, the jury returned a split verdict. The defendant was found not guilty on the charge of illegally voting but was convicted of the lesser offense of making a false affirmation on voter registration form (i.e., signing the registration form knowing that he was a convicted felon *despite* listing his felony conviction on that same form). In this case, the defendant was reported to have received no jail time and only a sentence of probation.

The cases dropped or dismissed, as well as the low sentences (i.e., probation but no jail time) for cases resulting in a conviction or a guilty plea, offered strong ammunition to critics of the OECS. In many cases, people had made innocent mistakes about their status to vote but were prosecuted vigorously. The results of these initial prosecutions suggested that perhaps the millions of dollars appropriated to the OECS, the assignment of two dozen investigators and law enforcement officers, and the time and resources expended by the judicial system were not a wise use of state resources.

The OECS's early activities were not limited to cases concerning convicted felons who claimed to have voted by mistake and confusion about whether the civil liberties of these individuals had been restored in Florida. A review of the OECS's annual reports, available at the Florida Secretary of State's website, reveals that the office appeared to be very busy in its first nine months of its existence (April 2022-December 2022). In its 2023 report (covering OECS activities in 2022), starting on page 10 and spanning the next eighty pages, is a spreadsheet listing every complaint/case referred. Annotations include details on each complaint such as the county of the alleged violation, the election laws allegedly violated, whether the complaint was referred to a different state agency, and the current status and/or resolution of each complaint. The spreadsheet itemizes 3,026 complaints (Florida Department of State, 2023, 6, 10–90). The report appears to show that well over half the complaints were forwarded to the Florida Law Enforcement Department or to another state agency for action.

The OECS listed that it handled a wide range of voter fraud-related cases, ranging from individuals attempting to vote in two different states at the same time to a felon and undocumented immigrant allegedly voting under an alias and creating false documentation suggesting he was a citizen of the United States, among many other similar type cases (Florida Department of State, 2023, 10–90). By early 2024, OECS was claiming that at least sixty cases were viewed as serious enough to execute an arrest warrant on the subject individual. Of these cases, OECS claimed "at least 25" convictions or guilty pleas (LaGrone, 2024).

OECS has also claimed that it prevented or caught alleged perpetrators in several larger election fraud/voter fraud schemes. For example, in 2023, working with the Pinellas County Supervisor of Elections, OECS uncovered a fraud scheme that supporters claim serves to justify the existence of state election security agencies. In this case, state authorities identified two men (foreign nationals from Russia and Uzbekistan residing in Florida) who were purportedly behind sending at least 132 fraudulent voter registration forms to Pinellas County, Florida, in February and March 2023 (United States Department of Justice, 2025). According to the official press release by the United States Department of Justice, the registration "applications were submitted in names other than their own, in envelopes with return and address labels that were identically formatted, including containing the same typographical error, and bore various indicia of fraud including, among other things, repeating dates of birth and addresses and nearly sequential social security numbers" (United States Department of Justice, 2025). The Department of Justice alleged that the defendants had also submitted change of address forms to route mail to several addresses controlled by the defendants.

In February 2025, the Department of Justice announced the arrest of the two alleged perpetrators, who were both charged with conspiracy to submit false voter registration forms (United States Department of Justice, 2025). In April 2025, one of the two individuals arrested submitted a guilty plea, admitting that he hired his co-defendant and others to "submit more than 100 fraudulent voter registration applications to the Pinellas County Supervisor of Elections in February and March 2023" (United States Attorney's Office, 2025). Florida touted this case as an accomplishment of the OECS, which provided background support, although the case was prosecuted by the federal government and not the state of Florida.

Other cases touted as successes for the OECS involve fraud related to petitions, as Florida allows for amendments to its state constitution through citizen petition/ballot initiatives. Based on a complaint received in late 2022, the OECS helped facilitate the prosecution of an individual accused of submitting dozens of fake/fraudulent signatures on a petition to add a proposed state constitutional amendment to the ballot for the next election (Florida Department of State, 2023, 90). Similarly, in 2024, the OECS, working with Georgia law enforcement, helped facilitate the arrest of an individual from Georgia for running a petition scam in Florida. In this case, according to the Florida Department of Law Enforcement (FDLE), the defendant submitted "71 invalid constitutional initiative forms throughout Florida" relating to an initiative to legalize the personal use of marijuana (Florida Department of Law Enforcement, 2024). The defendant was charged with eight counts of criminal offenses relating to petition fraud, including the "criminal use of a deceased individual's information, criminal use of personal identification information and false swearing, submitting false voter registration information" (Florida Department of Law Enforcement, 2024). The FDLE stated that "seventeen people have been charged with petition fraud following FDLE investigations, including fraud on the marijuana, casino and abortion initiatives involving more than 34,000 invalidated petitions" (Florida Department of Law Enforcement, 2024).

Critics of the OECS have claimed that the low number of cases prosecuted and the even lower number of convictions each year are miniscule compared to the overall number of registered voters in the state (over 13 million registered voters in Florida in 2025), and therefore that this work is not a good use of taxpayer resources. Critics further argue that while pursuing voter fraud cases is an important state interest, it could be just as effectively accomplished in the same way investigations were handled before the creation of the OECS, namely by local city or county law enforcement and referral to state attorneys' offices where appropriate. Dr. Dan Smith, an election law expert and a professor of political science at the University of Florida, assessed OECS's overall accomplishments as "not terribly impressive. We had those types of numbers [handled] quietly behind closed doors prior to the creation of this office" (LaGrone, 2024). Smith also opined that "honestly, it's an entity that doesn't need to exist, shouldn't exist, and has proven itself basically useless" (LaGrone, 2024).

Opponents also claim that the operation of an agency like the OECS may chill some eligible voters from voting. OECS agents arrived at one voter's front door to question him about whether he signed a petition to put an issue on the Florida ballot to amend the constitution. The voter reported that an agent not only questioned him about his signature but also showed him a folder containing about ten pages of personal information about the voter. He later said, "The experience left me shaken" (Rozsa, 2024).

Some potential voters who are formerly convicted felons may decide not to vote out of an overabundance of caution, even if the person believes that he or she has served the terms of their incarceration and probation and made complete restitution to the state (for court fees) or other injured parties. Additionally, the changes made in 2019 to a 2018 constitutional amendment are confusing to many lawyers, let alone laypersons. The Florida Rights Restoration Coalition (FRRC) has noted that Florida has never published a centralized database allowing those with past felony convictions to determine for themselves their eligibility to vote. Because of the lack of definitive database, the FRRC alleges "former felons have refrained from registering to vote or voting for fear of making a mistake and facing prosecution" (Perry, 2023). A Brennan Center for Justice report stated in its resource entitled "10 Reasons Courts Should Toss Florida's Flimsy 'Voter Fraud' Prosecutions": "now the state is prosecuting people ... for honest mistakes about their eligibility [and] intimidating potentially eligible voters" (Brennan Center for Justice, 2022). As Democratic Florida representative Dianna Hart stated, "we have scared thousands of people around the state from exercising their God-given right to have a voice in their government" and "this is a fear tactic, and it's voter suppression, plain and simple" (Saunders, 2023).

Supporters of the OECS say that even if the agency only brings and wins a small number of cases each year, its existence is justified if the overall effect is the deterrence of future election related crimes from occurring. Republican Florida representative Juan Alfonso Fernandez-Barquin claimed that the OECS "further protects the integrity of our most sacred right, the right to vote, [and] ensures fraud will be investigated and prosecuted to the full extent of the law, the way it should" (Saunders, 2023). According to Florida Governor Ron DeSantis and other supporters, if the existence of such an agency renews or strengthens the populace's faith in the election system, it is worth the effort.

Other states have been watching the experiment in Florida play out over the last couple of years, and several states are considering similar type laws and/or agencies. Georgia, Texas, and Ohio have all taken steps to come more in line with Florida's position. In 2022, Georgia's legislature promulgated a law giving the Georgia Bureau of Investigation (GBI) the authority to initiate the investigation and prosecution of election crimes, creating an "election police" function within GBI. Texas contributed additional resources (both budget and staff) to its Election Integrity Unit in the Attorney General's Office. In Virginia, the state Attorney General's office established an "election integrity unit" with more than twenty assigned staff members (Schneider and Vozzella, 2024). Finally, Ohio also announced an Election Integrity Unit within its Secretary of State's Office, albeit on a much smaller scale than OECS (Barber, 2022).

Further Reading

Barber, Benjamin. "Southern States Create Election Police Forces." *Facing South*, April 7, 2022. https://www.facingsouth.org/2022/04/southern-states-create-election-police-forces

Brennan Center for Justice. "10 Reasons Courts Should Toss Florida's Flimsy 'Voter Fraud' Prosecutions." November 7, 2022. https://www.brennancenter.org/our-work/research-reports/10-reasons-courts-should-toss-floridas-flimsy-voter-fraud-prosecutions

Cohen, Miles. "Florida Voter Has Election Fraud Charges Touted by DeSantis Dismissed." ABCNews, October 21, 2022. https://abcnews.go.com/US/voter-fraud-charge-dismissed-florida-arrest/story?id=91858299

Fineout, Gary. "Florida: DeSantis Signs Bill Creating One of the Nation's Only Election Police Units." *Politico*, April 25, 2022. https://www.politico.com/news/2022/04/25/desantis-florida-election-police-units-00027577

Florida Department of Law Enforcement. "FDLE Announces Arrest of Georgia Man for Petition Fraud." September 12, 2024. https://www.fdle.state.fl.us/News/2024/September/FDLE-announces-arrest-of-Georgia-man-for-petition

Florida Department of State. "Office of Election Crimes and Security." Accessed July 19, 2025. https://dos.fl.gov/offices/election-crimes-and-security/

Florida Department of State, Office of Election Crimes and Security. "Annual Report." January 15, 2023. https://files.floridados.gov/media/706232/dos-oecs-report-2022.pdf

Hasen, Rick. "Florida: 2 DeSantis Election Fraud Cases End with Guilty Pleas in Hillsborough; Both Men Received Six Months of Probation. Their Attorneys Called the Prosecutions Political." *Tampa Bay Times*, March 30, 2023. https://electionlawblog.org/?p=13531

LaGrone, Katie. "Data Shows Florida's Election Crimes Office Still Struggling to Find Staff, Accomplishments Raise Questions." ABC Action News WFTS Tampa Bay, August 1, 2024. https://www.tampabay28.com/news/state/data-shows-floridas-election-crimes-office-still-struggling-to-find-staff-accomplishments-raise-questions

Levin, Sam. "First Case in DeSantis Voter Fraud Crackdown Ends with Split Verdict." *The Guardian*, February 8, 2023. https://www.theguardian.com/us-news/2023/feb/08/florida-desantis-election-crimes-nathan-hart

Perry, Mitch. "Voting Rights Group Files Lawsuit against DeSantis on Felon Voting Eligibility; Florida Rights Restoration Coalition: State's Amendment 4 Compliance Is 'a National Embarrassment.'" *The Florida Phoenix*, July 19, 2023. https://

floridaphoenix.com/2023/07/19/voting-rights-group-files-lawsuit-against-desantis-on-felon-voting-eligibility/

Rosza, Lori. "DeSantis Election Police Question People Who Signed Abortion Ballot Petition." *The Washington Post*, September 9, 2024. https://www.washingtonpost.com/nation/2024/09/09/desantis-election-abortion-referendum-fdle/?_pml=1

Saunders, Jim. "Statewide Prosecutor Bolstered in Election Cases." WLRN South Florida, February 10, 2023. https://www.wlrn.org/state/2023-02-10/statewide-prosecutor-bolstered-in-election-cases

Schneider, Gregory S., and Laura Vozzella. "Youngkin Stokes Fear of Vast Noncitizen Voting in Virginia. Records Don't Show It." *Washington Post*, October 9, 2024. https://www.washingtonpost.com/dc-md-va/2024/10/09/youngkin-noncitizen-voters-virginia/

Soule, Douglas. "Voter Fraud Charges Dropped against 69-Year-Old Florida Woman Arrested at 3 a.m." *Tallahassee Democrat*, October 17, 2023. https://www.tallahassee.com/story/news/politics/2023/10/17/florida-voter-fraud-case-dropped-against-69-year-old-arrested-at-3-a-m/71217722007/

United States Attorney's Office, Middle District of Florida. "Foreign National Pleads Guilty to Conspiring to Submit over 100 Fraudulent Voter Registrations." April 29, 2025. https://www.justice.gov/usao-mdfl/pr/foreign-national-pleads-guilty-conspiring-submit-over-100-fraudulent-voter

United States Department of Justice, Office of Public Affairs. 2025. "Russian and Uzbek Nationals Charged with Conspiracy to File False Voter Registration Applications." February 3, 2025. https://www.justice.gov/opa/pr/russian-and-uzbek-nationals-charged-conspiracy-file-false-voter-registration-applications

5

Mail-in Ballots, Ballot Drop Boxes, Voter Identification Requirements, and Early Voting

Voting options have increased in the last half century. In addition to voting in person on Election Day, states allow voting by mail, casting ballots via drop boxes, and/or early voting. Policies regarding who can vote by mail, where drop boxes are placed, what identifications are required and/or accepted, and when voting is permitted can either broaden participation or, if misapplied or confusing, reinforce structural barriers that suppress the vote.

Through restrictive legislation, potential voter suppression by states can be seen with each of these types of voting. The use of absentee mail-in ballots and voter drop boxes illustrates this conundrum. These options offer convenience for voting, which undoubtedly increases participation. However, concerns regarding ballot integrity and voter fraud have led some to believe that restrictions on the unfettered use of mail-in ballots and voting drop boxes are needed. Limitation of these voting methods also means that at least some voters will be dissuaded from voting if their circumstances make it difficult to travel to a polling place on Election Day.

The problem can also be seen with early voting practices and stricter voting identification laws. Early voting provides citizens with greater flexibility as to when to vote. This is especially important for those with limitations on their availability to vote on Election Day. Extending the voting period over a week or two helps to ameliorate adverse conditions like long lines on Election Day as well. As such, early voting encourages voting by making the experience more accessible and pleasant. This is said to increase participation not only as it relates to a current election in which a voter might experience difficult or unpleasant conditions, but future elections as well. Scholarship supports the proposition that those who experience adverse conditions will have a greater probability of not voting at all in subsequent elections (and vice versa, the better the experience, the more likely the person will vote in the next election). However, the longer the early voting period is extended, the higher the cost to the state, as each day of early voting requires additional state resources to facilitate.

Strict voter identification laws (either for voter registration, in person-voting, or both) are framed as fraud-prevention measures. They ensure that a person is who he or she says they are and prevent duplicate registration and/or voting. They also decrease the likelihood of a person voting multiple times in a single election. But strict requirements on the type of identification can suppress participation by groups less likely to hold the qualifying identification. This includes individuals and groups who are unable to obtain the required documentation because of costs or transportation. Strict identification laws restrict the act of voting when the required documentation is hard to obtain. For instance, 87 percent of eligible voters have a driver's license. This means that 13 percent of the voting population lacks this type of identification that often satisfies the strict voter identification requirements. Certain groups like the elderly and poor are disproportionately restricted/suppressed by strict identification requirements. Limiting the number or use of drop boxes in urban areas has the same impact.

The practices of mail-in ballots, ballot drop boxes, voter identification requirements, and early voting illustrate how seemingly neutral rules (i.e., time, place, and manner of voting rules) can inadvertently affect the ability or willingness of various groups to participate in voting. In addition, these practices can be manipulated to adversely impact and suppress different groups and selectively burden those with the least scheduling flexibility, without overtly seeming to do so.

Q25: How do restrictions on voting by mail or absentee voting impact voter participation?

Answer: Restrictions to voting by mail or absentee voting by their very nature limit the total number of possible votes submitted. Certain groups are more adversely impacted than others based upon socioeconomic conditions and day-to-day limitations on one's time and resources. These groups include the elderly, the poor, and the working class, who may not have dependable transportation to a physical election site or the flexibility to be present at that site on Election Day, and therefore, might not be able to vote if they lacked the flexibility in terms of the modality of voting or limitations on the diverse methods to voting.

The Facts: Absentee ballots, sometimes referred to as "mail-in ballots," have long been a central feature of voting in elections. Historically, absentee ballots were used by voters "absent" on Election Day (such as military personnel or travelers). At a minimum, all states are required by federal law to offer absentee ballots to military and overseas voters per the Uniformed and Overseas Citizens Absentee Voting Act of 1986. Absentee voting has expanded into a widespread practice used by millions of regular Americans in each election cycle in the last quarter century as well. The ability to vote by mail was especially important in facilitating the vote during the COVID-19 pandemic when almost half (46%) of all votes (65 million) were via absentee/mail-in ballots (Pew Research Center, 2020). This compares to only about 21 percent of the votes cast this way in 2016.

Terminology varies between the states. Traditionally, beyond the military, "absentee voting" implied that an excuse was needed (e.g., absenteeism caused by illness or travel), whereas "vote-by-mail" can refer to states approving of universal absentee ballot ballots to all voters. Prior to 2020's liberal and extensive use of absentee ballots, a handful of western states like Colorado, Oregon, and Washington had already long conducted all elections by mail. These states would even proactively mail ballots to every registered voter at the beginning of an election cycle.

With encouragement from President Donald Trump, many states with Republican-led leadership started to push for significant reductions/limitations to the use of absentee ballots between 2021 and 2025 after widespread usage in 2020. Then, on August 18, 2025, President Trump called for the complete elimination of absentee ballots. He claimed that he would be signing an Executive Order recommending that states discontinue their absentee ballot practices. Article I, Section 4 of the US Constitution gives states the exclusive authority to set and regulate the "time, place, and manner" of elections for the House and Senate. The president has the power to cajole states into possibly adhering to his desires but cannot mandate the change. Alternatively, President Trump might be able to pressure the Republican members in Congress to pass legislation overriding the wishes of the states, as Article I, Section 4 (clause 2) specifies Congress may overrule "time, place, and manner" determinations by the states in instances Congress deems necessary.

Because of the delegation of power to states under Article I, Section 4, there is no single nationwide standard and a wide divergence of practices pertaining to the use of absentee ballots. This includes the types of absentee ballots used. Most states allow "no-excuse absentee voting," meaning any registered voter can request an absentee ballot without providing a reason. States such as California, Colorado, Nevada, Oregon, Washington, and Vermont (among a few others) automatically mail ballots to all active registered voters, effectively operating universal vote-by-mail systems (McReynolds, 2020). Arizona long had a Permanent Early Voting List (allowing any voter to get mail ballots routinely), and Virginia (after 2020 reforms) lets voters opt to automatically receive mail ballots for every election if a voter so opted as well. This approach has been praised for increasing voter participation, particularly among groups facing mobility or scheduling barriers.

By contrast, approximately one-third of states still require voters to provide a qualifying reason for requesting an absentee ballot. A qualifying reason includes such things as illness, disability, military service, or religious observance. For example, Texas and Mississippi restrict absentee ballots to voters meeting such criteria (NCSL, 2025). Critics argue that these limitations create unnecessary barriers that still disproportionately impact other groups (e.g., the poor and the elderly). Defenders claim that reason-based approach to absentee ballots preserves in-person voting as chief means of voting and that it also reduces opportunities for fraud.

Regardless of the state and/or the type of absentee ballot, the voter must first apply for an absentee ballot through their state's election office. The only exception is for military members, as federal law (the Uniformed and Overseas Citizens Absentee Voting Act) mandates that absentee ballots must be sent to and accepted from all military personnel. Once approved, the ballot is mailed to the voter who completes it and returns it either by mail, in person at a designated drop box, or at an election office. State laws differ on deadlines for requesting and returning absentee ballots, signature verification requirements, whether the absentee ballot must be notarized, and when ballots must be received. Some states specify the absentee ballots must be received before or on Election Day while others say ballots postmarked by Election Day but received later may be also be counted (National Conference of State Legislatures, 2025).

Studies have shown that the use of no-excuse absentee ballots improves voter participation and limits turnout inequities. The convenience of voting at home "on one's own time" especially helped young people, lower-income individuals working long or inflexible hours, the elderly, and others facing barriers to getting to a polling place. For instance, older Americans were more inclined to vote by mail. A majority of voters over sixty-five did so in 2020, while younger voters (under thirty-five) were slightly less likely (roughly 42–44% voted by mail) (Pew Research Center, 2020).

A 2021 study of Colorado's switch to all-mail elections (which started in 2014) found a "resounding success at expanding and equalizing democratic access" (Democracy Docket, 2021). Turnout in Colorado increased by an estimated 9.4 percent overall after all-mail voting was implemented. In this 2021 study, the greatest turnout gains were among groups that historically vote at lower rates. Voters under forty saw their turnout jump by about 16.6 percent. Likewise, turnout rose about 10 percent among the lowest-income voters which was significantly more than among the most affluent voters. The same pattern held across race and education. Black, Latino, Asian American, and Native American voters' turnout increased more sharply (on the order of 10–13% increases) (Democracy Docket, 2021).

And while citizen access to no-excuse absentee ballot has improved overall participation in voting, minority groups do not necessarily have an advantage in this means of voting. Research shows that Black voters in 2020 were somewhat less likely to vote by mail (about 38% did so) than white voters (45%) or Hispanic voters (51%), whereas Asian American voters had the highest mail voting rate (around 66%) (Pew Research Center, 2020).

Surveys after 2020 showed that Republicans, influenced by fraud rhetoric, were far more skeptical of mail voting than Democrats. Pew Research reported that two-thirds of Trump voters reported voting in person, compared with 42 percent of Biden voters (Pew Research Center, 2020). Additionally, nearly four-in-ten Trump voters (37%) say they voted in person on Election Day while just 17 percent of Biden voters say they cast their ballot at a polling place on Election Day (Pew Research Center, 2020). Yet, despite this partisan difference, there is some research to suggest that mail-in ballots do not greatly sway partisan voter turnout (Thompson et al., 2020). Additional research establishes that the availability of options to vote before election day does not confer a consistent advantage to either political party despite partisan rhetoric attempting to influence voter choices about one voting method over another (e.g., mail-in voting versus in-person) (Gronke et al., 2008; Yoder et al., 2020).

Some critics, many fueled by unsubstantiated claims of widespread voter fraud in the 2020 presidential election and in the months and years thereafter, have argued that mail-in ballots should be restricted because there is allegedly less ballot security with them than in-person voting. However, the fundamental finding from studies and audits is that mail voting has been secure, with negligible rates of fraud (Brennan Center for Justice, 2024; Cassidy, 2021; Minnite, 2010). A 2021 Associated Press review found fewer than 475 cases of potential voter fraud in six key states (Arizona, Georgia, Michigan, Nevada, Pennsylvania, and

Wisconsin) out of 25.5 million votes cast in 2020, "a minuscule number" with no impact on the result (Cassidy, 2021).

Some critics have claimed that how mail-in ballots are collected (if not mailed or put in a drop box by the voter him or herself) creates the possibility of fraud. Specifically, they point to the practice of third-party ballot collection (pejoratively termed "ballot harvesting"). Under this practice, many voters (especially elderly or disabled) entrust a family member, friend, or another third party to deliver their sealed ballot. This practice is often also crucial for rural voters who lack home mail service and have transportation limitations. Some states (e.g., California) allow this practice. California law permits any person to collect and return a voter's completed ballot so long as the voter has authorized it. But under California law, paid collectors must be disclosed, and coercion is illegal. Other states have criminalized the practice after 2020. States like Georgia and Texas passed laws in 2021 to make it a crime for most individuals outside of a voter's family or household to handle that voter's absentee ballot. In Arizona, a 2016 law (upheld by the US Supreme Court in *Brnovich v. DNC*, 594 U.S. 647 (2021)) likewise bans third-party collection of mail ballots by anyone not a caregiver or family member.

Limited research has shown few (if any) instances of fraud occurring with this practice. Research on Native American reservations, for instance, examined the practice of third-party collection and delivery of mail-in ballots. The finding was that organized ballot collection on reservations greatly facilitated legitimate voting without any corresponding evidence of fraud (University of Utah, 2024).

Restrictions on voting are sometimes justified on the grounds that cutting back on voting options will save a state money. For example, this claim is often made in relation to early voting (see Question 28). However, some research suggests that mail-in ballots actually save money and resources. One study in Colorado examined the costs of the 2010 election under different models and found significant savings from all-mail elections. If all Colorado counties had conducted the 2010 election entirely by mail (instead of a mix of polling places and absentee voting), the average cost per voter would have dropped by an estimated $1.05, a reduction of almost 19 percent (from $6.70 down to $5.65 per registered voter) (Pew Research Center, 2012).

States like Georgia and Florida have enacted tighter deadlines for absentee ballots as well as restrictions on who can return absentee ballots, practices critics argue disproportionately affect those with disabilities and minority voters (Gardner, 2021). These policies can also adversely impact poorer voters who might not be able to travel farther distances to get to a polling location or might not have time to vote (depending on ability to get time off from work).

Further Reading

Biggers, Daniel R., and Michael J. Hanmer. "Who Makes Voting Convenient? Explaining the Adoption of Early and No-Excuse Absentee Voting in the American States." *State Politics & Policy Quarterly*, *15*, no. 2 (2015), 192–210.

Brennan Center for Justice. "Mail Ballot Security." June 28, 2024. https://www.brennancenter.org/our-work/research-reports/mail-ballot-security

Burden, Barry C., David T. Canon, Kenneth R. Mayer, and Donald P. Moynihan. "Election Laws, Mobilization, and Turnout: The Unanticipated Consequences of Election Reform." *American Journal of Political Science*, *58*, no. 1 (2014), 95–109.

Carter, Sara, Andrew Garber, Catherine Silvestri, and Connie Wu. "How Voting Laws Have Changed in Battleground States since 2020." Brennan Center for Justice, August 15, 2024. https://www.brennancenter.org/our-work/research-reports/how-voting-laws-have-changed-battleground-states-2020

Carter, Tracey B. "One's Health versus One's Right to Vote: How the COVID-19 Pandemic Changed the Legal Landscape of Absentee/Mail-in Voting in the United States from the 2020–2024 Election Cycles." *University of Florida Journal of Law & Public Policy*, *35*, no. 1 (2024), 1–57.

Cassidy, Christina A. "Far Too Little Vote Fraud to Tip Election to Trump, AP Finds." *AP News*, December 14, 2021. https://apnews.com/article/voter-fraud-election-2020-joe-biden-donald-trump-7fcb6f134e528fee8237c7601db3328f

Democracy Docket. "In Colorado, All-Mail Voting Is a Step toward Equity." August 24, 2021. https://www.democracydocket.com/analysis/in-colorado-all-mail-voting-is-a-step-toward-equity/

Fortier, John C. *Absentee and Early Voting: Trends, Promises, and Peril.* AEI Press, 2006.

Gardner, Amy. "Florida Republicans Rushed to Curb Mail Voting after Trump's Attacks on the Practice. Now Some Fear It Could Lower GOP Turnout." *Washington Post*, May 3, 2021. https://www.washingtonpost.com/politics/florida-republicans-mail-voting/2021/05/02/4c133920-a9bf-11eb-8c1a-56f0cb4ff3b5_story.html

Gronke, Paul, Eva Galanes-Rosenbaum, Peter A. Miller, and Daniel Toffey. "Convenience Voting." *The Annual Review of Political Science, 11* (June 2008), 437–55.

Hasen, Richard L. *Election Meltdown: Dirty Tricks, Distrust, and the Threat to American Democracy*. Yale University Press, 2020.

Hasen, R. L. *Cheap Speech: How Disinformation Poisons Our Politics—and How to Cure It*. Yale University Press, 2022.

Hernson, Paul S., and Charles Stewart, III. "The Impact of COVID-19, Election Policies, and Partisanship on Voter Participation in the 2020 U.S. Election." *Election Law Journal, 22*, no. 2 (June 2023), 135–49.

McReynolds, J. "How Vote-at-Home with Vote Centers Can Work." Stanford-MIT Healthy Elections Project, August 25, 2020. Executive Research Summary of Report. https://www.lawfaremedia.org/article/healthy-elections-project-releases-2020-research-compendium

Minnite, Lorraine C. *The Myth of Voter Fraud.* Cornell University Press, 2010.

National Conference of State Legislatures (NCSL). "Voting Outside the Polling Place: Absentee, All-Mail and Other Voting at Home Options." August 1, 2025. https://www.ncsl.org/elections-and-campaigns/voting-outside-the-polling-place

Pew Research Center. "Cost Savings from All-Mail Balloting." January 3, 2012. https://www.pew.org/en/research-and-analysis/articles/2012/01/03/cost-savings-from-all-mail-balloting

Pew Research Center. "The Voting Experience in 2020." November 30, 2020. https://www.pewresearch.org/politics/2020/11/20/the-voting-experience-in-2020/

Thompson, Daniel M., Jennifer Wu, Jesse Yoder, and Andrew B. Hall. "Universal Vote-by-Mail Has No Impact on Partisan Turnout." *Proceedings of the National Academy of Sciences, 117,* no. 25 (2020), 14052–6.

University of Utah, College of Social and Behavior Science. "Exposing Myths about Ballot Collection on Native American Reservations." August 14, 2024. https://attheu.utah.edu/research/exposing-myths-about-ballot-collection-on-indian-reservations/

Yoder, Jesse, Cassandra Handan-Nader, Andrew Myers, Tobias Nowacki, Daniel M. Thompson, Jennifer A. Wu, and Chenoa Yorgason. "The Expansion of Voting before Election Day, 2000–2024: Universal Vote-by-Mail Has No Impact on Partisan Turnout or Vote Share." *PNAS, 117,* no. 25 (June 2020), 14052–6.

Yoder, Jesse, Cassandra Handan-Nader, Andrew Myers, Tobias Nowacki, Daniel M. Thompson, Jennifer A. Wu, Chenoa Yorgason, and Andrew B. Hall. "How Did Absentee Voting Affect the 2020 U.S. Election?" *Science Advances, 7,* no. 52 (December 2021), 1–43.

Q26: Are ballot drop boxes secure and fraud resistant?

Answer: Yes. Recent elections have illustrated that ballot drop boxes have been secure with no major documented instances of fraud. A relatively new phenomenon utilized just in the last twenty-five years, the use of drop boxes has become the preferred mode of submitting absentia and mail-in ballots since 2020 in the majority of states. In the 2020 election, about 41 percent of mail voters nationwide returned their ballots via drop box, roughly the same share that returned ballots through US mail (Pew Research Center, 2020). Despite the success of this method of voting and its abundant use in 2020, conspiracy theories and unfounded rumors were spread by Republicans after the 2020 presidential election about the integrity of ballot drop boxes. As such, some states with Republican leadership (e.g., Georgia, Texas, Florida) have spearheaded efforts for the limitation of the use of drop boxes in their states.

The Facts: Prior to the 2020 presidential election, very few states allowed the use of ballot drop boxes. The origins of the use of drop boxes for elections can be traced to the state of Oregon in the late 1990s. In 1998, Oregon voters approved a ballot measure mandating vote by mail for all future elections. The first all-mail general election was held in November 2000, and the use of ballot drop off boxes was a part of this new electoral approach for the state. As part of the new law, Oregon required each county to establish secure drop sites where voters could deposit their completed mail-in ballots in lieu of using the US Postal Service. This made Oregon the earliest adopter of ballot drop boxes. These boxes were secure receptacles, typically placed inside courthouses, outside government buildings, or at election offices. The keys and locks to the boxes were safeguarded, and protecting the "chain of custody" for transporting ballots to the voting tabulation area involved steps as rigid and strict as would be taken in the treatment of "chain of custody" of evidence in a criminal case.

Starting in 2005, Washington state followed Oregon's example and began to phase out traditional polling places and conduct elections through all-mail ballots as well. As with Oregon, Washington also provided secure ballot drop boxes across the state for its residents who were leery of using the US Postal Service. In fact, the use of drop boxes was by far the preferred mode of submitting ballots in Washington state as well. In 2016, 56.9 percent of all statewide ballots were submitted via drop boxes (Hufford, 2020). Colorado soon followed suit, and since that time, 70 percent of voters in some Colorado counties deposit their vote in drop boxes (Sherman, 2021). Because of the success and the convenience of ballot drop boxes, as well as the heightened security and faith in the integrity of these boxes, several states throughout the western United States soon adopted their use, including Utah, Arizona, Montana, New Mexico, and California.

Florida embraced the use of ballot drop boxes until it decided to limit their usage in 2021. In the early 2000s, a few county election officials in Florida offered secure drop off boxes at election offices and early voting locations for the first time. By 2018, most counties provided official drop boxes for their residents. The proliferation of the usage of drop boxes had also expanded to other states by this time, including Hawaii, Nevada, Ohio, Georgia, Maryland, Michigan, and New Jersey, among others. Approximately one in every six voters cast their ballot through the use of a drop box nationwide by 2016. During this period, election officials praised drop boxes as a secure convenience for voters and a practice that had been utilized for over a decade without any controversy or documented fraud (Sherman, 2020; Sherman, 2021).

Drop boxes were ubiquitous in several states from 2016 to 2020. In Washington, for example, a 2017 state statute specified that there should be at least one ballot drop box per every 15,000 registered voters and at least one drop box in every city or town with a post office. Only eight states (Arizona, California, Colorado, Hawaii, Montana, New Mexico, Oregon, and Washington) expressly permitted ballot drop boxes by statute in 2020. Yet, in practice, many more states use ballot drop boxes regularly, either through statewide practice (without specific state level statutory language) or on a county-by-county basis as approved by county-level election officials. At least sixteen states permitted the practice in the absence of state statutory authorization (Hufford, 2020).

Despite the popularity of drop-boxes in the above-mentioned West Coast states, during the 2016 presidential election, only 16 percent of voters across the country voted by submitting their ballot into a drop box (Hufford, 2021). In large part because of the coronavirus pandemic, comfort with the practice greatly improved as evidenced by the fact that approximately forty states allowed for the use ballot drop boxes in the 2020 presidential election. Citizens quickly embraced this option. Many voters believed that using drop boxes was more convenient and had better security measures in place than regular mail. Usage of drop boxes during the 2020 election shot up to over 40 percent of voters.

In the aftermath of the 2020 election, however, the use of ballot drop boxes became the focus of conspiracy theories regarding security and fraud. After President Biden's electoral victory in 2020, President Trump and some of his supporters began claiming, without corroborative evidence, that Democratic political operatives were stuffing drop boxes with fraudulent ballots with the intention of stealing the presidential election. Before that point, there were few, if any, complaints involving the integrity of ballot drop boxes. Boxes were used widely in many Republican-led states. But when President Trump began referring to use of the ballet drop boxes as "a voter security disaster" (Sherman, 2020), Republican-led states began revising their state laws to restrict the use of the drop boxes. Some of these states included Florida, Texas, and Georgia, among others.

These unfounded security claims received further public attention through right-wing media outlets that amplified the complaint (still without any serious evidence borne out through official governmental or academic studies). One example of such media coverage is a film entitled *2000 Mules*. The premise of this movie was that there was a coordinated ballot stuffing scheme involving drop boxes in each of several swing states. Despite the inflammatory claims in the film, various investigations (ranging from law enforcement to the media, to academics, to journalists) found no evidence to corroborate these claims. Yet this type of accusation sowed distrust among many voters, and no amount of neutral research and government public service announcements could reverse that damage. In a vivid illustration of misinformation and its negative effects, accusations of ballot drop box fraud and abuse in the 2020 election were made in North Carolina, angering many voters. The main problem with these assertions was that North Carolina did not even use drop boxes in the 2020 election (Izaguirre and Cassidy, 2022).

The erosion of public trust in turn led to more state governments eliminating the use of ballot drop boxes after 2020. As stated previously, forty states utilized ballot drop boxes in the 2020 election, but by 2025, the number dropped to approximately twenty-eight states (plus the District of Columbia). Roughly a dozen states now not only do not use but also expressly prohibit the use of drop boxes, typically claiming concerns of fraud of the chief reason for their discontinuation. Other states either have ambiguous laws that do not clearly approve of or prohibit the use of drop boxes or allow for their use in limited local elections only, which would then leave it to the choice of individual counties within the state as to whether to utilize them or not.

According to a voting rights expert at the Brennan Center for Justice, ballot drop boxes are more secure than the typical regular mailboxes that would otherwise be utilized for absentee and mail-in ballots. A single drop box weighs more than 600 pounds and has security and tamper proof mechanisms built into the receptacle. "They are tamper proof, bomb proof, fireproof and in many places equipped with cameras, or by government offices. They have more security features then mailboxes do, and they are opened only by qualified election workers" (Sherman, 2020). Combined with strict chain of custody procedures from the drop box to the tabulation center, drop boxes could be said to be more secure than mail-in voting.

Numerous investigations and reports have concluded that no evidence has been found to support Republican claims of compromised security regarding drop boxes. There are too many such reports to be discussed here, but one example comes from a major Associated Press (AP) survey of states based on an independent investigation. The resulting AP report concluded that "none of the election offices in states that allowed the use of drop boxes in 2020 reported any instances in which the boxes were connected to voter fraud or stolen ballots" (PBS News, 2022). The nationwide study concluded that there was "no problem that could have affected the results, including from fraud, vandalism or theft" (Izaguirre and Cassidy, 2022).

That said, some incidents regarding drop boxes have occurred. Two drop boxes were targeted by arsonists, in Boston and Los Angeles. In both instances, firefighters were able to extinguish the flames, and election workers contacted affected voters (whose ballots were damaged) and allowed them to re-cast their ballot (Izaguirre and Cassidy, 2022). In another incident, a group of people armed and clothed in tactical gear allegedly positioned themselves to stake out drop boxes in the name of securing them and preventing ballot harvesting (the collection and delivery of ballots on behalf of other voters). They allegedly confronted and harassed voters, which could be considered the equivalent of intimidating voters on their way to a polling place, a federal criminal offense (Sievers, 2022).

Scholarship has repeatedly substantiated that ballot drop boxes improve voter turnout. For example, a political science study analyzed the introduction of thirty new ballot drop boxes in Washington's King County (an area that includes Seattle), specifically looking at the effect of these boxes on voter turnout. The study found that the increased convenience in voting via access to drop boxes modestly increased voter participation, particularly in lower-turnout contests (i.e., off-year elections and primaries) (Collingwood et al., 2018). Conversely, limitations in this mode of voting operate to suppress the vote. For example, even within states that use drop boxes, urban counties with large minority populations of voters may be allotted only a handful of drop boxes, forcing residents to travel long distances to polling locations or endure long lines to deliver ballots. Rural or predominantly white counties may receive comparatively greater access relative to population size. These disparities turn a tool of accessibility into one of exclusion. By limiting drop box locations or access hours, policymakers can effectively suppress turnout among certain groups (e.g., minorities, students, and working-class voters) that might not be in support of the positions or candidates of these policymakers.

Further Reading

Brown, Brielle A. "Where's My Ballot? Why Congress Should Amend H.R.1 to Include a National Mandate of Drop Boxes for Federal Elections to Help Protect the Black Vote." *Drexel Law Review, 14*, no. 2 (2022), 405–49.

Collingwood, Loren, and B. Gonzalez O'Brien. "Is Distance to Drop Box an Appropriate Proxy for Drop Box Treatment? A Case Study of Washington State." *American Politics Research, 49*, no. 6 (2021), 604–17.

Collingwood, Loren, William McGuire, Benjamin Gonzalez O'Brien, Katherine Baird, and Sarah Hampson. "Do Drop Boxes Improve Voter Turnout? Evidence from King County, Washington." *Election Law Journal: Rules, Politics, and Policy, 17*, no. 1 (2018), 58–72.

Flower, Stephen. "Ballot Drop Boxes Are Often the Subject of False Claims. Here's What to Know." NPR, October 25, 2024. https://www.npr.org/2024/10/25/nx-s1-5163635/ballot-drop-boxes-explainer

Greenberger, Michael, and Jason M. Roberts. "Dropbox Allocation and Use among Georgia Voters in the 2020 Election." *Election Law Journal, 23*, no. 1 (2023), 55–68.

Hufford, Alex. "The Rise of Ballot Drop Boxes Due to the Coronavirus." LawFare, August 27, 2020. https://www.lawfaremedia.org/article/rise-ballot-drop-boxes-due-coronavirus

Hufford, Alex. "Ballot Drop Boxes in the 2020 Elections." Stanford-MIT Healthy Elections Project, March 10, 2021. https://web.mit.edu/healthyelections/www/sites/default/files/2021-06/Ballot_Drop_Boxes.pdf

Izaguirre, Anthony, and Christina A. Cassidy. "No Major Problems with Ballot Drop Boxes in 2020, AP Finds." AP News, July 17, 2022. https://apnews.com/article/voting-rights-2022-midterm-elections-covid-health-wisconsin-c61fa93a12a1a51d6d9f4e0a21fa3b75

McGuire, William, Benjamin Gonzalez O'Brien, Katherine Baird, Benjamin Corbett, and Loren Collingwood. "Does Distance Matter? Evaluating the Impact of Drop Boxes on Voter Turnout." *Social Science Quarterly, 101*, no. 5 (2020), 1789–809.

PBS News. "No Major Problems with Ballot Drop Boxes in 2020, AP Survey Finds." PBS News, July 17, 2022. https://www.pbs.org/newshour/politics/no-major-problems-with-ballot-drop-boxes-in-2020-ap-survey-finds

Pew Research Center. "The Voting Experience in 2020." November 20, 2020. https://www.pewresearch.org/politics/2020/11/20/the-voting-experience-in-2020/

Sherman, Amy. "Ballot Drop Boxes Have Long Been Used without Controversy. Then Trump Got Involved." Politifact, October 16, 2020. https://www.politifact.com/article/2020/oct/16/ballot-drop-boxes-have-long-been-used-without-cont/

Sherman, Amy. "Ballot Drop Boxes Were Popular in 2020. Then They Became a GOP Target." Politifact, May 19, 2021. https://www.politifact.com/article/2021/may/19/ballot-drop-boxes-were-popular-2020-then-they-beca/

Sievers, Caitlin. "More Reports of Voter Intimidation at Valley Ballot Drop Boxes Are Being Referred to Prosecutors." *AZMirror*, October 24, 2022. https://azmirror.com/2022/10/24/more-reports-of-voter-intimidation-at-valley-ballot-drop-boxes-are-being-referred-to-prosecutors/

Q27: What is the status of universal voter identification laws?

Answer: Not all states have fully adopted the requirement of proof of voter identification to cast a ballot, but at the time of this writing, a majority of states (72%, or thirty-six states) have done so. Further, among the states that have adopted the requirement of proof of voter identity, twenty-three (46%) only accept government issued photo identification cards.

The Facts: Few voting practices embody the tension between security and suppression more vividly than the requirements of voter identification laws. Proponents understandably argue that requiring a government-issued photo identification improves electoral integrity and prevents fraud. However, the actual incidence of in-person voter fraud is statistically negligible, while the burdens imposed by strict photographic identifications are real. Millions of eligible voters lack the types of identification required by some states, and studies have shown that these individuals are disproportionately Black, Hispanic, the elderly, and poor. Obtaining proper identification can involve time, money, and sometimes overcoming bureaucratic hurdles. These burdens can be particularly challenging for those who lack ready access to transportation or lack necessary underlying documents (e.g., notarized birth certificates).

The debate in states about "strict photo identifications" for purposes of voting is one that has been particularly contentious, especially in the years since the 2020 election. In recent polling, Americans appear overwhelming in favor of requiring government issued photo identification cards to vote. As one example, a Gallup poll administered in October 2024 reported that 84 percent of Americans (including a majority of Republicans, Democrats, and Independents) all supported the notion of requiring a voter identification card to vote (Gallup, 2024).

For much of the country's history, producing a photo identification card to vote was not required. In small towns throughout America, in little villages and hamlets of one hundred people or so, there was not a need for photographic identification, because in the words of the television show *Cheers* theme song, they were places where "everyone knows your name" (and face). President Jimmy Carter often reminded people of this fact, stating that in small towns across America "everyone knew everybody else." As such, no voter identification was needed. In 2005, President Carter co-chaired the bipartisan Commission on Federal Election Reform with former Secretary of

State James Baker, and Carter's early experiences in Plains, Georgia, informed the final report language when it stated:

> And in the old days and in small towns where everyone knows each other, voters did not need to identify themselves. But in the United States, where 40 million people move each year, and in urban areas where some people do not even know the people living in their own apartment building let alone their precinct, some form of identification is needed. (Report on the Commission of Federal Election Reform, 2005, 18)

Even in the small town where Carter grew up, with the 2020 census reporting a population of 573 individuals, election officials would be hard pressed to recognize every voter by their face alone.

One of the chief arguments in favor of the universal adaptation of each person presenting a government issued identification card to vote is the prevention of voter fraud. In *Crawford v. Marion County*, 553 U.S. 181 (2008), the Supreme Court decided a case dealing with Indiana's voter identification law. Justice John Paul Stephens, writing for the majority of the Court, specified that a state had an "unquestionably relevant" interest in requiring proof of voter identification. The majority opinion in *Crawford* also stated that while no specific impersonation/identification fraud was proven to have existed in Indiana (in the record of the lower court proceedings in that specific case), "flagrant examples of such fraud in other parts of the country … have been documented throughout this Nation's history by respected historians and journalists" and that such fraud could impact election results in close elections. As the Commission on Federal Election Reform made clear: "In close or disputed elections, and there are many, a small amount of fraud could make the margin of difference" (Report on the Commission of Federal Election Reform, 2005, 18).

Another argument put forward in support of universal voter identification laws is that such a requirement would instill and/or bolster confidence in the overall electoral system. Attacks on the integrity of the electoral process and claims of fraud and "stolen" elections have been particularly ubiquitous in American political discourse since the 2020 presidential election and have damaged the country's collective faith in the electoral process. People have also been animated by multiple claims made by President Donald Trump regarding the 2016, 2020, and 2024 presidential elections. As such, supporters feel that any security steps like voter identification laws, so long as they are implemented in such a way as to not intentionally disenfranchise voters (or implemented in a way to not disparately impact certain groups), could go a long way toward instilling public confidence in elections. Phrased another way, any step that could be taken to ameliorate or diminish such criticisms and increase faith in the voting system is a goal worth pursuing.

The Commission on Federal Election Reform, in the section of its final report dealing with "Photo Identifications," acknowledged this and stated, "The perception of possible fraud contributes to low confidence in the system. A good ID system could deter, detect, or eliminate several potential avenues of fraud—such as multiple voting or voting by individuals using the identities of others or those who are deceased—and thus it can enhance confidence" (Report on the Commission of Federal Election Reform, 2005, 18–9). Further, the Committee concluded that "the electoral system cannot inspire public confidence if no safeguards exist to deter or detect fraud or to confirm the identity of voters. Photo IDs currently are needed to board a plane, enter federal buildings, and cash a check. Voting is equally important" (Report on the Commission of Federal Election Reform, 2005, 18). Even if electoral fraud is extremely rare, laws seemingly protecting electoral integrity give the American citizen comfort. As explained by another source,

> Even if voter ID laws do not reduce voter fraud, it is possible that their widespread implementation might increase public confidence in election integrity. Here are some activities in American daily life that typically require a valid photo ID: buying alcohol or tobacco; opening a bank account; applying for food stamps, welfare, Medicaid and Social Security; renting and buying a house or car; flying on an airplane; getting married; purchasing a firearm; adopting a pet; applying for a hunting or fishing license; renting a hotel room; securing mobile phone service through a major carrier; visiting a casino; donating blood; and applying for unemployment benefits. (Everything Policy Brief, 2024)

As to the argument that photo identification laws could disenfranchise eligible voters, the Carter-Baker Commission itself identified that requiring voters to have photographic identification cards would most likely disproportionately affect the young, the elderly, the poor, and Black Americans (Anderson, 2020, 53). While the Commission viewed such criticism as "serious and legitimate," it also believed that the risk of disenfranchisement could be minimized or eliminated through thoughtful legislation on the topic (Report on the Commission of Federal Election Reform, 2005, 19).

So, what would a potentially thoughtful attempt by the state look like? Indiana's 2006 Voter Identification Law provides one example. That law mandated that individuals must present a government-issued photo identification to vote. To avoid claims of the law being "void because of vagueness," the law provided a list of what types of identifications would be acceptable, which included an Indiana driver's license, an Indiana identification card, a military identification card, or a passport. In an effort to not unintentionally disenfranchise the indigent, Indiana law provided that an official state identification card would be provided (solely at the state expense) to those individuals who could not afford it on their own (Seigel, 2016). Finally, the law carved out several exceptions or accommodation for those who could not produce an identification card at the time of election. Those exceptions included a provision that allowed individuals sixty-five years or older, or disabled, to submit an absentee ballot through the mail without proof of identification. The law also allowed those individuals who could not produce identification cards on election day to be able to cast a provision ballot (a requirement of federal law introduced through the Help America Vote Act of 2002), and that ballot would be counted so long as the voter could produce a valid identification card, or signed an affidavit attesting to the fact that they could not afford the costs associated with obtaining such an identification card (e.g., cost to travel to a government office to receive a free state provided identification card). The only major drawback was that these voters would not have their provisional ballots counted if the voter failed to provide that additional information within ten days (Seigel, 2016).

The Indiana law and related proposals for nationwide photographic identification cards were not without critics. The NAACP and the ACLU challenged the Indiana legislation in court, claiming that there was no concrete evidence of fraud in Indiana, which is what purportedly prompted the legislation (Anderson, 2020, 56). According to Carol Anderson, a professor and author of a well-received book in this topical area, "the state's offer of 'free ID' was a brilliant smokescreen that masked that the actual documents required to obtain an Indiana's driver's license or a [free] state identification were not so easy to get and often came with costs borne solely by the would-be voter" (Anderson, 2020, 57). In Marion County, Indiana, individuals were caught in an "obviously Catch-22 of classic proportions," in that the health department required a driver's license to get a copy of a birth certificate and a birth certificate was needed as proof to obtain a driver's license (Anderson, 2020, 57). Presumably, though, this problem might be avoided by submitting an affidavit in support of the voter's provision ballot.

Despite its faults, the constitutionality of Indiana's law was upheld by the Supreme Court in a 6–3 decision in the *Crawford* case. Since its passage in 2006, the Indiana voting law has been described as a "success story," "a triumph," and a law that has "stood the test of time" (Seigel, 2016). As Indiana law professor and election law expert Michael J. Pitts stated in 2016, the "Indiana law is written in such a way that it's relatively easy to get around showing ID if you don't have one" (Seigel, 2016).

But this arguably positive solution in Indiana has not necessarily been reflected in other states. The NAACP legal defense fund completed a study that found that more than 100,000 registered voters in Alabama could not vote because they did not have the photo identification required by the state (Anderson, 2020, 68). According to Anderson, "with no viable public transportation, no access to vehicles, and the closest DMV sometimes nearly 50 miles away and open for only a few days a month," voters were facing what then-Attorney General Eric Holder called a modern day "poll tax" (Anderson, 2020, 69).

Anderson discussed another probative study that showed that "turnout gaps between white and ethnic minority voters are far higher in states where people must show ID during or after voting" (Anderson, 2020, 70). According to Anderson, "there is a 4.9% percent gap between Latino and white voters in states that do not require an ID, but this 'leaps to 13.2 percent' difference in states like Texas, North Carolina, Georgia, and Wisconsin" (Anderson, 2020, 70). For Black Americans, the gap "rises from 2.9 percent to 5.4 percent; among Asians, the gap increases from 6.5 to 11.5 percent" (Anderson, 2020, 70). Finally, "in Wisconsin, 8.3 percent of white voters who were surveyed said they were 'deterred' from voting in the 2016 election because of voter ID laws; the number more than tripled for African Americans (27.5 percent)" (Anderson, 2020, 70).

Largely Republican-recommended voter identification verbiage proliferated around the nation after 2004, leading to state legislation that would require all prospective voters to present government-issued photo identification documents at the polls. Opponents of these laws pointed out that in every state there were thousands of eligible voters who did not possess the requisite government-issued identification cards. According to the Carter-Baker Commission, in their report issued well over two decades ago, as many as 19 million potential voters nationwide (at the time of the report) did not possess either a driver's license or a state-issued photo identification. Even if a state created procedures for those individuals to obtain photo identifications, as was proposed in a number of states, the procedures themselves were inherently burdensome and potentially more costly for economically worse off groups. As reflected in the Carter-Baker Commission and in the US Supreme Court's majority opinion in *Crawford v. Marion County*, the voters most likely to be adversely affected by lacking a driver's license are typically the young, elderly, poor, and Black Americans—

groups that, on average, are more likely to vote Democrat than Republican. So, for at least some Democrats, photo identification requirements appear to be simply a new thinly disguised form of voter suppression.

Opponents of strict voter identification laws have argued that in-person voter fraud is astronomically rare. In a well-cited 2014 peer-reviewed study, political scientists John S. Ahlquist, Kenneth R. Mayer, and Simon Jackman found that in-person voter impersonation is essentially nonexistent in modern US elections (Ahlquist et al., 2014). Another 2014 peer-reviewed study by Ray Christensen and Thomas J. Schultz, examining elections in Florida, Ohio, and Utah (including both polling places and mail-in voting modalities), also concluded that voter-impersonation fraud is extremely rare, uncovering no new instances of people impersonating other voters aside from two isolated cases already known to authorities (Christensen and Schultz, 2014). Law Professor Justin Levitt found impersonation to be present in only "31 credible instances out of one billion ballots casted" between 2000 and 2014, a statistically trivial number that is unlikely to sway an election (Levitt, 2014).

Opponents of identification laws argue, then, that concerns over in-person voter fraud are "much to do about nothing." University of Kentucky Law Professor Joshua Douglas wrote that "in-person voter impersonation—the only kind of election fraud a voter ID would prevent—is virtually nonexistent" and that fixating on strict photo identification requirements "is a waste of time and money" (Douglas, 2017). Rather, according to Professor Levitt, the types of voter fraud more susceptible to potential abuse include absentee ballots, election worker misconduct, and mail-in voting, none of which are impacted by more rigid voter identification laws (Levitt, 2014).

Strict voter identification laws, opponents claim, needlessly risk disenfranchising potentially hundreds of thousands of otherwise eligible voters in response to a largely imaginary threat. In defending its voter ID law, the state of Indiana claimed that only 1 percent of the voting population of the state lacked a government identification card, calling the number of voters without identification "negligible" (Anderson, 2020, 57). However, that 1 percent amounted to 43,000 eligible disenfranchised voters in Indiana in 2006 (Anderson, 2020, 57). In fact, according to a written testimony to the United States Senate Committee on the Judiciary Subcommittee on the Constitution, Civil Rights and Human Rights in 2011, perhaps as much as 11 percent of eligible voters nationwide do not have a government-issued identification card (Brennan Center for Justice, 2011). This percentage equates to approximately 20 million voters.

Many states stop issuing state driver licenses after a certain age. These and other senior citizens who no longer drive do not have a valid driver's license. Many indigent individuals do not have a license or passport. Homeless individuals often lack proper identification because of no set living address. Perhaps unsurprisingly, the lower a person's annual earnings, the less likely they are to have the appropriate photo identification needed to satisfy the strict photo identification laws required by the states. Some studies have indicated that, among people earning under $25,000 per year, as many as 20–30 percent lack photo identification that would satisfy state requirement (Everything Policy Brief, 2024).

Even in those states wherein "free" state identification cards are offered to those who cannot afford to pay the processing fees or where other accommodations are made to assist voters, like provisional ballots, opponents still claim there are logistical and practical barriers to voting. The government office issuing free identification cards might be miles from a person's home, an obstacle for those without a driving license or who cannot afford transportation. Many states with mandatory voter photo identification laws do not exempt senior citizens from these requirements, and seniors often face challenges involving transportation. Many seniors are on fixed incomes, and paying perhaps $25–$30 for a certified and/or notarized birth certificate (needed to establish one's identity to obtain a state identification card) might constitute a financial hardship. Other citizens might not be able to leave work to travel to the appropriate government office without lost wages or personal time.

These logistical and financial barriers for certain groups of people create a dual system of treatment of individuals regarding the right to vote, a right which should exist equally to all. The Supreme Court, in *Crawford v. Marion County*, acknowledged that a "somewhat heavier burden" falls on a smaller number of people such as the elderly or the poor or those who have problems obtaining their original birth certificate (for whatever reason). The dissenting Justices in the *Crawford* decision, Justices Stephen Breyer and David Souter, also pointed out that the law created some real-world disadvantages to the vulnerable citizens in Indiana and treated those individuals differently as to the right to vote.

Requiring a government-issued photo identification card is not the only way to prevent voter fraud and voter impersonation. In those fourteen states that do not require proof of identification to vote, other efforts are made to ensure no voter fraud occurs. Depending on the state, voters might be required to sign a poll book, affidavit, or oath (under "pains and penalty of perjury") attesting one's identity before voting. Another historically popular way to verify voter identity without requiring that the voter provide an identification card or other paper documentation is to check the voter's signature against the signature on the registration record.

Further Reading

Ahlquist, John S., Kenneth R. Mayer, and Simon Jackman. "Alien Abduction and Voter Impersonation in the 2012 U.S. General Election: Evidence from a Survey List Experiment." *Election Law Journal: Rules, Politics, and Policy, 13*, no. 4 (2014), 460–75.

Anderson, Carol. *One Person, No Vote: How Voter Suppression Is Destroying Our Democracy*. Bloomsbury Publishing, 2020.

Brennan Center for Justice. "Testimony of The Brennan Center for Justice at NYU School of Law before the United States Senate Committee on the Judiciary Subcommittee on the Constitution, Civil Rights and Human Rights: New State Voting Laws: Barriers to the Ballot?" September 8, 2011. https://www.brennancenter.org/our-work/research-reports/new-state-voting-laws-barriers-ballot

Christensen, Ray, and Thomas J. Schultz. "Identifying Election Fraud Using Orphan and Low Propensity Voters." *American Politics Research, 42*, no. 2 (2014), 311–37.

Crawford v. Marion County Election Board, 553 U.S. 181 (2008).

Douglas, Joshua A. "The False Promise of Voter ID." *Governing Magazine*, March 29, 2017. https://www.governing.com/gov-institute/voices/col-false-promise-photo-id-voting.html

Everything Policy Brief. "Voter Identification." October 31, 2024. https://www.everythingpolicy.org/policy-briefs/voter-identification

Gallup. "Americans Endorse Both Early Voting and Voter Verification." October 24, 2024. https://news.gallup.com/poll/652523/americans-endorse-early-voting-voter-verification.aspx

Government Accountability Office. "Elections: Issues Related to State Voter Identification Laws [Reissued on February 27, 2015]." GAO-14–634, September 19, 2014. https://www.gao.gov/assets/gao-14-634.pdf

Levitt, Justin. "A Comprehensive Investigation of Voter Impersonation Finds 31 Credible Incidents out of One Billion Ballots Cast." *The Washington Post*, August 6, 2014. https://www.washingtonpost.com/news/wonk/wp/2014/08/06/a-comprehensive-investigation-of-voter-impersonation-finds-31-credible-incidents-out-of-one-billion-ballots-cast/

Report on the Commission of Federal Election Reform. *Building Confidence in U.S. Elections*. September 2005. https://capitalresearch.org/app/uploads/baker-carter-commission-2005-election-doc.pdf

Seigel, Josh. "After Voter ID Defeats, Lessons from Indiana's Law That 'Has Stood Test of Time.'" *The Daily Signal*, October 7, 2016. https://www.dailysignal.com/2016/08/07/after-voter-id-defeats-lessons-from-indianas-law-that-has-stood-test-of-time/

Q28: How commonplace is the practice of early voting, and how does it impact voter turnout?

Answer: Early voting offers citizens multiple days or weeks ahead of Election Day to cast their ballots rather than limiting participation to a single weekday. Early voting can mean the difference between voting and staying home for voters working hourly jobs or caring for children and family members. Expanding early voting is associated with higher turnout and also helps to ameliorate long lines and long waits on Election Day. Reductions in early voting days or hours, on the other hand, can adversely and disproportionately impact certain demographic groups.

Overall, states have provided more early voting opportunities since 2000, although several big electoral states reduced their early voting opportunities in 2024. States have generally recognized the advantage of early voting both for the voter and the state. For the voter, early voting increases the access to the ballot box. The state benefits in being able to better manage long lines and crowds and in having sufficient time to deal with logistical challenges that might arise, such as malfunctioning voting equipment. In their decisions regarding early voting, states are also considering the overall cost to provide early voting (as well as the increased potential for fraud)and the need for volunteers and volunteer poll watchers to staff polling places for extended periods of time.

The Facts: The purpose of early voting is to make access to the ballot box more inclusive and ease the crowds and wait times on the day of the election. Because Election Day is a weekday (Tuesday), it can be difficult for some voters to get to the polls. Allowing for some type of early voting (either in person or via absentee ballot) gives people more choices and flexibility.

Early voting benefits many groups that may otherwise experience voter suppression. For example, it can help poorer voters who might not have the ability to leave work on election day itself. Many college students have either classes or part-time jobs, or both, on weekdays, making it hard to vote. This is in part why several states have opened early voting sites on college campuses, and studies indicate this boosts student participation. In Florida, the introduction of on-campus early voting in 2018 helped mitigate the usual drop-off in turnout among younger voters in the midterm election (Schur et al., 2024). By locating polling places where students live and by offering flexible voting times, early voting reforms can draw in new voters who might otherwise skip the polls. Political scientists who studied voting trends found that the limitation or restriction of early voting reduced turnout among young voters in 2012 (Schur et al., 2024).

Voters have cited a variety of benefits in early voting, including avoiding long lines, more choices of time during the work week, avoidance of personal illness or sickness, and avoiding bad weather, among other things that might have prevented individuals from voting in the past (Marley et al., 2024). The people most affected are those with the least flexibility. Typically, this includes college-aged students and hourly workers who may be unable to vote in the narrow window that remains. As such, restrictive early voting laws risk disenfranchising these eligible voters.

The Center for Election Innovation and Research has reported that early voting provides benefits to states as well, finding that "research has demonstrated that more options to vote before election day mean more opportunities to identify and counteract any human error, machine breakdown, power outage, cyberattack, rumor campaign, or other potential issue that may arise" (Yoder et al., 2024). Early voting can also help states manage crowds at polling stations. However, extending the number of days of early voting and allowing for weekend voting also costs states more money (Schraufnagel et al., 2022).

Early voting has been a relatively recent phenomenon. In the 1990s, about 90 percent of voters cast their ballots on Election Day. By 2000, the votes cast on Election Day had dropped to about 60 percent, while early voting surged to about 40 percent. Only twenty-four states provided for early voting in 2000 compared with forty-seven states (and the District of Columbia) in 2024 (CBS News, 2024; Yoder et al., 2024).

Since many states passed legislation allowing for early or no-excuse absentee ballot voting in recent decades, a much greater slice of the total number of votes cast occurs prior to the day of the actual election. In the 2024 presidential election, early voting numbers equaled roughly 47 percent of the total number of votes cast in the 2020 election (Marley et al., 2024). This amounted to more than 74 million early votes (Marley et al., 2024). According to the Center for Election Innovation and Research, 97 percent of registered voters had the ability to cast their votes early in 2024, as opposed to only 40 percent in the 2000 election (CBS News, 2024). To take just two swing states as examples, in Georgia, roughly 80 percent of the entire vote cast in 2020 was cast in early voting alone in 2024

(Marley et al., 2024). In North Carolina, approximately 72 percent of all votes cast in the 2024 election were cast by way of early voting or absentee ballots (Doran, 2025).

The 2020 election was particularly noteworthy in its twofold impact on the practice of early voting. First, partly because of the COVID-19 pandemic, most states lifted previous restrictions on no-excuse mail in ballots and/or widened the ability for early voting at a diverse array of locations and modalities. This led to record numbers of ballots being cast before election day in 2020. Approximately 69 percent of all ballots were cast before Election Day (by mail or early in-person) compared with only 40 percent in 2016 (Yoder et al., 2024). While this greatly advanced the variety of ways people could vote, secondarily, it also contributed to a kick-back in a handful of states that sought to roll back some of this flexibility in the 2024 election by restricting early voting in some way (either by removing the amount of time or limiting the locations for early voting).

In the wake of the 2020 election, two opposing trends emerged among the states regarding early voting. Some states moved to expand early voting access permanently. Other states passed legislation scaling back and restricting early voting laws. According to a Brennan Center for Justice report, in 2021 alone, twenty-five states passed sixty-two laws that expanded voting access, outpacing the thirty-three restrictive laws passed in nineteen states that year (Brennan Center for Justice, 2021). However, between 2021 and 2024, at least thirty states passed new laws that make it harder to vote (Brennan Center for Justice, 2021). This doubled the pace of restrictive legislation compared to the previous decade (American Bar Association, 2024).

By 2024 and 2025, this divide had grown larger. Citing several Brennan Center for Justice Reports in 2021 and 2023, one analysis noted a "stark divide between states. On one side are those broadening democratic participation … on the other are those making it harder to vote," often in states where voting was already difficult (Hapgood, 2023). In other words, states that already had restrictive voting rules tended to impose even more constraints after 2020 while states with more accessible systems mostly moved further toward expansion (Brennan Center for Justice, 2021). This has produced a patchwork of laws in which a voter's ability to vote early (and how many days early and methods available to the voter) increasingly "depends on the state in which [that] voter happens to reside" (Brennan Center for Justice, 2021).

As stated, research suggests that early voting increases participation among groups that might otherwise face difficulties voting on a single designated day or because of especially unflexible work schedules during the working week. Those with caregiving responsibilities might also benefit from weekend or extended voting hours as they might otherwise struggle to take time off on a Tuesday. During the 2020 election in Texas, officials in Harris County (Houston) launched measures that included 24-hour voting centers. Proponents of the around the clock voting locations were aimed at those "who work all day, have children to care for, or any other situation that makes going to the polls in the middle of the day difficult" (Champion, 2021). These extended hours proved popular and contributed to record turnout for people voting early. In fact, the early voting alone in Harris County was more than the entire number of votes cast in the county in the entire 2016 presidential election (Champion, 2021).

These expansive 2020 laws were largely repealed in Texas in 2021 (through Texas Senate Bill 1). One reason may have been that providing twenty-four-hour voting facilities increased costs for the state. Yet, alternatively, restricting early voting in Texas has also been characterized as "a clear attempt to limit access to the vote" (Champion, 2021). The change in law, critics said, would disenfranchise many voters who had benefited from the expanded hours in 2020, including shift workers and others with non-traditional schedules, thereby adversely impacting working-class voters.

Another example of the impact of cutting early voting can be seen in the allowance (or not) of voting on Sundays. Early voting on Sundays has been defended as a way to broaden inclusivity by making the ballot box more accessible to people who cannot get to the polls during the work week. Also, Sunday voting was essential to the "Souls to the Polls" movement, wherein many Black churches organized voting drives to encourage people to vote immediately after Sunday church services. The Brennan Center for Justice has published research that suggested Black Americans are more likely to vote on Sundays than white voters, and Black voters would therefore be more adversely impacted by the removal of Sunday voting. In Georgia in the 2020 general election,

> Black voters (who make up 30 percent of the registered electorate) accounted for 36.5 percent of Sunday voters, but just 26.8 percent of early in-person voters on other days. On the other hand, 60 percent of the voters who voted early on other days were white, though that was true of just 47 percent of Sunday voters (53 percent of registered voters in Georgia are white). Barring counties from holding early in-person voting on Sundays would disproportionately impact Black Georgians. (Morris, 2021)

Limited research on this issue tends to support the proposition that these voters will not migrate to another day during the work week should Sunday or weekend voting be prohibited. For instance, in 2011, Florida's legislature reduced the early voting period for the 2012 election from fourteen days down to eight days and eliminated the final Sunday before the election. In "Race, Party, and the Consequences of Restricting Early Voting in Florida in the 2012 General Election," two political science researchers who analyzed the voting data concluded that the voters who would have voted on Sundays do not as a general matter move to another day or modality of voting. The researchers also concluded that those who previously voted on Sundays would be more likely not to vote in subsequent elections. After Sunday voting was removed in Florida in 2012, those Black voters who voted on Sundays in the 2008 election were especially likely to not vote at all in subsequent elections (Herron and Smith, 2014).

Another striking example was North Carolina's attempt to curtail early voting (and limit Sunday voting) in 2013. That year, shortly after the Supreme Court's *Shelby County v. Holder* decision that gave the green light to previously restricted states under the Voting Rights Act, North Carolina passed a wide-ranging bill that, among other provisions, reduced the early voting period from seventeen days to ten days and eliminated one of the two Sundays for early voting. These changes to the law were challenged in the courts, and the intent and impact of these changes were scrutinized. A federal appellate court struck down the law as unconstitutional, finding that it was crafted "with almost surgical precision" (Anderson, 2020) in disproportionately affecting Black Americans with discriminatory intent. New early voting restrictions (reduction of early voting from six weeks to three weeks and the outright prohibition on Sunday voting) were again proposed in North Carolina in 2025 (Doran, 2025). The 2025 proposal in North Carolina closely mirrored the overturned 2013 law and raised the possibility that it would once again suppress turnout in the Black community.

The research and examples from Texas, Florida, and North Carolina illustrate how reducing early voting opportunities might be viewed as voter suppression by some, in that the states are ultimately undermining access and means that voters had come to rely on in previous elections and increased the likelihood that these voters would not return to vote via another method or time. Therefore, limiting early voting (whether by reducing the days available, cutting evenings/weekends, or restricting convenient locations) tends to shrink the electorate. Further, scholarship suggests that that "when someone votes in one election, they are more likely to vote in subsequent elections" (Bitzer et al., 2023, 278; Coppock and Green, 2015; Gerber et al., 2003). Similarly, when a voter chooses a method to cast their vote, they are likely to continue to use that same method in future elections. And the opposite is also true, namely that a negative experience in one of these factors (fewer polling locations, farther distances to travel, how long are the lines and wait time, friendly or not friendly environment, etc.) might reinforce the behavior/decision to just avoid voting in the future election (Bitzer et al., 2023; Coppock and Green, 2015; Gerber et al.,2003). According to two well-published scholars in this area, "The ability to cast an early ballot may alter the composition of the electorate (along partisan, demographic, or socioeconomic lines) and create a potential electoral (dis)advantage for Republicans or Democrats" (Biggers and Hanmer, 2015).

Beyond Texas, Florida, and North Carolina, voting trends can be equally followed and analyzed in other states via useful databases. Several recent analyses by nonpartisan organizations like the Brennan Center for Justice and the Voting Rights Lab provide detailed state-by-state breakdowns of these legislative changes (Carter et al., 2024; Voting Rights Lab, 2024). The American Bar Association's 2024 voting rights report and state fact sheets from the Congressional Black Caucus Foundation also document the impact of post-2020 laws on early voting hours and accessibility across different regions (American Bar Association, 2024; Congressional Black Caucus Foundation, 2024).

Further Reading

American Bar Association. "Ninth Annual State of Voter Rights: Election 2024: State of U.S. Voting Rights." October 10, 2024. https://www.americanbar.org/groups/crsj/resources/on-demand/ninth-annual-state-of-voting-rights/

Anderson, Carol. *One Person, No Vote: How Voter Suppression Is Destroying Our Democracy*. Bloomsbury Publishing, 2020.

Bentele, Keith, and Erin O'Brien. "Jim Crow 2.0? Why States Consider and Adopt Restrictive Voter Access Policies." *Perspectives on Politics, 11*, no. 4 (2013), 1088–116.

Biggers, Daniel R., and Michael J. Hanmer. "Who Makes Voting Convenient? Explaining the Adoption of Early and No-Excuse Absentee Voting in the American States." *State Politics & Policy Quarterly, 15*, no. 2 (2015), 192–210.

Bitzer, Michael, Tyler Dukes, and Christopher A. Cooper. "Substitution Effect, Turnout Effect, or Both? Changes in Distance to the Early Voting Site and Voter Turnout." *Election Law Journal, 22*, no. 3 (2023), 278–85.

Brennan Center for Justice. "Voting Laws Roundup: October 2021." October 4, 2021. https://www.brennancenter.org/our-work/research-reports/voting-laws-roundup-october-2021

Brennan Center for Justice. *The Impact of Voter Suppression on Communities of Color.* January 10, 2022. https://www.brennancenter.org/our-work/research-reports/impact-voter-suppression-communities-color

Brennan Center for Justice. "Voting Laws Roundup: October 2023." October 19, 2023. https://www.brennancenter.org/our-work/research-reports/voting-laws-roundup-october-2023

Carter, Sara, Andrew Garber, Catherine Silvestri, and Connie Wu. "How Voting Laws Have Changed in Battleground States since 2020." Brennen Center for Justice, August 15, 2024. https://www.brennancenter.org/our-work/research-reports/how-voting-laws-have-changed-battleground-states-

Carter, Tracey B. "One's Health versus One's Right to Vote: How the COVID-19 Pandemic Changed the Legal Landscape of Absentee/Mail-in Voting in the United States from the 2020–2024 Election Cycles." *University of Florida Journal of Law & Public Policy, 35,* no. 1 (2024), 1–57.

CBS News. "Map Shows Which States Offer Early Voting and Mail-in Ballots for the 2024 Election." October 17, 2024. https://www.cbsnews.com/news/map-early-voting-mail-ballot-states/

Champion, Ellis. "Texas Republicans Target Harris County Early Voting." Democracy Docket, February 25, 2021. https://www.democracydocket.com/news-alerts/legislation-alert-texas-republicans-target-harris-county-early-voting/

Congressional Black Caucus Foundation. "Election 2024: Voting Rights Facts Sheets." Accessed August 21, 2025. https://www.cbcfinc.org/black-civic-engagement-hub/voting-rights-scorecard/voting-rights-fact-sheets/

Coppock, Alexander, and Donald P. Green. "Assessing the Correspondence between Experimental Results Obtained in the Lab and Field: A Review of Recent Social Science Research." *Political Science Research and Methods, 3,* no. 1 (2015), 113–31.

Doran, Will. "New GOP Bill Would Slash Early Voting in NC, Ban Sunday Voting." WRAL, February 6, 2025. https://www.wral.com/story/new-gop-bill-would-slash-early-voting-in-nc-ban-sunday-voting/21845129/

Equal Justice Initiative. "Supreme Court Leaves Intact Decision Striking Down North Carolina Voter Law That Targeted African Americans." May 17, 2017. https://eji.org/news/supreme-court-leaves-intact-decision-striking-down-north-carolina-voter-law-targeted-african-americans/

Gerber, Alan S., Donald P. Green, and Ron Shachar. "Voting May Be Habit Forming: Evidence from a Randomized Field Experiment." *American Journal of Political Science, 47,* no. 3 (2003), 540–50.

Gronke, Paul, and Daniel Krantz Toffey. "The Psychological and Institutional Determinants of Early Voting." *Journal of Social Issues, 64,* no. 3 (2008), 503–24.

Hamel, Brian T., Jan Leighley, and Robert Stein. "Why Making Voting Easier Isn't Enough: Early Voting, Campaigns, and Voter Turnout." *American Politics Research, 52,* no. 4 (2024), 343–54.

Hapgood, Katherine. "See Which States Are Expanding—or Restricting—Voting Rights." The Center for Public Integrity, October 27, 2023. https://publicintegrity.org/politics/elections/who-counts/see-which-states-are-expanding-or-restricting-voting-rights/

Herron, Michael C., and Daniel A. Smith. "Race, Party, and the Consequences of Restricting Early Voting in Florida in the 2012 General Election." *Political Research Quarterly*, *67*, no. 3 (2014), 646–65.

Herron, Michael C., and Daniel A. Smith. "Souls to the Polls: Early Voting in Florida." *State Politics & Policy Quarterly*, *14*, no. 4 (2014), 391–410.

Marley, Patrick, Yvonne Wingett Sanchez, Joel Achenbach, and Molly Hennessy-Fiske. "Early Voting Turnout High as Nearly 47% of 2020 Electorate Cast Ballots." *The Washington Post*, November 2, 2024. https://www.washingtonpost.com/politics/2024/11/02/early-voting-election-2024/

Morris, Kevin. "Georgia's Proposed Voting Restrictions Will Harm Black Voters Most." Brennan Center for Justice, March 6, 2021. https://www.brennancenter.org/our-work/research-reports/georgias-proposed-voting-restrictions-will-harm-black-voters-most

Schraufnagel, Scot, Michael J. Pomante, II, and Quan Li. "The Cost of Voting in the American States: 2022." *Election Law Journal*, *21*, no. 3 (2022), 220–8.

Schur, Lisa, Joseph Dietrich, Michael Herron, Douglas Kruse, Whitney Quesenberry, Melissa Rogers, Jean Schroedel, Daniel Smith, and Cameron Wimpy. "Ensuring Voting Access across the Electorate: Best Practices and New Areas for Research." *MIT Election Data and Science Lab*, 2024. https://electionlab.mit.edu/sites/default/files/2024-04/voting-access-usability.pdf

Voting Rights Lab. "Election Watch 2024: Changes to In-Person Voting since 2020." September 17, 2024. https://votingrightslab.org/2024/09/17/election-watch-2024-changes-to-in-person-voting-since-2020/

Yoder, Kyle, April Tan, and Stefan Martinez-Ruiz. "The Expansion of Voting before Election Day, 2000–2024." The Center for Election Innovation & Research, July 2024. https://electioninnovation.org/research/expansion-voting-before-election-day/

6

Impacts of Restrictions and Conditions of Polling Places on Voting

Polling place locations play a central role in determining the accessibility of voting. Abundant polling locations increase access, and voters at these locations can cast ballots with ease. A restricted number of polling locations suppress participation. Closing polling places typically results in longer travel distances, confusion about where to vote, and higher costs of participation in terms of time and resources. These closures often disproportionately affect individuals with fewer transportation options or inflexible work schedules. The unavailability of convenient polling place locations creates significant obstacles and disincentives to vote, particularly for low-income individuals (Voting Rights Lab, 2020).

Various recent scholarly studies reinforce a long-standing finding of political science research that the "cost" of voting increases with inconvenience, and distance or travel time is a tangible cost that can deter voting. For example, his 2020 article "A Precinct Too Far: Turnout and Voting Costs," economics professor Enrico Cantoni found that even a modest increase in distance traveled significantly lowers turnout. According to Cantoni, a quarter of a mile increase in distance to the polling place caused a 2–5 percent drop in ballots cast in those elections (Cantoni, 2020). In their 2025 article "The Direct Cost to Voters of Polling Site Closures and Consolidations," political scientists Scott Abramson and Sharece Thrower looked at polling place reassignment after a natural disaster occurred (i.e., a tornado). The authors found that reassigning voters to a new, farther polling site caused in-person turnout to drop by about 5.65 percentage points on average, with nearly all of this decline the result of the longer travel distances required (Abramson and Thrower, 2025).

Thus, the farther one must travel, the more likely a person will decide to forego voting. However, this problem can be alleviated somewhat if states allow the use of no-excuse absentee and mail-in ballots, eliminating the need for travel. If a state does not permit no-excuse absentee ballots, it may institute other assistance measures such as free transportation on election day, so that at least one hurdle to voting (the cost of transportation to and from a polling place) is removed.

Fewer polling locations and restricted early voting periods also lead to crowded polling places and longer waiting times. Underfunded and/or understaffed polling places can also contribute to this problem, as fewer election workers and volunteers in certain polling precincts mean that there are fewer people around to help manage crowds and facilitate voting. Fewer resources and longer lines also correlate to a less accommodating and voter friendly environment, which may lead voters to give up before casting their ballot and stay home from the polling place all together when the next election occurs. Though their impact may be more subtle than other forms of disenfranchisement, these factors have measurable effects on turnout, as documented in numerous studies. Voters in predominantly minority or lower-income precincts wait in line at polling places significantly longer to cast ballots than those in wealthier or predominantly white precincts.

Evidence supports the contention that polling stations tend to be less accessible (whether measured by distance, crowding, or efficiency) in poor and minority communities than in wealthier, white ones. Therefore, voter suppression resulting from the number of polling places and the conditions at polling places is disproportionate in those communities.

Further Reading

Abramson, Scott, and Sharece Thrower. "The Direct Cost to Voters of Polling Site Closures and Consolidation." *Political Science Research and Method* (2025), 1–22. doi: 10.1017/psrm.2025.10034

Cantoni, Enrico. "A Precinct Too Far: Turnout and Voting Costs." *American Economic Journal: Applied Economics, 12*, no. 1 (2020), 61–85.

Voting Rights Lab. "Polling Place Consolidation: Negative Impacts on Turnout and Equity." July 2020. https://votingrightslab.org/wp-content/uploads/2023/12/Polling-Place-Consolidation-Negative-Impacts-on-Turnout-and-Equity.pdf

Q29: Which states have closed polling places, and how has this suppressed the vote?

Answer: Over 1,000 polling places have been closed nationwide since the 2013 *Shelby County v. Holder* decision, which struck down the Voting Rights Act's "preclearance" requirement. Prior to that ruling, jurisdictions with histories of racial discrimination in voting (locations primarily concentrated in the south and southwest) had to get federal approval before closing or moving polling places. In the three years following *Shelby*, there were reportedly 868 fewer polling places in previous preclearance jurisdictions (Anderson, 2020, 119).

Proponents of the shuttered polling places largely justify the closures as cost-cutting measures and point to the need to streamline and centralize voting locations in their state. For example, places like Arizona have instituted fewer, centralized voting locations in place of hundreds of individual precincts within the state. Opponents have argued that the closing of these polling places is a thinly veiled attempt to suppress voting among certain communities, as it can often require people to travel greater distances to vote, disproportionately impacting the less affluent, the elderly, and/or minority communities.

The Facts: On June 25, 2013, the Supreme Court had handed down its decision in *Shelby County v. Holder*, eliminating the preclearance requirement for states with histories of racial discrimination. Once that protection was removed, a tsunami of poll closures followed. Many states, like Alabama and Louisiana, had already passed legislation that was then held, ready to be implemented at the moment when preclearance requirements were removed by statute or invalidated by the Supreme Court. Preemptively passed legislation ran the gamut of election policies and procedures, containing changes to voter identification laws, the use of mail-in ballots, the number and location of polling places, and so on.

The Leadership Conference on Civil Rights identified 1,688 polling place closures from 2012 to 2018 in states and counties that were formerly under federal oversight, nearly double the number of closures identified in the immediate aftermath of *Shelby*. An updated analysis found that by the 2018 midterm elections, there were 1,173 fewer polling places in these jurisdictions than just four years earlier even though voter turnout was higher (Leadership Conference on Civil and Human Rights, 2025). The movement to close hundreds of polling places hit the voters of several states especially hard. Texas alone closed 750 polling locations in the years after *Shelby*. Other states with large numbers of closures included Arizona, Georgia, and Louisiana, all of which are home to sizable minority and low-income populations (Leadership Conference on Civil and Human Rights, 2025).

The pattern of polling place closures observed in recent years does not appear to be random. A political party wishing to suppress voter turnout for supporters of the opposition party can strategically arrange for polling stations (or drop boxes) to be located less conveniently, thereby depressing voter participation in targeted areas. This tactic alone may make the difference in a close election. As noted in an article in the *Election Law Journal*, "scholars and practitioners of election administration know that site placement matters. All else being equal, voters are more likely to vote when they live closer to a polling place. Likewise, it is clear that voters are sensitive to administrative changes to their polling places" (Bitzer et al., 2023, 284; see also, Curiel and Clark, 2021). Political scientists have long believed that the "cost" of casting a vote increases with voter inconvenience, and distance or travel is a tangible cost that can deter participation. As one expert noted, "the important things are not the [polling] hours of operation but the location of the polling place and the distance and travel time it takes a voter to get there" (Paterson, 2018).

The farther a person must travel to vote, the less likely the person will in fact vote. As polling locations close, greater distances to new polls present distinct problems related to the ability to get transportation to the new location. Many voters lack transportation to travel an extra distance, and working voters may not be able to take the extra time from work to make the longer drive. Voters in communities with fewer transportation choices appear to be impacted the hardest. Recent research found that increasing distance to the polling site had a disproportionate negative impact for individuals in high-poverty areas (Bagwe, et al., 2022). Another academic study found that lower-income workers (with less time off and shorter work breaks) had a lower turnout rate than their more affluent voter counterparts (Charles and Stephens, 2013).

In Georgia, a one-mile increase in distance led to a significant drop in overall turnout only among voters living in the poorest communities, while higher-income area voters appeared to be able to offset the inconvenience of distance due to vehicle ownership (Bagwe et al., 2022). Participation by lower-income voters using public transportation tended to drop as much as 3 percent per extra mile traveled (Bagwe et al., 2022). A 2025 article recounted that prospective voters without vehicles faced obvious and significant obstacles to in person voting, and the problem got worse when the distance or travel time to the polling stations increased (Ganemtore, 2025). A Michigan study illustrated the strong correlation between vehicle ownership, wealth, and increased participation at the polls (especially when polling places are moved miles away from a voter's neighborhood). The researchers documented that in the 2018 election, 66 percent of registered voters who had access to a car cast a ballot, compared with only 36 percent of those with no personal/private vehicle (de Benedictis-Kessner et al., 2020). In Alabama, "13.8 percent of Black households in Alabama as compared to 4 percent of white households … have no access to a vehicle" (Anderson, 2020, 126).

Even relatively small distances can have an impact. One study in 2024 found that a voter being just a single minute closer by car to the voting location increased the voter's likelihood of voting by approximately 2 percent in Atlanta, Georgia. In a working research paper presented at the American Political Science Association annual meeting, academic authors Gaurav Bagwe, Juan Margitic, and Allison Stashko, in studying voter behavior involving 15 million voters in Georgia and in Pennsylvania, found that for each additional mile a voter traveled to that person's assigned precinct or polling place, there was a corresponding reduction in the probability of voting by roughly 0.5–1.7 percent (Bagwe et al., 2022). A 2015 study suggested that for every one-tenth of a mile increase to a polling place, a registered Black voter's participation (and vote) declines by 0.5 percent (Anderson, 2020, 119).

Eliminating polling locations has been shown to have a clear voter suppressive effect that is more pronounced among Black voters as opposed to white voters in the same state (Curiel and Clark, 2021; Morris and Miller, 2021). An empirical research analysis found that voters of color are disproportionately impacted by the closure of polling places (Cantoni, 2020). Data from Milwaukee, Wisconsin, for the 2020 presidential election, which took place during the COVID-19 epidemic, showed that "polling place consolidation reduced overall turnout by about 8.7 points and reduced turnout among the Black population in the city by about 10 points" (Morris and Miller, 2021, 597). The study concluded that "polling place consolidation even accompanied by widespread absentee voting in the face of an emergency may result in disenfranchisement, particularly among Black voters" (Morris and Miller, 2021, 597).

In the 2016 election, seventeen states (plus the District of Columbia) had fewer in-person polling locations in heavily populated Black, Latino, and Native American communities than they did in 2012. In Georgia, several counties in 2015–16 proposed closing polling sites predominantly in Black neighborhoods (plans that civil rights advocates successfully challenged as discriminatory). In Lake County, Indiana, which includes a very large minority population and a large working-class population, the county accounted for 170 polling place closures after *Shelby*. In Manatee County, Florida, officials closed 38 percent of polling sites prior to the 2014 elections, and the burden fell disproportionately on minority voters: "Black and Latinx voters were significantly more likely to be reassigned to new polling places as a result of [the] closures" (Voting Rights Lab, 2020). Poll closures and subsequent reassignments typically meant longer travel distances or travel to unfamiliar locations. In Florida, a study found that voting sites in the state were farther away from minority voters compared with white voters (Abbasi et al., 2023). Such examples illustrate a broader trend: low-income communities (often with large minority populations) have seen more than their share of polling place shutdowns, whereas affluent or predominantly white areas have been less likely to lose voting sites (Voting Rights Lab, 2020).

Data from North Carolina seems to support these voting trends as well. When North Carolina passed the Uniform and Expanded Early Voting Act in 2018, it reduced the total number of early voting locations in seventy of the state's one hundred counties. Scholars studying the impact of this law found that the poll closures had the effect of suppressing the vote: "We find that voters whose early voting sites were changed and particularly those whose sites were moved farther away were less likely to vote in the next election and more likely to choose another method of voting if they did cast a vote. These effects appear to be magnified among racial minorities" (Bitzer et al., 2023, 278). At one point, in Sparta, Georgia, local officials voted to move a polling station in a predominantly Black community seventeen miles away from the community (Anderson, 2020, 119).

The same effect of voter suppression holds true with regard to ballot drop boxes in some states. Several studies have shown that longer distances to locations where voters can drop off their ballots correlate with a reduced likelihood of voting altogether (Collingwood et al., 2018; McGuire et al., 2020). In Texas, the placement of ballot boxes disproportionately increased the distance traveled by nonwhite voters versus white voters in the state (Karner and Rowangould, 2021).

While the focus of this analysis has been the closure of polling stations and its suppressive effect on poor and minority voters, brief mention should also be made of the accessibility of services for securing requisite voter photo identification. Sparsely located Department of Motor Vehicle (DMV) offices in a state where a government issued driver's license is required to vote can also problematic for some individuals. For example, within hours of the *Shelby County v. Holder* decision, Texas enacted SB 14, which made government-issued photo identifications a new requirement under state law. However, approximately one-third of the counties in Texas, including counties that are heavily minority populated, lack a DMV. "Republican legislators recognized that it would require some citizens to travel up to 250 miles round-trip to obtain a license" (Anderson, 2020, 69). It is not hard to imagine individuals staying home rather than traveling such distances to obtain a government-issued photo identification to vote.

In Georgia, the Department of Justice Civil Rights Division found that only about one-third of the state's counties had a DMV office and there was not a single DMV in the entire city of Atlanta. Of the fifty-six locations throughout the state, only five were accessible via public transportation (Anderson, 2020, 61). Similarly, in Alabama, the governor closed DVM offices in six counties where Black Americans made up more that 70 percent of the population and another eleven DVM offices in counties wherein Black Americans made up more than half of the residents (Anderson, 2020, 125). The governor justified the closing of thirty-one driver's license offices in mostly Black counties by claiming that financial exigencies required paring down the number of DMVs (Anderson, 2020, 67). According to several scholars, "the impact was devasting," and the state effort ensured that "almost a third of Alabama's voting age population lived more than 10 miles away from the nearest-license-issuing office that was open more than two days per week" (Anderson, 2020, 125).

As discussed, traveling great distances to polling locations has a great effect of suppressing votes and otherwise discouraging potential voters from exercising their most precious right to vote. Due to the somewhat subtle nature of this type of disenfranchisement, voting rights advocates and concerned citizens need to be vigilant in evaluating seemingly benign or innocuous policy changes by election officials. In 2018, Georgia state officials decided just weeks before the midterm elections that Randolph County, purportedly one of the state's poorest, must close seven of its nine polling stations. This plan would have forced county residents (many of whom were Black and low-income) to travel ten or more miles to cast a ballot. Further, public transportation in the county was largely nonexistent, and many people lacked their own personal vehicles. It looked like a large segment of the voting population would not be able to vote because of the revised location of polls. Fortunately, however, after intervention by civil rights groups and a large public outcry, the county board of elections backed off the proposal, keeping the original polling stations open (Young, 2018). Had this allegedly simple measure been passed without notice, the communities impacted (overwhelming poor, Black neighborhoods) would have lost significant voting clout, as turnout would likely have plummeted due to the added travel burden (Young, 2018).

Further Reading

Abbasi, Mohsen, Suresh Venkatasubramanian, Sorelle A. Friedler, Kristen Lum, and Calvin Barrett. "Measuring and Mitigating Voting Access Disparities: A Study of Race and Polling Locations in Florida and North Carolina." *Proceedings of the 6th ACM Conference on Fairness, Accountability, and Transparency (FAccT 2023)*, (2023), 1038–48.

Anderson, Carol. *One Person, No Vote: How Voter Suppression Is Destroying Our Democracy*. Bloomsbury Publishing, 2020.

Bagwe, Gaurav, Juan Margitic, and Allison Stashko. "Polling Place Location and the Costs of Voting." American Political Science Association Annual Meeting (Paper Presentation), July 5, 2022. https://jmargitic.github.io/JM/Margitic_JMP.pdf

Bitzer, Michael, Tyler Dukes, and Christopher A. Cooper. "Substitution Effect, Turnout Effect, or Both? Changes in Distance to the Early Voting Site and Voter Turnout." *Election Law Journal, 22*, no. 3 (2023), 278–85.

Brady, Henry E., and John E. McNulty. "Turning Out to Vote: The Costs of Finding and Getting to the Polling Place." *American Political Science Review, 105*, no. 1 (2011), 115–34.

Cantoni, Enrico. "A Precinct Too Far: Turnout and Voting Costs." *American Economic Journal: Applied Economics, 12*, no. 1 (2020), 61–85.

Charles, Kerwin Kofi, and Melvin Stephens, Jr. "Employment, Wages, and Voter Turnout." *American Economic Journal: Applied Economics, 5*, no. 4 (2013), 111–43.

Collingwood, Loren, and B. Gonzalez O'Brien. "Is Distance to Drop Box an Appropriate Proxy for Drop Box Treatment? A Case Study of Washington State." *American Politics Research, 49*, no. 6 (2021), 604–17.

Collingwood, Loren, William McGuire, Benjamin Gonzalez O'Brien, Katherine Baird, and Sarah Hampson. "Do Drop Boxes Improve Voter Turnout? Evidence from King County, Washington." *Election Law Journal: Rules, Politics, and Policy, 17*, no. 1 (2018), 58–72.

Curiel, John A., and Jesse T. Clark. "Disparities in Poll Closures in the Age of COVID-19: A Case Study of Wisconsin." *Election Law Journal: Rules, Politics, and Policy, 20*, no. 4 (2021), 345–63.

de Benedictis-kessner, Justine, and Maxwell Palmer. "Got Wheels? How Having Access to a Car Impacts Voting." *Democracy Docket*, October 16, 2020. https://www.democracydocket.com/opinion/got-wheels-how-having-access-to-a-car-impacts-voting/

Dyck, Joshua J., and James G. Gimpel. "Distance, Turnout, and the Convenience of Voting." *Social Science Quarterly, 86*, no. 3 (2005), 531–48.

Ganemtore, Yasmine. "How Ease of Access to Polling Locations Impacts Participation in Elections." *Fair Elections Center*, May 19, 2025. https://fairelectionscenter.org/media/polling-locations-blog/

Haspel, Moshe, and H. Gibbs Knotts. "Location, Location, Location: Precinct Placement and the Costs of Voting." *Journal of Politics, 67*, no. 2 (2005), 560–73.

Karner, Alex, and Dana Rowangould. "Access to Secure Ballot Drop-off Locations in Texas." *Findings*, May 2021. https://findingspress.org/article/24080-access-to-secure-ballot-drop-off-locations-in-texas

Leadership Conference on Civil and Human Rights. "Democracy Diverted: Polling Place Closures and the Right to Vote." 2025. https://civilrights.org/democracy-diverted/

McGuire, William, Benjamin Gonzalez O'Brien, Katherine E. Baird, Benjamin Corbett, and Loren Collingwood. "Does Distance Matter? Evaluating the Impact of Drop Boxes on Voter Turnout." *Social Science Quarterly*, *101*, no. 5 (2020), 1789–809.

Morris, Kevin, and Peter Miller. "Voting in a Pandemic: COVID-19 and Primary Turnout in Milwaukee, Wisconsin." *Urban Affairs Review*, *58*, no. 2 (2021), 597–613.

Paterson, Blake. "Bipartisan Furor as North Carolina Election Law Shrinks Early Voting Locations by Almost 20 Percent: Nearly Half of the State's Counties Are Shutting Down Polling Places, in Part Because of a Law Passed in June." Electionland from ProPublica, September 14, 2018. https://www.propublica.org/article/bipartisan-furor-as-north-carolina-election-law-shrinks-early-voting-locations-by-almost-20-percent

Rowangould, Dana, Lou Jiehong, Alex Karner, and Deb A. Niemeiter. "Does Access to Voting Locations Affect the Choice to Vote?" *Transportation Research Interdisciplinary Perspectives*, *24* (January 2019), 1–9. https://www.sciencedirect.com/science/article/pii/S2590198224000150

Teale, Chris. "There Are 100,000 Fewer Election Day Polling Places in 2024." *Route Fifty*, March 24, 2024. https://www.route-fifty.com/management/2024/03/there-are-100000-fewer-election-day-polling-places-2024/394959/

Voting Rights Lab. "Polling Place Consolidation: Negative Impacts on Turnout and Equity." July 2020. https://votingrightslab.org/wp-content/uploads/2023/12/Polling-Place-Consolidation-Negative-Impacts-on-Turnout-and-Equity.pdf

Young, Sean. "Letter to Randolph County Board of Elections and Registration." ACLU Georgia, August 14, 2018. https://www.acluga.org/sites/default/files/field_documents/aclu-ga-ltr-re-randolph-polling-place-closures-8-14-18.pdf

Q30: Are there longer waits and lines in urban polling stations than in small towns and suburban areas?

Answer: Yes. Numerous studies have shown that affluent communities (which tend to be in small towns or suburbs) face significantly fewer logistical problems with their voting places, including fewer long lines, more expansive voting hours, and so on. Conversely, poorer, more urban communities are more likely to experience problems at the polls, particularly in states that have closed polling stations (resulting in fewer, more geographically distant polling locations) or reduced hours. This discrepancy, then, has the tendency to disproportionately suppress the low-income and minority vote (Klain et al., 2020). Affluent, predominantly white precincts typically have minimal wait times (often under five minutes), with many voters experiencing no lines at all. Low-income or minority precincts often face wait times that extend to twenty or thirty minutes. These inequities, not always intended by the state, are usually attributed to differences in polling resources (e.g., number of machines, poll workers, polling locations, etc.).

The Facts: Studies have shown that the consolidation of polling places discussed in Question 29 has not only suppressed the vote due to obstacles such as longer distances to travel, but has also produced longer lines at the polling stations that remained opened. In 2012, four thousand voters stood in a line in downtown Cincinnati stretching one-quarter of a mile in length. In 2016, Maricopa County, Arizona, reported wait times of five hours or more (Anderson, 2020, 117). While one might be tempted to argue that longer wait times is a minor inconvenience and does not adversely impact the vote, studies suggest that the problem does indeed depress voter turnout, especially among already underrepresented groups.

In 2012, for example, of the ten Florida precincts with the longest delays, 70 percent of the voters were Latino or Black. On average, Black Americans had to wait in line twice as long as whites. Nationwide, in 2012, whites who lived in white neighborhoods had the shortest wait times of all citizens, approximately seven minutes (Anderson, 2020, 117). In mostly white suburban precincts, many voters report minimal wait time (often under five minutes), with some voters experiencing no lines. Conversely, many low-income or minority polling places reportedly face long lines on average of twenty to thirty minutes, with some voters waiting far longer than thirty minutes (Klain et al., 2020; West, 2019).

This inequity can be attributed to two main factors: the location and the condition of polling places. First, a lower density of polling locations in urban areas (fewer polling sites per capita) leads to larger crowds at each site. Second, longer lines can be the result of inferior polling place resources in disadvantaged areas, such as fewer polling workers and/or machines.

Even if a voter decides not to leave a long line and go home, they will still likely have a relatively negative voting experience, and those same voters may think twice about voting in the next election cycle. Research suggests that voters who encounter problems or poor conditions in voting will in fact often stay home in the next election. In Florida, for instance, in looking at the voting records for two general elections in 2012 and 2016, researchers found that "minority voters incurred disproportionately long wait times in 2012 and that in-person voters who waited excessively in 2012 had a slightly lower probability—approximately one percent—of turning out to vote in 2016" (Cottrell et al., 2020, 109). Encountering waits of four to five hours in a poor urban area, compared to ten to fifteen minutes in an affluent suburb, may cause voters to conclude that voting is not worth the cost. While this suppression of the vote may not always be as intentional as what occurred in the aftermath of ratification of the Fifteenth Amendment, or more recently in the Civil Rights Era of the 1950s–60s, it operates to disenfranchise voters just the same.

In December 2004, the *Columbus Dispatch* published a detailed analysis highlighting how long lines and machine shortages affected Democratic precincts in Franklin County, a very heavily populated district and home to approximately 60,000 students at The Ohio State University in Columbus. Multiple reports indicated four to five hours of waiting at the polls. Machine allocation disparities appeared to favor Republican areas, as urban Democratic precincts received fewer machines in 2000 than their Republican counterparts (Niquette, 2004). This type of voting machine disadvantage also led to extremely long lines in other cities, such as Cleveland (Keyssar, 2000, 270–9). A report published by *Vanity Fair* titled "Ohio's Odd Numbers" indicated that some voters endured waits as long as ten to eleven hours. Most of these voters were minorities or voters on college campus precincts (Hitchens, 2006).

Other national-level studies (spanning multiple election years) have examined disparities in how long Americans wait to vote, comparing predominantly minority or low-income precincts to more affluent, predominantly white precincts. A group of academic scholars published an article entitled "Waiting to Vote" with the Brennan Center for Justice in 2020. The study centered on data from the 2018 general election, which had a very high turnout for a midterm election. Many voters encountered hours-long lines and endured malfunctioning equipment. The study combined survey data on voter experiences to compare the experiences of different groups in different regions of the country. The authors estimate that about three million Americans waited thirty minutes or more to cast their ballots, with a disproportionate number of these delays occurring in locations with large nonwhite populations. Black and Latino voters experienced significantly longer waits on Election Day compared to white voters. Roughly 6.6 percent of Latino voters and 7 percent of Black voters reportedly waited over thirty minutes or more to vote. Only 4.1 percent of white voters waited over thirty minutes. Additionally, overall, Latino voters waited 46 percent longer on average than white voters, and Black voters waited 45 percent longer than white voters (Klain et al., 2020, 3–4).

A study conducted by the Massachusetts Institute of Technology (MIT) and the Bipartisan Policy Center, published in *Fulcrum*, reinforced the inequality that exists between different groups in waiting to vote. This study, using polling place data for the 2018 election, analyzed over 3,000 precincts, spanning eleven states and the District of Columbia. Its main findings were that in polling stations or precincts with less than 10 percent of the minority population, voters had an average wait time of 5.1 minutes, while in polling places or precincts with more than 90 percent minority population, voters averaged a wait time of 32.4 minutes (West, 2019).

Another study of the 2018 election found that voters in areas with household incomes above their state's median cast ballots roughly thirty-two seconds faster than those in lower-income areas, a difference that can build up over the course a polling day. Further, for every $10,000 increase in median income, voters spent about eleven fewer seconds checking in to vote. The authors of the study suspected that the longer lines and longer wait periods in poorer and minority neighborhoods were likely the result of having fewer resources (e.g., older voting machines and/or fewer poll workers per voter) (Pitzer et al., 2021).

Another group of scholars analyzed cellphone data to determine waiting periods to vote during the 2016 election. Their study utilized anonymous cellphone data from over 150,000 voters waiting in line at approximately 40,000 different polling places nationwide. The resulting data appeared to show that residents of predominantly Black neighborhoods waited 29 percent longer to vote than those in predominantly white neighborhoods and were significantly more likely to spend over thirty minutes at the polling place (Chen et al., 2022). Approximately 74 percent of the Black voters spent thirty minutes or more waiting in line (Chen et al., 2022). These scholars noted that the dramatic differences in wait time might be the result of an uneven allocation of polling resources (i.e., fewer poll workers and fewer voting machines) (Chen et al., 2022).

Author and professor Stephen Pettigrew, in his 2017 article entitled "The Racial Gap in Wait Times: Why Minority Precincts Are Underserved by Local Election Officials," brought national attention to this issue. He even presented his research to the United States House of Representatives. Using nationwide survey data from 2006 to 2014, Pettigrew found that voters in predominantly minority precincts experienced significantly longer lines than those in white precincts. In the 2012 election, a voter in a majority-minority precinct waited twice as long on average as a voter in a majority-white precinct. Nonwhite voters were about three times more likely to wait over thirty minutes (and six times more likely to wait over an hour) compared to white voters. Pettigrew, in describing the 2012 national election, indicated that "1 in 10 voters waited in line for more than 30 minutes to cast a ballot. About 3.5 million voters waited in excess of an hour, with some standing in line for longer than five hours" (Pettigrew, 2017, 527). In subsequent testimony in front of the United States House of Representatives

Subcommittee on Elections for the Committee on House Administration, Pettigrew characterized the long lines as an indirect form of suppression and a way to interfere with the fair access to voting (Pettigrew, 2021). In another published article, Pettigrew postulated that for every additional hour a voter waits in line to vote, their probability of voting in the subsequent election drops by one percentage point (Pettigrew, 2021).

Social scientists Charles Stewart III and Stephen Ansolabehere replicated Pettigrew's findings, reporting that long lines were a national problem that adversely impacted voting and resulted in potential indirect (unintentional) suppression. Their research, conducted in part through the auspices of the Caltech/MIT Voting Technology Project, illustrated that the average wait for white voters was about half as long as the average wait for nonwhite voters in 2012 (Stewart and Ansolabehere, 2015). This study helped prompt the Presidential Commission on Election Administration to recommend that no voters should wait more than thirty minutes to vote. The authors were careful to note, however, that their data and study was not an exhaustive nationwide analysis and that further research was required:

> Chronic long lines appear to beset only a handful of states and counties. Research that compares states that are similar demographically, but which have significantly different average wait times, would advance our understanding of how laws and practices facilitate expeditious service at polling places. (A wide-ranging comparison of California and Florida—states with similar demographics and ballot lengths but dramatically different average wait times—would seem the logical place to start). (Stewart and Ansolabehere, 2015, 52)

In a scholarly analysis entitled "The 2018 Voting Experience: Polling Place Lines," researchers looked at 3,119 polling places across the country in the 2018 midterms and compared results to 2014. The analysis found that although most voters had short waits, long lines were concentrated in certain communities. The share of voters waiting more than thirty minutes doubled from 3 percent in 2014 to 6 percent in 2018. According to the researchers, the worst delays were disproportionately in precincts with "high minority populations, high population density, and low incomes" (Weil et al., 2019, 4). Phrased another way, voters in heavily minority and poorer areas were significantly more likely to endure extended wait times than those in whiter, more affluent areas. Precincts that were over 90 percent nonwhite had some of the longest waits. This study underscored that racial and economic factors together predicted where lines were longest in 2018 (Weil et al., 2019). There is also a clear (and logical) correlation between longer wait times and population density of the area served (Kimball, 2013).

In another regional study, two academic authors examined twenty polling places around St. Louis during the 2018 election, finding evidence that poll site quality varied substantially from place to place. Polling place quality was impacted by such factors as parking availability, poll worker assistance, signage, and wait times at each site. The scholars correlated those factors with the surrounding census tract's profile and reported demographics for each area. Their findings "indicate that voting infrastructure and the environment at polling sites are associated with the predominant race and income level of the census tracts in which they are located" (Pitzer et al., 2021, 175). This meant that polling places serving low-income and predominantly minority communities tended to have worse infrastructure or longer processing times than those in more affluent or white areas. These differences were not merely cosmetic; they had real consequences. The study found that deficient polling conditions (e.g., inadequate staffing or equipment) were linked to lower voter turnout in the affected precincts (Pitzer et al., 2021).

As a result of a reduction in the number of polling locations in many locations after 2013, as discussed in Question 29, poorer precincts now frequently contend with having to serve more and more voters with the same (or fewer) resources. One analysis noted that jurisdictions previously covered by the Voting Rights Act's preclearance had, by 2018, on average 10 percent more registered voters assigned per polling place compared to jurisdictions not under VRA oversight (Voting Rights Lab, 2020). In other words, the polling places in these disproportionately low-income and minority areas were more strained and crowded on Election Day than those in other communities (Voting Rights Lab, 2020).

While the argument is sometimes made that long lines result from antiquated equipment found in poorer polling precincts, this disparity has been greatly reduced in recent years. In the aftermath of the 2000 presidential election, the differences in performance between old punch card machines and computer voter machines were put on full display. Because of this, Congress enacted the Help America Vote Act in 2002 provided funding to modernize outdated voting equipment. Therefore, while fewer machines or fewer poll workers certainly result in longer lines, drastically outdated machines are probably not as much of a factor. Problems with malfunctioning machines may still be an issue, however, and these problems may be more difficult to address at very busy polling locations, thereby contributing to longer lines.

Further Reading

Anderson, Carol. *One Person, No Vote: How Voter Suppression Is Destroying Our Democracy*. Bloomsbury Publishing, 2020.

Brennan Center for Justice. "Racial Disparities in Election Day Experiences." June 3, 2020. https://media.carnegie.org/filer_public/05/c6/05c6d6bd-af08-4fdd-bf2a-972b1330017f/6_02_waitingtovote_final.pdf

Chen, M. Keith, Kareem Haggag, Devin G. Pope, and Ryne Rohla. "Racial Disparities in Voting Wait Times: Evidence from Smartphone Data." *Review of Economics and Statistics, 104*, no. 6 (2022), 1341–50.

Cottrell, David, Michael C. Herron, and Daniel A. Smith. "Voting Lines, Equal Treatment, and Early Voting Check-In Times in Florida." *State Politics & Policy Quarterly, 21*, no. 2 (2020), 109–38.

Dyck Joshua, J., and James G. Gimpel. "Distance, Turnout, and the Convenience of Voting." *Social Science Quarterly, 86*, no. 3 (2005), 531–48.

Herron, Michael C., and Daniel A. Smith. "Precinct Closing and Wait Times in Florida during the 2012 General Election." *Election Law Journal, 14*, no. 3 (2015), 220–38.

Herron, Michael C., and Daniel A. Smith. "Precinct Resources and Voter Wait Times." *Electoral Studies, 42*, no. 2 (2016), 249–63.

Herron, Michael C., Daniel A. Smith, Serra Wendy, and Joseph Bafumi. "Wait Times and Voter Confidence: A Study of the 2014 General Election in Miami-Dade County." In *Races, Reforms, & Policy: Implications of the 2014 Midterm Election*, ed. Sisco Tauna, Galdieri Christopher, and Lucas Jennifer, University of Akron Press, 2017, pp. 107–22.

Hitchens, Christoper. "Ohio's Odd Numbers." *Vanity Fair*, October 16, 2006. https://www.vanityfair.com/news/2005/03/hitchens200503

Keyssar, Alexander. *The Right to Vote: The Contested History of Democracy in the United States*. Basic Books, 2000.

Kimball, David. "Why Are Voting Lines Longer for Urban Voters?" SSRN, March 29, 2013. https://ssrn.com/abstract=2255009

Klain, Hannah, Kevin Morris, Rebecca Ayala, and Max Feldman. "Waiting to Vote: Racial Disparities in Election Day Experiences." Brennan Center for Justice, June 2020. https://votingrightslab.org/wp-content/uploads/2023/12/Polling-Place-Consolidation-Negative-Impacts-on-Turnout-and-Equity.pdf

Mukherjee, Elora. "Abolishing the Time Tax on Voting." *Notre Dame Law Review, 85*, no. 1 (2009), 177–246.

Niquette, Eric. "Columbus Dispatch: Voting Machine Imbalance." December 12, 2004. https://www.dailykos.com/stories/2004/12/12/79408/-

Paterson, Blake. "Bipartisan Furor as North Carolina Election Law Shrinks Early Voting Locations by Almost 20 Percent." *Propublica*, September 24, 2018. https://www.propublica.org/article/bipartisan-furor-as-north-carolina-election-law-shrinks-early-voting-locations-by-almost-20-percent

Pettigrew, Stephen. "The Racial Gap in Wait Times: Why Minority Precincts Are Underserved by Local Election Officials." *Political Science Quarterly, 132*, no. 3 (2017), 527–47. https://onlinelibrary.wiley.com/doi/full/10.1002/polq.12657

Pettigrew, Stephen. "The Downstream Consequences of Long Waits: How Lines at the Precinct Depress Future Turnout." *Electoral Studies, 71* (2021), 1–17.

Pettigrew, Stephen. "Voting in America: The Potential for Polling Place Quality and Restrictions on Opportunities to Vote to Interfere with Free and Fair Access to the Ballot." United States House of Representatives Subcommittee on Elections for the Committee on House Administration, June 11, 2021. https://www.govinfo.gov/content/pkg/CHRG-117hhrg45527/html/CHRG-117hhrg45527.htm

Pitner, Barrett Holmes. "Early Voting Lines Are so Long, People Are Fainting. That Harms Democracy." *The Guardian*, October 19, 2016. https://www.theguardian.com/commentisfree/2016/oct/19/early-voting-lines-georgia

Pitzer, Kyle, Gena Gunn McClendon, and Michael Sherraden. "Voting Infrastructure and Process: Another Form of Voter Suppression?" *Social Service Review, 95*, no. 2 (2021), 175–209. https://www.journals.uchicago.edu/doi/10.1086/714491

Stewart, Charles, III, and Stephen Ansolabehere. "Waiting to Vote." *Election Law Journal: Rules, Politics, Policy, 14*, no. 1 (2015), 47–53. https://www.liebertpub.com/doi/full/10.1089/elj.2014.0292

University of Maryland School of Public Policy: Center for Global Sustainability. "Does Access to Voting Locations Affect the Choice to Vote?" February 6, 2024. https://cgs.umd.edu/research-impact/publications/does-access-voting-locations-affect-choice-vote

Voting Rights Lab. "Polling Place Consolidation: Negative Impacts on Turnout and Equity." July 2020. https://votingrightslab.org/wp-content/uploads/2023/12/Polling-Place-Consolidation-Negative-Impacts-on-Turnout-and-Equity.pdf

Weil, Michael, Charles Stewart III, Tim Harper, and Christopher Thomas. "The 2018 Voting Experience: Polling Place Lines." Bipartisan Policy Center and MIT Data, November 2019. https://bipartisanpolicy.org/download/?file=/wp-content/uploads/2019/11/The-2018-Votin-Experience.pdf

West, Geoff. "Voting Today? Here's Why Some Will Face Longer Lines than Others; Non-whites Face Longest Delays at the Polls." *Fulcrum*, 2019. https://thefulcrum.us/voting-wait-times

Q31: What disparities exist between voting resources at polling places in affluent and poor communities?

Answer: Multiple reports and studies since the 2000 election have provided evidence of disparities in allocated poll resources in the United States. Affluent neighborhoods tend to have more voting machines per capita, newer equipment, and more poll workers, while disadvantaged communities often face reduced resources.

The Facts: Historically, local election funding played an oversized role in supplying resources for polling stations, allowing affluent communities to afford and purchase better voting machines, whereas poorer communities struggled with outdated equipment. This problem was put on full display to the country in the 2000 presidential election, particularly in relation to the close Florida contest. Researchers found that poor communities in the state were more likely to use outdated punch card machines that resulted in a significantly higher rate of uncounted votes compared to affluent communities that had more modern equipment. The United States House of Representatives commissioned a study that concluded that voters in high-poverty, heavily minority districts were more likely to have their ballots go uncounted because of the disparity in resources (Ritter, 2020).

Another well-known and well-documented instance of disparity of resources between affluent (largely suburban and rural) versus poorer (largely urban) precincts was seen in Franklin County, Ohio, in the 2004 presidential election. According to an exposé/study published in *The Columbus Dispatch*, the predominantly Democratic urban precincts in Columbus had fewer voting machines in 2004 than they did in 2000, while many more affluent suburban precincts received more machines than they had in 2000. The result was that in the poor precincts there were far more voters per machine than in the more affluent communities. According to the *Columbus Dispatch*, heavily Democratic precincts had about 20 percent more registered voters per machine than Republican leaning areas, leading to longer wait times. This uneven distribution was acknowledged by Franklin County officials, although they indicated that it was the result of misjudgments regarding estimated turnout and not based upon some insidious motivation to discriminate based upon race or party affiliation. The *Columbus Dispatch* concluded that it was troubling evidence of disparity, even if officials did not intentionally create it (Niquette, 2004).

A more recent example comes from Georgia's 2018 gubernatorial election. In Fulton County, which encompasses the metro-Atlantic urban area, voters experienced long lines on Election Day in part because a number of voting machines were either broken or were provided to precincts in insufficient numbers needed to accommodate the high turnout. Democratic candidate for governor, Stacey Abrams, claimed that Georgia officials orchestrated voter suppression by allocating inadequate voting equipment to the predominantly minority precincts (Gardner, 2019). Republican Governor Brian Kemp denied this charge. Yet, even if there was no specific intention to pawn off older equipment to poorer districts, the inoperative equipment, coupled with fewer machines and fewer poll workers, could have contributed to the unintentional suppression of votes.

A study by the Bipartisan Policy Center and the Massachusetts Institute of Technology also determined that Georgia's predominantly minority communities had some of the longest wait times in the nation in 2018 (Gardner, 2019). Professor Stephen Pettigrew, an election data expert, testified to Congress in 2021 that he believed that precincts with minority voters received fewer voting machines, voting staff, and poll watchers, on average, which directly contributed to the racial gap in wait times at the polls. These gaps persist even when comparing neighborhoods of similar size or within the same city. Pettigrew characterized the poor polling-place conditions in minority or low-income areas as a form of voter suppression. While the intention of election officials may not have been to suppress the vote of certain groups, the result was clear (Pettigrew, 2021).

Several other studies support Pettigrew's assertions. Professor Kyle Pitzer and coauthors, for example, examined Saint Louis polling places in 2018, determining that the voting infrastructure and process at those polling sites tracked with the income level of the community in which they were located. Professors Michael Herron and Daniel A. Smith came to similar conclusions in examining how the allocation of polling place resources (such as voting machines and poll workers) affected waiting times. Their findings indicated that precincts serving higher minority populations often had fewer resources per voter (Herron and Smith, 2016). Other research noted that in areas studied, predominantly white precincts had on average far more voting machines and poll workers per voter (roughly twenty voters per machine) than predominantly minority precincts, which had much higher ratios (ninety voters per poll worker) (Pettigrew, 2017; Pettigrew, 2021).

In a study sponsored by the Brennan Center for Justice, another group of scholars addressed the problem of disparity of treatment between different groups in a report entitled "Waiting to Vote: Racial Disparities in Election Day Experiences." This national analysis of voter surveys and resource data regarding the 2018 general election concluded that the economic prosperity (or lack thereof) of different polling precincts directly impacted the voting conditions at the respective precincts. Counties that had shrinking incomes over the prior decade tended to have fewer poll workers and machines per voter. On average, a county with falling median income had eighty-two voters per poll worker and 590 per polling place, whereas a county with income growth had about seventy-four voters per worker and 470 per polling place. This, according to the report, resulted in longer lines. Voters in the worst-resourced counties (lowest per-voter availability of polling stations/workers) waited two to three times longer to vote than those in the best-resourced counties (Klain et al., 2020).

Similarly, the authors believed that the overall racial composition of precincts also appeared to correlate with differences in resources. Counties with fewer white voters over time ended up with significantly fewer voting resources per voter than those wherein there were more white voters. According to the researchers, an average county that "became less white" had about eighty voters per poll worker and 550 voters per polling place, compared to sixty-three voters per worker and 390 per polling place in counties that grew whiter over the decade (Klain et al., 2020).

Further Reading

Anderson, Carol. *One Person, No Vote: How Voter Suppression Is Destroying Our Democracy*. Bloomsbury Publishing, 2020.

Gardner, Amy. "Study: Heavily Minority Precincts Endured Longer Wait Times to Cast Ballots in 2018." *The Washington Post* November 4, 2019. https://www.washingtonpost.com/politics/study-heavily-minority-precincts-endured-longer-wait-times-to-cast-ballots-in-2018/2019/11/04/f8433e1c-fef7-11e9-8501-2a7123a38c58_story.html

Herron, Michael, and Daniel A. Smith. "Precinct Resources and Voter Wait Times." *Electoral Studies, 42* (2016), 249–63.

Klain, Hannah, Kevin Morris, Rebecca Ayala, and Max Feldman. "Waiting to Vote: Racial Disparities in Election Day Experiences." Brennan Center for Justice, June 30, 2020. https://www.brennancenter.org/our-work/research-reports/waiting-vote

Niquette, Eric. "GOP Strongholds Saw Increase in Voting Machines." *Columbus Dispatch*, December 12, 2004. https://www.dailykos.com/stories/2004/12/12/79408/-

Pettigrew, Stephen. "The Racial Gap in Wait Times: Why Minority Precincts Are Underserved by Local Election Officials." *Political Science Quarterly, 132*, no. 3 (2017), 527–47.

Pettigrew, Stephen. "Voting in America: The Potential for Polling Place Quality and Restrictions on Opportunities to Vote to Interfere with Free and Fair Access to the Ballot." United States House of Representatives Subcommittee on Elections for the Committee on House Administration, June 11, 2021. https://www.govinfo.gov/content/pkg/CHRG-117hhrg45527/html/CHRG-117hhrg45527.htm

Pitzer, Kyle, Gena Gunn McClendon, and Michael Sherraden. "Voting Infrastructure and Process: Another Form of Voter Suppression?" *Social Service Review*, *95*, no. 2 (2021), 175–209. https://www.journals.uchicago.edu/doi/10.1086/714491

Ritter, Michael. "Exploring Voting Equipment and Inequality in the 2016 U.S. General Election." *MIT Election Date + Science Law*, October 5, 2020. https://electionlab.mit.edu/articles/exploring-voting-equipment-and-inequality-2016-us-general-election-part-2

7

Maintenance of Peace and Security at Polling Places

The security and peaceful operation of polling places are essential to a successful election. Election officials, partisan poll watchers, and occasionally, the police, are often seen at polling locations. In particular, the presence of partisan poll watchers and police officers at polling places can significantly influence how comfortable (or uncomfortable) a voter may feel when voting.

In most states, partisan poll watchers are empowered by state law to provide oversight and accountability in the election process. As part of this role, poll watchers may challenge voter eligibility by crosschecking the voter's name against existing registration lists. Poll watchers may also scrutinize or question whether the voter has the necessary identification to vote. In some states, poll watchers may even arrive at the polling precinct with a list of names to challenge if those people show up to vote. That list, for example, might include all known felons in the state, and the partisan poll watchers can seek to disqualify those individuals immediately.

Poll watchers can be a great asset and assistance in helping election officials, including answering basic questions from voters. Some poll watchers try to assist as many people to vote as possible regardless of party affiliation. However, when poll watchers are acting in an especially partisan and/or aggressive manner, voters may feel intimidated or apprehensive. Some poll watchers will only challenge potential voters from the opposing political party. Overzealous partisan poll watchers may unnecessarily increase the number of otherwise eligible voters who are denied the ability to cast their vote or who must settle for filling out a provisional ballot. The specter of an aggressive poll watcher could cause a voter to not cast a vote, thereby suppressing the vote in that instance. Even the perception of being closely watched can chill participation, potentially causing some to leave the polls without voting rather than risk confrontation.

Acts of intimation, either before or during voting, can dissuade people from voting. While partisan poll watchers in each state have varying degrees of power and authority, none of the states allow poll watchers to engage in the intimidation of voters. Thus, voter intimidation laws apply just as equally to partisan poll watchers than as they do to average citizens and voters.

The presence of law enforcement at polling stations presents another possible problem. Law enforcement officers may be needed to maintain peace and security, but some groups find the idea of law enforcement officers at polling stations intimidating, especially in light of law enforcement abuse of voters in the 1950s and 1960s. For these individuals, the presence of police often carries with it a history of intimidation, especially for minority communities and individuals with prior interactions with the criminal justice system. For these groups, seeing uniformed officers near the ballot box can evoke fear of questioning, harassment, or even arrest, discouraging them from entering the polling place. This dynamic is especially troubling in areas where the local community and local law enforcement do not have a strong rapport or relationship.

In most states, police officers are permitted to be present at polling stations to preserve and maintain the peace or when called upon by election officials to deal with a potential problem. State and local law enforcement officers may have the right to be at the polls for the purpose of helping election officials ensure a safe voting environment; for example, if private citizens try to interfere with the right to vote of others, election officials may call law enforcement in to protect the public and to ensure no one's vote is being suppressed. However, there are a great number of restrictions on the use of police officers at polling locations in the various states around the country. And just like average citizens and partisan poll watchers, under no circumstances may police officers intimidate voters, prevent people from voting, or target particular racial or ethnic groups.

Beyond the basic federal criminal offense regarding voter intimidation, additional laws exist to protect election workers themselves. It is the election worker who ultimately ensures that the election is run fairly and in an equitable fashion free from discrimination or intentional disenfranchisement. As such, election workers are rightly afforded special protection given their important role in the electoral system.

Q32: Are partisan poll watchers needed in elections, or do they contribute to voter suppression?

Answer: Partisan poll watchers in elections reflect a tension between positive and negative forces. On the one hand, ensuring election transparency by serving as neutral observers can be a useful service. However, occasionally, poll watchers engage in overzealous "policing" of voters to ensure that the voter is indeed qualified to vote. Left unchecked by state law, or even empowered by state law, poll watching can quickly turn from neutrally observing voting practices to hyper-partisanship in trying to disqualify as many voters from the other party as is possible. The practice of enabling poll watching straddles a fine line between ensuring that poll watchers can monitor voting practices freely (to help prevent fraud) and, in worse case scenarios, preventing poll watchers from intruding on the voting process and impeding voters from accessing the ballot box.

The Facts: Partisan poll watchers are citizen observers appointed by political parties or campaigns to ensure no irregularities occur at polling places. Poll watchers often also assist election officials and precinct workers in determining voter eligibility when voters show up to vote on Election Day. In its purest and most ideal form, poll watching improves the integrity of the voting on Election Day by providing an "extra set of eyes" on the process. Official poll watchers must be credentialed in advance and are legally forbidden from disrupting voting. While some states even allow them to challenge a voter's eligibility (e.g., if the person is suspected of not residing in the precinct or voting twice), such challenges are then handled by election officials under strict procedures set by the state.

The general concept of poll watching dates back a couple of hundred years in the United States. Elections in the eighteenth and nineteenth centuries were often chaotic and vulnerable to fraudulent practices. Because of the turbulent nature of these elections, official monitors were employed to help curb practices like vote-buying and to try to discourage violence during the voting process (RetroReport, 2020; Tanfani and Renshaw, 2020). Over time, political parties began appointing their own watchers to ensure their party was not impermissibly disadvantaged in the voting process. The core idea was that each side's presence would deter outright cheating by allowing them to "keep an eye on the voting—and each other—to make sure things go smoothly" (Tanfani and Renshaw, 2020).

Over time, state laws formalized the independent poll watching practice. By the twentieth century, virtually all states explicitly allowed partisan poll watchers under state specific rules (Carter Center and National Conference of State Legislatures, 2016). The partisan poll watchers, sometimes called "observers" or even "challengers" in some states, are vested with different powers depending on the state. In most states, poll watchers are empowered to note irregularities in the voting process and report those irregularities to local election officials.

However, in many other states, state law authorizes poll watchers to directly challenge voter eligibility through prescribed legal procedures set forth in each state's election statutes. As the National Conference of State Legislatures (NCSL) explains, poll watchers "closely monitor election administration and may keep track of voter turnout for their parties," but they are "prohibited from interfering in the electoral process" (NCSL, 2025). In practice this means watchers can observe and question procedural matters, but they cannot touch ballots, move equipment, or obstruct voters (National Conference of State Legislatures, 2025).

Georgia and Texas both recently revised their laws regarding poll watching, expanding protections for poll watchers. In Georgia, state election laws were revised in 2024 to empower partisan poll watchers to flag and challenge voters with "nonresidential" addresses. Official Georgia Code Annotated Section 21-2-230(b) now provides that if a voter's registration address is nonresidential (P.O. box, business, shelter, dormitory, etc.), a poll watcher or any eligible elector may cite that fact as probable cause to challenge the voter's eligibility. Further, election officials in Georgia must "immediately consider such challenge" and uphold it if probable cause exists. This approach represents a more aggressive type of poll watching compared to those jurisdictions who just allow their poll watchers to observe and make notes of irregularities for possible further scrutiny by election officials.

Texas Senate Bill 1 passed in 2021 and is now codified at Texas Election Code, Title 3 (Election Officers and Observers), §§ 32.075, 33.0015–33.063. The new law indicates that poll watchers are "entitled to observe any activity conducted at the location at which the watcher is serving." Watchers may "sit or stand near enough to see and hear the election officers" conducting that activity, and "a watcher may not be denied free movement where election activity is occurring" within the polling place. Senate Bill 1 (S.B. 1) made it a Class A misdemeanor for an official to knowingly obstruct a watcher's view or distance them in a way that makes observation ineffective. S.B. 1 also made it a criminal offense for an election official to refuse to accept a qualified watcher. If an election officer intentionally or knowingly refuses to accept a watcher for service when the watcher has met the legal requirements, that officer commits a Class A misdemeanor.

Recent revisions to Texas law also made it harder to remove poll watchers. Under Texas Election Code § 32.075(g), an election judge may not remove a duly accepted watcher for a violation of election law unless the violation is observed by an election judge or clerk. Further, subsection (h) of the same statutory provision provides that a presiding judge may call a law enforcement officer to remove a poll watcher only if the watcher commits a breach of the peace or some other violation of law (for example, threatening violence or a clear criminal act).

In part because of these new Texas rules, thousands of voter complaints were submitted during the 2022 midterm election. The complaints included reports of harassment and intimidation by poll watchers. In one Texas county, the NAACP filed a lawsuit involving poll watchers intimidating and "shadowing" Black voters, leading a federal judge to bar those watchers from following voters in the polling place (Downen, 2022).

North Carolina is another state that has loosened its restrictions on partisan poll watchers. Passed in 2023, North Carolina General Statute § 163-45.1 empowers poll watchers in the state to do the following: take notes (including electronically); listen to conversations between voters and election officials when those conversations concern election administration (for example, name search, eligibility questions, or challenge procedures); move about the voting place, including the designated curbside-voting area (without compromising privacy); leave and re-enter the voting enclosure; communicate by phone outside the voting enclosure (calls are not permitted while inside); witness opening and closing procedures at the voting place; and obtain copies of the "voted-voter list" at least three times per day (timing set by the State Board) or inspect records to create such a list in counties that use an authorization-to-vote document instead of poll books. Because the rules were loosened in North Carolina to let observers circulate more freely, officials documented multiple instances of watchers hovering too close to voters and workers and even tailing election staff to their cars. Dozens of incidents were recorded in 2022 of poll watchers intimidating voters or confronting election officials (Coster et al., 2024).

However, partisan poll watchers engaging in voter intimidation and voter suppression is not new. For example, in the late 1800s, during Reconstruction after the Civil War, some states' "challenger" laws were weaponized to harass Black voters. One case involved white men claiming to be United States Marshals and menacing Black voters with guns to scare them away from a polling place. Decades later, during the Civil Rights era of the 1950s and 1960s, Black Americans and other minority groups still faced voter intimidation tactics by poll "watchers" and mere "observers" (RetroReport, 2020).

Even more recently, in 1981, the Republican National Committee (RNC) deployed an unofficial "Ballot Security Task Force," with its armed 200 off-duty officer members wearing black armbands and carrying two-way radios to patrol polling sites in minority neighborhoods of New Jersey (Pilkington, 2020).

The appearance of this force, along with signs warning voters that "this area is being patrolled by the National Ballot Security Task Force" (despite the fact that no official organization by that name existed), reasonably chilled a number of voters. According to reporting, "black voters who were waiting in line were asked for their registrations by the 'officers,' and then turned away" (Pilkington, 2020). Further, "some Latino voters were chased from the polling stations by the daunting patrolmen" (Pilkington, 2020).

This task force was characterized as "one of the most egregious examples of election intimidation in America's long history of voter suppression" (Pilkington, 2020). Their tactics were so heavy handed that the RNC was required by an unprecedented thirty-year judicial consent decree to get its poll watching procedures pre-approved by a court order. This requirement finally came to an end in 2018.

Leading up to the 2020 presidential election, Republican leaders vowed to again to be aggressive in the use of partisan poll watchers, indicating that they would employ 50,000 poll watchers spread out across fifteen key swing states (Pilkington, 2020). The RNC also laid bare its ambitious plans to recruit 100,000 volunteers to serve as election attorneys and poll watchers leading up to the 2024 presidential election. Then, Danielle Alvarez, a senior advisor for President Donald Trump's campaign, told NBC News, "Our unprecedented election integrity program has recruited over 200,000 volunteers to Protect the Vote—these patriots have volunteered their time to bring transparency and accountability to our election process" (Cohen, 2024).

As the 2020 presidential election marked the first time since the 1980s that the RNC was free from the consent decree requiring oversight of its polling watching activities, President Donald Trump openly urged supporters to "go into the polls and watch very carefully" and even suggested that law enforcement might help as well (RetroReport, 2020). The Trump campaign set up an "army" of volunteers to monitor ballot drop box locations for irregularities such as illegal ballot harvesting (Tanfani and Renshaw, 2020). Some of these volunteers watching and/or guarding ballot drop boxes showed up armed and in military-style apparel.

In response to the beefed-up Republican poll-watcher push, Democrats have also maintained an active partisan poll-watching program. However, some have noted that the philosophical approach to poll watching differs as between the Republican and Democratic parties. The Republican Party, in its official guidance to volunteers, often depicts poll watching as a deterrence measure against fraud. Republican volunteers were encouraged to act as the party's "eyes and ears" at voting sites and to report any suspicious activity via hotlines and legal teams (Coster et al., 2024). In one GOP training session in North Carolina, a party official urged watchers to "Be aggressive. … The more assertive and aggressive you are in watching and reporting, the better the quality of the election" (Coster et al., 2024).

By contrast, Democrats tend to emphasize voter protection regardless of party affiliation, and the Democratic Party's instructions to poll watchers are to help facilitate as many possible legal voters as possible. The chief concern of Democratic Party in instructing poll watchers is not flagging cases of potential fraud, but in making sure eligible voters can vote and not be interfered with. Internal training materials for Democratic poll watchers instruct volunteers to "be polite, respectful, and helpful," to cooperate with poll workers, and "always work to resolve conflicts, not create them. … Avoid confrontation with election officers and others" (North Carolina Democratic Party, 2024). In short, while both parties' official guidance insists that watchers must follow the law and never harass voters (which is a federal criminal offense), the tone and focus often differ between Republican and Democratic programs, namely the prevention of fraud and providing inclusive voter assistance, respectively.

Further Reading

Carlson, Kathy. "Tennessee Poll Watchers See 'Democracy at Work.'" *Tennessee/Lookout*, August 3, 2022. https://tennesseelookout.com/2022/08/03/tennessee-poll-watchers-see-democracy-at-work/

Carter Center and National Conference of State Legislatures. "A Guide to Election Observer Policies in the United States." October 2016. https://www.cartercenter.org/resources/pdfs/peace/democracy/cc-us-election-observation.pdf

Cohen, Matt. "Poll Watching Is a Crucial Part of Elections—How Did It Become Controversial?" October 18, 2024. https://www.democracydocket.com/analysis/poll-watching-is-a-crucial-part-of-elections-how-did-it-become-controversial/

Coster, Helen, Alexandra Ulmer, and Tim Reid. "US Election Experts Worry about Republican Poll Watchers in Swing States." Reuters, October 24, 2024. https://www.reuters.com/world/us/be-aggressive-republican-poll-watchers-battleground-states-worry-us-election-2024-10-24/

Downen, Robert. "Texas Avoided Election Violence: Advocates Say Voters Still Need More Protection." *The Texas Tribune*, November 11, 2022. https://www.texastribune.org/2022/11/11/texas-midterms-violence-pollwatchers-threats/

Garber, Andrew. "How Poll Watchers Can Help or Hinder Fair Elections." Brennan Center for Justice, June 26, 2024. https://www.brennancenter.org/our-work/research-reports/how-poll-watchers-can-help-or-hinder-fair-elections

National Conference of State Legislatures (NCSL). "Poll Watchers and Challengers." June 9, 2025. https://www.ncsl.org/elections-and-campaigns/poll-watchers-and-challengers

North Carolina Democratic Party. "2024 Poll Observer Manual." 2024. https://www.orangedems.com/wp-content/uploads/2024/02/PollObserverManual_2024_02.pdf

Pilkington, Ed. "In 1981 a 'Task Force' Intimidated Voters at the Polls. Will Republicans Revert to Their Old Tactics?" *The Guardian*, August 24, 2020. https://www.theguardian.com/us-news/2020/aug/24/in-1981-a-task-force-intimidated-voters-at-the-polls-will-republicans-revert-to-their-old-tactics

RetroReport. "Transcript: Poll Watchers and the Long History of Voter Intimidation." November 1, 2020. https://retroreport.org/transcript/transcript-poll-watchers-and-the-long-history-of-voter-intimidation/

Tanfani, Joseph, and Jarrett Renshaw. "Challengers, Observers and Electioneering: The History and Rules of U.S. Poll Watching." Reuters, October 7, 2020. https://www.reuters.com/article/world/challengers-observers-and-electioneering-the-history-and-rules-of-us-poll-wa-idUSKBN26S1IH/

Q33: Is it permissible to station police at polling locations?

Answer: Yes. Police officers may be utilized to enforce laws or maintain peace and order at voting locations. Historically, the use of police during elections has been cause for great concern among certain groups. Since 2000, the norm has been to maintain minimal police visibility at polls. When police or armed agents do appear in the voting context, given previous historical practice, their presence can trigger controversy and accusation of voter suppression. Voter suppression by the presence of police can refer to wholesale groups of individuals harassed or intimidated by law enforcement but also applies to any person who has had a negative experience with police at the polls at some point in their lives and to individuals who believe that law enforcement blindly follows the dictates of incumbent political leaders. Civil rights advocates and election administrators emphasize that any security provided by police at polling stations must be implemented in a way that does not scare off lawful voters.

The Facts: Police (and other armed officers) were historically used at polling sites in ways that intimidated minority voters. In the Jim Crow era and other periods, armed officers, on-duty or off-duty, targeted Black voters and other voters of color, creating an atmosphere of fear at the polls. Throughout the South, Black voters were threatened and intimidated when trying to vote or register to vote at police stations. Intimidation could take terrifying forms, such as "snarling, fangs-bared German shepherds, straining to rip open the flesh of unarmed black people with the full encouragement of law enforcement" (Anderson, 2020, 121). The numerous incidents of violence included "state police and horseback-mounted sheriff deputies trampling, tear gassing, and whipping men, women, and children on Selma's Edmund Pettis Bridge" (Anderson, 2020, 121).

Historical events such as the Colfax massacre, the Eufaula Election Massacre, the Spring Hill insurrection, and Wilmington insurrection have seeped into the collective consciousness of Americans (Beckman and Merriam, 2024). The fact that some of these horrific events occurred at the hands of local law enforcement (e.g., local sheriffs) and local government officials help to explain a reluctance to have law enforcement anywhere near the ballot box unless necessary. Given such history during elections, as well as past and recent police violence against minorities more generally, it is not unreasonable for some Black voters to feel apprehensive or intimidated by the presence of police officers stationed at polling locations even in 2025.

But voter intimidation resulting from the placement of law enforcement at polls is not just a historical matter. According to author Carol Anderson, even in modern times, the placement of police officers at voting sites has intentionally been done to suppress the Black vote. For example, "exploiting the toxic relationship between law enforcement and African Americans is one way, as when Mississippi and then Florida posted sheriffs at polling places to reduce the turnout rate" (Anderson, 2020, 93 and 292). In Jacksonville, Florida, in 2000, the police presence was ubiquitous in predominantly Black neighborhoods: "Police officers stationed themselves conspicuously around the buildings and at entry points as if this were Mississippi in the 1950s all over again" (Anderson, 2020, 35–6). Florida's election saw "police hovering around the polls" throughout the state (Anderson, 2020, 45).

Other sources agree with Anderson's assessment. According to *Facing South*, the official publication of the Institute for Southern Studies, police officers have been intentionally utilized in a way that suppressed the vote among certain groups of voters:

> Voting rights advocates are concerned that the existence of such forces play into a history of voter suppression, particularly in communities of color. Historically, law enforcement played a major role in voter suppression. In the 1960s, police

> officers were frequently deployed to stop Black people from voting. In the early 1980s, New Jersey Republicans used off-duty police officers to patrol polling places in largely Black and Latino communities, triggering similar concerns of voter intimidation. (Barber, 2022)

In some instances, without necessarily intending to suppress the vote, officials have seemed to be oblivious to the possible negative impact police presence might have on some groups. In Macon, Georgia, for example, election officials decided to move the polling place for the predominantly Black voting precinct to the local sheriff's office (Anderson, 2020, 119). It was only when a voter pointed out the problems with this, given Florida's history before the Civil Rights Movement, that the city changed its plans.

Yet, despite deeply rooted misgivings about law enforcement involvement in elections, the use of local police officers may be needed to maintain security and peace at polling locations, and states have an interest and responsibility in ensuring a smooth election process. Many states have enacted statutes to keep law enforcement away from voting sites, except in very limited circumstances. Election officials can always summon police or sheriff's deputies if there is a disturbance, violence, or a threat to public safety at a voting site. The key distinction is that police are not preemptively posted at polls as a matter of routine but are essentially on standby and not on site unless needed. These laws vary by state, but they share a common goal of preventing voter intimidation while still being able to maintain the peace.

In New Jersey, for example, the state strengthened its restrictions on police at polling places in 2021, by enacting Public Law 2021, chapter 459, codified at New Jersey Statutes § 19:6-16. This law prohibits police from being present at polls except in very limited cases. Under this provision, local police departments "shall not assign police officers to any district board [polling place] … to enforce election laws, maintain order, [or] serve at the polling place" during an election. Officers may only come if called in for a specific emergency or disturbance, or to transport election materials, but may not otherwise remain within 100 feet of a poll. The statute even forbids officers from wearing their uniforms or carrying exposed weapons at polling sites on Election Day.

California criminalizes unauthorized police (or security) presence at voting sites. California Elections Code § 18544 makes it a felony for any "uniformed peace officer, private guard, or security personnel" (or anyone armed with a firearm) to be stationed in the immediate vicinity of a polling place without written authorization from elections officials. Similarly, Pennsylvania's Election Code flatly forbids on-duty police from being within 100 feet of a polling place while voting is underway, unless they are there to vote or are responding to a specific request to restore order. Pennsylvania statute Title 25, § 3047 provides that "no police officer in commission, whether in uniform or in citizen's clothes, shall be within one hundred feet of a polling place" during an election, "unless called upon to preserve the peace" or for other narrow exceptions. It also explicitly bars any police officer from "unlawfully us[ing] or practic[ing] any intimidation, threats, force or violence" or in any way influencing voters within the 100-foot zone. A few other states (e.g., Florida, Ohio, North Carolina, and Wisconsin) have declared that if police officers are present, they must take orders from the presiding election judge or the clerk of elections in charge.

The primary reason for these prohibitions is to prevent voter intimidation. Even if conducted with good intentions, a visible law enforcement presence can be perceived as intimidating. Voters should not feel they are being watched by authorities while casting a ballot. Indeed, many state statutes were born from past abuses. For example, Pennsylvania's 100-foot ban on police traces back to partisan police intimidation in the early twentieth century. New Jersey's recent law was motivated by modern worries that uniformed officers at polls might deter turnout in some neighborhoods. The Brennan Center for Justice, in an October 2020 report, summarized the reasoning behind police restrictions at voting sites well: "State and local laws and practices place limits on the role of law enforcement" at polling places, because armed officers' "mere presence in polling places could raise reasonable fears" among voters of being harassed or profiled (Morales-Doyle et al., 2020).

In addition to state-level legal restrictions, federal law flatly precludes the use of federal law enforcement at polling places. 18 U.S.C. § 592 makes it a federal crime to deploy armed federal law enforcement or troops to any polling place "unless such force be necessary to repel armed enemies of the United States." That is, the law prohibits not only the presence of federal civil law enforcement but also the use of military personnel at the polls:

> Whoever, being an officer of the army or Navy, or other person in the civil, military, or Naval Service of the United States, orders, brings, keeps, or has under his authority or control any troops or armed men at any place where a general or special election is held, unless such force be necessary to repel armed enemies of the United States, shall be fined under this title or imprisoned not

> more than five years, or both; and be disqualified from holding any office of honor, profit, or trust under the United States.

Other federal statutes also prohibit the military from interfering in elections. For example, the Posse Comitatus Act of 1878 bans troops from being deployed on US soil to conduct certain state law enforcement activities. While there are a number of exceptions to the Posse Comitatus Act, none of those exceptions authorize use of the military at polling locations, again barring the need to "repel armed enemies of the United States."

That said, use of the National Guard has been authorized (legally) in non-law enforcement capacities during elections. For example, during the COVID-19 pandemic, several states faced severe poll worker shortages. In response, states like Wisconsin and Kentucky deployed National Guard members to serve as poll workers. These troops were mostly unarmed and in plain clothes, and they performed typical poll-worker tasks (setting up equipment, helping check in voters, etc.). Their deployment was done at the request of election officials and was carefully managed to avoid any perception of military enforcement of voting. This example demonstrates that there are benign ways to involve law enforcement or military personnel in elections, but should be utilized very cautiously and under the strict control of election officials.

Further Reading

Anderson, Carol. *One Person, No Vote: How Voter Suppression Is Destroying Our Democracy*. Bloomsbury Publishing, 2020.

Barber, Benjamin. "Southern States Create Election Police Forces." *Facing South*, April 7, 2022. https://www.facingsouth.org/2022/04/southern-states-create-election-police-forces

Beckman, James, and Eric Merriam. *Crimes against the State: Sedition, Rebellion, and Treason since America's Founding*. Bloomsbury, 2024.

Krasovic, Mark. "Armed Poll Watchers: New Jersey's Cautionary Tale Ahead of the 2020 Presidential Election." The Conversation, August 10, 2020.

Morales-Doyle, Sean, Daniel I. Weiner, Wendy Weiser, Mike German, and Elizabeth Goitein. "Voters Should Not Be Intimidated." Brennan Center for Justice, October 7, 2020. available at https://www.brennancenter.org/our-work/research-reports/voters-should-not-be-intimidated

Niven, David. "Policing Polling Places in the United States: The Negative Effect of Police Presence on African American Turnout in an Alabama Election." *Democracy and Security, 17* (2021), 1–14.

Q34: Are voters protected by law from intimidation, threats, coercion, and/or violence at the polling place?

Answer: Yes. Today, any attempt to threaten, coerce, or harass people to influence their vote is viewed as a very serious matter, and such conduct would be subject to state and/or federal investigation and possible prosecution for voter intimidation, as well as possible civil monetary liability. Voter intimidation is quite relevant to voter suppression and disenfranchisement, as intimidation may lead to non-participation by otherwise eligible voters.

The Facts: Historically, in the United States, there have unfortunately been many instances of threats and acts of intimidation and/or violence against prospective voters. For example, at the end of Reconstruction in the South, Black voters attempting to cast ballots were often met at polling places by white groups with the intent on blocking entrance into the voting precinct. During this time, numerous voters recounted being turned away from the polling place by verbal threats of possible violence or through shows of force by white vigilante groups blocking the entrance to the voting facility. Prospective Black voters were also turned away through similar displays of force or suggested violence in the 1940s and 1950s. Placing a sheriff outside the front door of a voting location in the South was often a sufficiently (and not-so-subtly) communicated message to Black Americans attempting to vote to "think twice" about casting their ballot.

Since the Civil Rights Movement of the 1950s and 1960s and the enactment of the Voting Rights Act of 1965 (which has a specific provision outlawing intimidation, coercion, and violence), such brazen acts against prospective voters dramatically decreased. Yet, anecdotal reports of intimidation and coercion have continued to be reported despite the grave seriousness of the offense under current state and federal criminal laws. A 2022 study found that two out of every five voters were worried about violence or acts of intimidation occurring at polling places (Sweren-Becker and Singh, 2024).

Voter intimidation, broadly speaking, is any action which threatens violence, coerces action (or inaction), or harasses people to influence their vote. Both federal law and various state criminal laws explicitly prohibit the intimidation of voters. Federal laws attempting to criminalize voter intimidation have existed since shortly after the Civil War and in the early 1870s, but these laws often had a checkered history of enforcement. The so-called Ku Klux Klan act of 1871, currently codified at 42 U.S.C. Section 1985(3), provides for civil liability for those engaged in conspiracies to intimidate voters, although the US Supreme Court has held that Section 1985(3) requires "class-based, invidiously discriminatory animus," meaning a conspiracy to intimidate voters based upon race or another protected classification. So, racially motivated conspiracies to threaten, harass, or deter minority voters can fall squarely within Section 1985(3), but the law is not considered a general voter-intimidation statute absent this discriminatory animus.

A key provision of the Voter's Rights Act of 1965 (Section 11(b)) expressly prohibits such behavior toward voters:

> No person, whether acting under color of law or otherwise, shall intimidate, threaten, or coerce, or attempt to intimidate, threaten, or coerce any person for voting or attempting to vote, or intimidate, threaten, or coerce, or attempt to intimidate, threaten, or coerce any person for urging or aiding any person to vote or attempt to vote, or intimidate, threaten, or coerce any person for exercising any powers or duties under … [various sections to the Voters Rights Act].

This provision in the Voters Rights Act also allows private citizens to civilly sue others to enforce the provision and collect civil damages (known as a private attorney general authorization). Another federal law that is equally clear in prohibiting interference with voters is 18 U.S.C. Section 594, which makes it a crime to intimidate or threaten voters in federal elections:

> Whoever intimidates, threatens, coerces, or attempts to intimidate, threaten, or coerce, any other person for the purpose of interfering with the right of such other person to vote or to vote as he may choose, or of causing such other person to vote for, or not to vote for, any candidate for the office of President, Vice President, Presidential elector, Member of the Senate, Member of the House of Representatives, Delegate from the District of Columbia, or Resident Commissioner, at any election held solely or in part for the purpose of electing such candidate, shall be fined under this title or imprisoned not more than one year, or both.

Prosecutions under 18 U.S.C. Section 594 are very rare (although they have been occasionally threatened by the government), in part because it is a misdemeanor offense with a maximum punishment of a year or less. Rather, prosecutors have preferred to bring criminal cases under a separate statute covering voter intimidation conduct that allows for felony convictions (incarcerations of more than a year). This statute can be found at 18 U.S.C Section 241, sometimes referred to as the civil rights conspiracy statute. It has been utilized successfully to prosecute conspiracies that aimed to oppress or intimidate citizens in exercising their voting rights or in the free exercise or enjoyment of any other right or privilege guaranteed by the Constitution. These laws together provide an adequate legal framework in the US judicial system to both address intimidation by government officials (i.e., those acts committed "under color of law") and hold private individuals accountable, both criminally and civilly. State governments have also passed statutes making it a criminal offense to harass or intimidate voters.

Accessing the number of acts of alleged intimidation that have occurred during each recent election is difficult for several reasons. First, prosecutions are often pursued on the state level, not handled federally, so accurate numbers would entail surveying all prosecutions and convictions in each of the fifty states, as well as federally. Second, if the offender is, for example, brandishing a weapon, he or she might be charged with "aggravated assault" or another state criminal offense instead of the specific charge of voter intimidation (and thus the incident might not be reported). Third, in virtually every election in recent years, there have been anecdotal accounts of aggressive (and sometimes even armed) individuals loitering near a voting precinct, acting in a boisterous and/or menacing fashion. There have also been occasional reports of overly aggressive poll watchers. In nearly all these incidents, however, when the conduct was reported to the authorities, the individuals allegedly engaged in those activities dispersed and/or discontinued any aggressive or menacing behavior, sometimes in response to authorities issuing warnings.

Intimidation tactics have taken an array of different approaches, from using threatening language against voters, to cyber-intimidation, to repeatedly driving large vehicles with huge partisan flags by voting locations, to armed individuals loitering just outside legal perimeters of voting precincts. In one documented case, a man was arrested in October 2020 and charged with voter intimidation for leaving a letter at a house that displayed a Harris–Biden campaign sign. The letter, which contained the word "warning" in red at the top of the page, stated in part: "This is a warning to anyone reading this letter if you are a Biden/ Harris supporter you will be targeted. We have a list of homes and addresses by your election signs. We are the ones with those scary guns, We are the ones your children have nightmares about" (Gaines, 2020). The letter also made threats to various politicians. In February 2021, for his voter intimidation conduct, the defendant was found guilty and sentenced to two years' incarceration followed by three years of supervised release ("Maryland News," 2021). He was also separately charged federally with threatening the lives of Joseph Biden, Kamala Harris, and others, to which he pled guilty (United States Attorney's Office, 2021). The United States Attorney stated, in part, that "conduct like this that threatens major candidates and fellow citizens only undermines our democracy and the principles upon which America was founded. We will not tolerate threatening conduct that seeks to intimidate, harass or dissuade Americans from exercising their right to vote" (Gaines, 2020).

In another example, from 2022, a private group of individuals recruited volunteers in Arizona to monitor drop boxes, purportedly in fear of "ballot stuffing" by the opponent. Some volunteers were armed and wore tactical style military gear. Multiple voters claimed that they were being intimidated and sued the organization that had reportedly organized and arranged the drop-box "monitoring" activities. The federal judge involved in the case issued a restraining order, specifying that the volunteers for the group could not come within 75 feet of a ballot drop box, that they must desist in yelling at or speaking to voters (unless they were spoken to or yelled at first), and that they could not openly carry firearms with 250 feet of a drop box. The judge also required the leader of the group to publicly post messages correcting false claims about Arizona ballot laws, making it clear that it is not necessarily illegal to drop multiple ballots in a drop box (Reuters, 2022).

In 2020, a group of demonstrators in Fairfax County, Virginia, purportedly disrupted early voting, forcing election officials to make the decision to move voter lines inside. Waving Donald Trump campaign flags while chanting and yelling, at a certain point, the demonstrators were alleged to have formed a line that voters had to circumnavigate to enter the polling place (Corasaniti and Saul, 2020).

The United States Department of Justice unsealed a criminal indictment in 2021 against two Iranian nationals for alleged voter intimidation and making interstate threats. The two defendants were said to have utilized thousands of hacked and stolen e-mail addresses to send messages to thousands of American voters. According to the Department of Justice, the senders of the message pretended to be members of the right wing "Proud Boys," and wrote in the text of the e-mails that "you will vote for Trump on Election Day or we will come after you" (United States Department of Justice, 2021).

A high-profile state-level voter intimidation case arose from a "robocall" scheme organized by two activists in October 2020. (A robocall is an automated telephone call that renders a pre-recorded message when the individual answers the call.) Robocalls were sent to approximately 12,000 Detroit area phone numbers that purportedly roughly correlated to Black areas in Detroit and Black voters. The phone message told voters to "beware of vote by mail" and that those voting by mail would have their personal data entered into a public database to be used by police to arrest people with outstanding warrants or by credit companies to collect debts (Michigan Department of Attorney General, 2024). The two defendants in the case were indicted for multiple felonies, including intimidation of voters and conspiracy to intimidate voters. Because of the appellate process and multiple appeals, the prosecution was still pending at the time of this writing. The two defendants were separately charged and indicted for the same scheme. One person pled guilty to telecommunications fraud in 2022 (Oladipo, 2024).

As mentioned earlier, the so-called Ku Klux Klan act of 1871, currently codified at 42 U.S.C. Section 1985(3), provides for civil liability for those engaged in conspiracies to intimidate voters. A very prominent example illustrating private citizens utilizing this statute/law to combat political intimidation pertained to the "Trump Train" highway confrontation in Texas in October 2020. As the Biden–Harris campaign bus was traveling down a highway in Texas, it was surrounded by approximately forty vehicles flying Trump flags, forcing the bus to a very low speed and restricting its movement, and allegedly, at one point, almost forcing the bus off the road (Guardian Staff, 2024). The occupants of the bus brought a lawsuit under the Ku Klux Klan act, claiming the drivers of the various vehicles were conspiring to intimidate voters and those on the bus. Only six defendants, as the alleged ringleaders of the confrontation, were sued. The federal lawsuit eventually went to a jury trial in September 2024. While the jury found five of the defendants to not be liable, the supposed main ringleader was held to be liable for intimidation, and the court ordered the defendant to pay $40,000 in damages (Guardian Staff, 2024).

Further Reading

Corasaniti, Nick, and Stephanie Saul. "Trump Supporters Disrupt Early Voting in Virginia." *Fairfax County Times*, September 21, 2020. https://www.fairfaxtimes.com/articles/trump-supporters-disrupt-early-voting-in-virginia/article_be07dda0-fc55-11ea-b8ab-4b39670e4fe8.html.

Gaines, Daniella. "Frederick Man Arrested for Threatening to Kill Biden, Harris." *Maryland Matters*, October 21, 2020. https://marylandmatters.org/2020/10/21/frederick-man-arrested-for-threatening-to-kill-biden-harris/

Guardian Staff. "Texas Jury Finds One 'Trump Train' Driver Liable for Encircling 2020 Biden-Harris Bus." *The Guardian*, September 25, 2024. https://www.theguardian.com/us-news/2024/sep/23/texas-court-clears-trump-train

"Maryland News: Frederick Man Charged with Voter Intimidation." *DC News Now*, February 24, 2021. https://www.dcnewsnow.com/news/local-news/maryland/frederick-man-charged-for-voter-intimidation/

Michigan Department of Attorney General. "Court of Appeals Upholds Attorney General's Criminal Charges in Voter Intimidation Robocall Case." December 16, 2024. https://www.michigan.gov/ag/news/press-releases/2024/12/16/court-of-appeals-upholds-attorney-generals-criminal-charges-in-voter-intimidation-robocall-case

Oladipo, Gloria. "Two Far-Right Conspiracy Theorists to Pay up to $1.25m for Robocall Campaign." October 10, 2024. https://www.theguardian.com/us-news/2024/apr/10/black-voter-robocall-jacob-wohl-jack-burkman-fined

Reuters News. "Federal Judge Issues Restraining Order against Arizona Group Accused of Voter Intimidation." November 2, 2022. https://www.reuters.com/legal/government/federal-judge-issues-restraining-order-against-arizona-group-accused-voter-2022-11-02/

Sweren-Becker, Eliza, and Jasleen Singh. *Guide to Laws against Intimidation of Voters and Election Workers*. Brennan Center for Justice, June 18, 2024. https://www.brennancenter.org/our-work/research-reports/guide-laws-against-intimidation-voters-and-election-workers

United States Attorney's Office, District of Maryland. "Maryland Man Pleads Guilty in Federal Court to Threatening 2020 Democratic Candidates for President and Vice President, Joe Biden and Kamala Harris, and Their Supporters during the Campaign." June 22, 2021. https://www.justice.gov/usao-md/pr/maryland-man-pleads-guilty-federal-court-threatening-2020-democratic-candidates-president

United States Department of Justice. *Federal Prosecution of Election Offices*. 4th edition. Washington, DC, 1984. https://www.ojp.gov/pdffiles1/Digitization/99354NCJRS.pdf

United States Department of Justice. "Two Iranian Nationals Charged for Cyber-Enabled Disinformation and Threat Campaign Designed to Influence the 2020 U.S. Presidential Election." *Press Release*, November 18, 2021. https://www.justice.gov/archives/opa/pr/two-iranian-nationals-charged-cyber-enabled-disinformation-and-threat-campaign-designed

Q35: Are election workers adequately protected from intimidation and violence?

Answer: The protection of election workers from violence and intimidation goes to the heart of a successful and smooth-running election. Attacks on and threats toward election workers jeopardize the functionality of the electoral process and adversely impact voter participation and access. If a group is able to bully or cajole non-partisan election officials with relative impunity, the ultimate effect may be that workers resign (and are potentially replaced by partisan activists) or workers may be intimidated into taking actions that disenfranchise voters or negate the will of voters (e.g., by not counting certain ballots, disallowing certain people to vote, biased certification of election results, etc.).

While there exists a bevy of laws meant to protect election and poll workers, there has also been an explosion of incidents of harassment and threatened violence against election workers since 2020. Some argue that the heightened threats and acts of intimidation against these workers beckon additional laws with harsher consequences for violation of those laws.

The Facts: At first blush, one might wonder what the protection of election workers and poll workers has to do with the topic of voter disenfranchisement or suppression of the vote. The connection is that there needs to be a non-partisan group of election workers who are free from threats and intimidation and, therefore, able to ensure that voters are able to vote properly, that legal ballots are accepted and counted, and that the results of an election are fairly tabulated and recorded. A violation of any of these requirements leads to disenfranchisement.

An unfortunate development in recent elections, since roughly 2016, is an increase of incidents of harassment or violence targeting election workers. The 2020 presidential election saw an explosion of incidents, relatedly largely to multiple repeated claims of a "stolen election." As such, the harassment and/or threats of violence to election workers went from a relatively rare occurrence prior to the 2020 presidential election cycle, to an unprecedented wave of threats of violence and even death threats to election workers. Since 2020, working as an election or poll worker went from a relatively obscure public service job to a potentially very dangerous job.

While there have always been a small number of individuals who might act belligerent or inappropriately toward an election worker, these numbers appeared to increase greatly nationwide during and after the 2020 election. A canvassing of the paucity of arrest records and news article archives involving such incidents from 2016 to 2019, as well as the near absence of prosecutions of defendants charged with harassing or threatening election workers during this period, reinforces how rare this problem was before 2020. Yet, after the 2020 election, arrests and prosecutions became much more frequent as well as more intense. Many offenses resulting in arrest involved threats of violence or death. In one threat made to a Nevada election worker by phone, the person said, "I hope you all go to jail for treason. I hope your children get molested. You're all going to f——die" (So and Szep, 2021). This person proceeded to call another three times over a fifteen-minute period, telling the election worker each time that "she was going to die" (So and Szep, 2021).

The United States Department of Justice reported a "significant increase" in threats to election officials after the 2020 election, with over 1,000 incidents of threats or harassment reported in the few months immediately following the election (Balser, 2022). Colorado Secretary of State Jena Griswold received approximately 1,800 death threats and threats of physical violence in just a one-year period (Richard, 2025). Griswold was also the subject other forms of harassment like "swatting attacks" (false emergency calls intended to provoke a large-scale police response) and harassing, abusive phone messages (So and Szep, 2021).

The dramatic increase in intimidation and threats directed at election officials and poll workers prompted the Department of Justice to form an Election Threats Task Force to combat the surge. By mid-2023, this task force had charged more than a dozen people for threatening election officials and workers. In a press-conference, then Attorney General Merrick Garland stated: "I will reiterate again today, these cases are a warning if you threaten to harm or kill an election worker or official or volunteer, the Justice Department will find you and we will hold you accountable" (Romero and Charalambous, 2024). Commentators, however, have criticized the productivity of the task force, given that there were more than 2,000 threats referred to the Federal Bureau of Investigation by election workers and the Justice Department opened just 100 investigations, charged twenty people, and landed just fifteen convictions (Romero and Charalambous, 2024).

Unfortunately, the threats and fears appear to have continued to increase each year. According to a Brennan Center of Justice survey conducted in early 2021, 17 percent of local election officials had been threatened and nearly one in three felt unsafe (Romero and Charalambous, 2024). Surveys conducted in May 2024 reveal that the problem has continued to grow, as 38 percent of local election officials reported experiencing threats, harassment, or abuse (Merrefield, 2024). Also, in 2024, over half of local election officials interviewed indicated that they were worried about the safety of their staff (Merrefield, 2024). In 2023, approximately one in five election workers feared being physically assaulted because of the job, and 45 percent feared for the safety of their election colleagues (Edlin and Norden, 2023).

Despite the drastic increase in intimidation and threats of violence to election workers since 2020, a patchwork of federal and state laws makes such behavior criminal. As explained by United States Attorney General Merrick Garland in 2022, "an important part of keeping the American people safe is protecting those who serve the public from violence and unlawful threats of violence … [and] … there is no First Amendment right to unlawfully threaten to harm or kill someone" (So and Lynch, 2022). Federal prosecutions for the intimidation and threats of election workers occur through a variety of different federal statutes depending on the circumstances. Intimidations and threats from afar, such as those communicated over the telephone, are in violation of 18 United States Code Section 875 (crime to threaten violence against someone through interstate commerce). Threats sent through the mail might be prosecuted under 18 United States Code Section 876 (crime to use the mail to make threatening communications). Another statute, 18 United States Code Section 245, makes it a crime to interfere with the duties of public officials administering elections. Also, as discussed elsewhere in this book, the Voting Rights Act of 1965 (52 U.S.C. Section 10307(b)) prohibits attempts to intimidate or threaten a person attempting to vote, and the so-called Ku Klux Klan act (42 U.S.C. Section 1985(3)) provides a civil case course of action against conspiracies to use force or threats of force to interfere with officials carrying out election duties. There are also analogous state criminal laws that mirror the federal laws discussed.

Despite this seeming plethora of applicable criminal laws, given the recent explosion of acts of intimidation and threats of violence, in 2022, a bipartisan group of senators introduced proposed legislation called the Election Worker Protection Act (Senate Bill 1318). This legislation would make it a federal crime to harass or intimidate election workers. This legislation had not been enacted as of 2025. Numerous states have recently introduced and passed laws making it a criminal act to maliciously publish election workers' personal information online (a tactic utilized to engage criminal actors in activities meant to intimidate election workers). Those state law efforts can be tracked through an online state-by-state guide provided by the nonprofit organization Public Citizen(see Public Citizen, 2025).

Further Reading

Balser, Jimmy. "Overview of Federal Criminal Laws Prohibiting Threats and Harassment of Election Workers." Congressional Research Service, Report: LSB10781, November 1, 2022. https://www.congress.gov/crs_external_products/LSB/PDF/LSB10781/LSB10781.4.pdf

Edlin, Ruby, and Lawrence Norden. "Poll of Election Officials Shows High Turnover amid Safety Threats and Political Interference." Brennen Center for Justice, April

25, 2023. https://www.brennancenter.org/our-work/analysis-opinion/poll-election-officials-shows-high-turnover-amid-safety-threats-and

Merrefield, Clark. "Reporting on Violence and Threats against US Election Workers: 6 Things to Know." *The Journalist's Resource,* June 18, 2024. https://journalistsresource.org/politics-and-government/poll-worker-threats-violence/

Public Citizen. "Tracker: State Legislation to Protect Election Officials." March 5, 2025. https://www.citizen.org/article/tracker-state-legislation-to-protect-election-officials/

Richard, Brandon. "Colorado's Top Election Official Received More than 1,800 Threats in Past Year." Denver7/ABC, June 17, 2025. https://www.denver7.com/news/local-news/colorados-top-election-official-received-more-than-1-800-threats-in-past-year

Romero, Laura, and Peter Charalambous. "DOJ Task Force, Formed in 2021 to Fight Election Threats, Has Brought Only 20 Cases." ABC News, September 5, 2024. https://abcnews.go.com/US/doj-task-force-formed-2021-fight-election-threats/story?id=113355654

So, Linda, and Jason Szep. "U.S. Election Workers Get Little Help from Law Enforcement as Terror Threats Mount." Reuters, September 8, 2021. https://www.reuters.com/investigates/special-report/usa-election-threats-law-enforcement/

So, Linda, and Sarah Lynch. "U.S. XCharges Texas Man for Threatening Georgia Election Officials." Reuters, January 21, 2022. https://www.reuters.com/world/us/us-charges-texas-man-threatening-georgia-government-officials-2022-01-21/

Index

About the Author

James A. Beckman is Professor of Legal Studies at the University of Central Florida, USA.